About the author

David Renton is currently a Senior Research Fellow at Sunderland University. Before that he worked as an Education Officer for the Trades Union Congress in London. He gained his M.A. in Modern History at Oxford University in 1995, and his Ph.D. at Sheffield University in 1998. He has lectured at Edge Hill College of Higher Education in Ormskirk, at Rhodes University in South Africa and at Nottingham Trent University. His books include: *Marx on Globalisation* (Lawrence & Wishart, 2001), *This Rough Game: Fascism and Anti-Fascism* (Sutton, 2001), *Liverpool: A Social History* (Hegemon Press, 2000), *Fascism, Anti-Fascism and the 1940s* (Macmillan, 2000), and *Fascism: Theory and Practice* (Pluto Press, 1999).

Dissident Marxism

Past voices for present times

DAVID RENTON

ZED BOOKS
London & New York

Dissident Marxism was first published in 2004 by
Zed Books Ltd, 7 Cynthia Street, London N1 9JF, UK,
and Room 400, 175 Fifth Avenue, New York, NY 10010, USA

www.zedbooks.co.uk

Copyright © David Renton, 2004

The right of David Renton to be identified as the author
of this work has been asserted by him in accordance with the
Copyright, Designs and Patents Act, 1988

Designed and typeset in Monotype Ehrhardt by Illuminati, Grosmont
Cover designed by Andrew Corbett
Printed and bound in the EU by Biddles Ltd, King's Lynn

Distributed in the USA exclusively by Palgrave Macmillan, a division of
St Martin's Press, LLC, 175 Fifth Avenue, New York, NY 10010

A catalogue record for this book is available from the British Library
Library of Congress Cataloging-in-Publication Data available

ISBN 1 84277 292 9 (Hb)
ISBN 1 84277 293 7 (Pb)

Contents

Acknowledgements

I would like to thank the many colleagues from different backgrounds who helped me to write this book. The most valuable advice I received came from Robert Molteno at Zed Books, who encouraged me to develop the argument, leading me away from a purely Western European perspective of intellectual history. The chapters on Paul Baran and Paul Sweezy, Walter Rodney and Samir Amin were included following his advice. Other friends were less successful in pressing me to include other dissidents from the same generation. Paul Mattick, Raya Dunayevskaya or Daniel Guérin – any one of these dissidents would have fitted easily into this book. The list of people I have chosen is far from definitive. I have deliberately excluded those whose contribution was expressed overwhelmingly at the level of theory (including Benjamin and Lukács). I have also avoided several figures (Lenin, Trotsky, Tony Cliff) about whom I have written previously or intend to write elsewhere. Yet whoever had been chosen, the main argument of this book – to defend a socialism based on the continuous rethinking of Marx – would have remained the same.

Several friends and comrades passed on comments on early versions of the chapter on Karl Korsch. They include John Rees of the *International Socialism Journal* and Esme Choonara. Gareth Dale loaned me his original copies of several of Korsch's articles in translation. David Camfield from *New Socialist* subjected the essay

to a vigorous thorough and helpful critique. I am also grateful to
Bob Pitt, who published an earlier version of the essay in his
magazine, *What Next?* With the material on Dona Torr and E.P.
Thompson, I received help from Chimen Abramsky, John Alexander, Barry Buitekant, Christine Collette, Keith Flett, Paul Foot,
Lindsey German, Royden Harrison, Eric Hobsbawm, Anthony
Howe, Yvonne Kapp, Victor Kiernan, Brian Pearce, Roger Simon,
Roger Spalding, Diana St John and Dorothy Thompson. I would
also like to thank David Cope of Left on the Shelf for helping me
to track down original copies of some of Torr's books. Early versions
of the chapter appeared in *History Workshop* and *Socialist Review*.

The chapter on Georges Henein was co-written with Anne
Alexander. It was read by Phil Marfleet, Donald LaCoss, Ann
Keen, Tony Cliff and Al Richardson. Pierre Broué published a
translation in *Cahiers Léon Trotsky*, and an essay based on the
research also appeared in *Revolutionary History*. Donald LaCoss of
the Chicago Surrealist Group also provided valuable comments.
Many friends helped with the chapter on Harry Braverman, including Edward Crawford of Marxists.org, Phil Gasper of the International Socialist Organisation and Sol Dollinger, a supporter of
American Socialist. The chapter was first published online, at Einde
O'Callaghan's site www.marxists.de. Mitch Dublin passed on
comments on the Walter Rodney chapter. The chapter on David
Widgery was strengthened by advice from a number of Widgery's
friends, including Paul Foot, Nigel Fountain, Syd Shelton, Ruth
Gregory and Sheila Rowbotham. A version of this chapter was
published in *Left History*. Mike Herbert helped to track down
source material. I am especially grateful to Widgery's widow, Juliet
Ash, for her support.

As well as those colleagues who read single chapters, a smaller
number of friends read the manuscript through, including Anne
Alexander, Peter Alexander, Ian Birchall, Keith Flett and Leo
Zeilig. Finally, I would like to thank a generation of friends that I
knew in Oxford in the early 1990s. Even when we disagreed, we
always worked together. These friends include Rachel Aldred, Anne
Alexander, Matthew Barratt, Jenni Borg, Chris Brooke, Palash
Dave, Jake Hotson, Bruce Howard, Sam James, Ben Kenward, Raj
Patel, Dave Pinnock, Robin Sen, Alexis Wearmouth and Matthew
Zepf. From them I learned anew the basic truth that Marxism was
not an academic science, but a creative art of change.

Introduction

The past few years have witnessed the birth of a new politics. The movement has revealed itself on the streets, in huge international protests. Seventy thousand marched against the World Trade Organisation at Seattle in 1999, 250,000 against the G8 at Genoa in 2001, 500,000 against a Europe of 'capitalism and war' in Barcelona in spring 2002. Similar numbers have taken part in protests in Brazil, Argentina and elsewhere. Commentators search for a title which catches the mood of 'the Seattle generation', 'anti-capitalism', 'the *new* New Left'. This new mood takes certain distinctive forms. First, it sees the world as a totality. Its supporters reject the single-issue politics of the 1980s and 1990s movement. The practice of separating campaigns for gender equality from issues of class, environment, music or race seems strange to the champions of the new style.[1] Second, the new politics is also organisationally libertarian. There is a suspicion of routine. All forms of structure are rejected, unless they conform to the immediate desires of the individual activist.[2] An enormous emphasis is placed on creativity. Third, the movement knows little history. The innocence of the new anti-capitalist movement is at once a strength and a weakness. The advantage is the open-mindedness of youth. Previously hostile traditions agree to meet, debate and sometimes even merge, ignoring the many past stupidities which have kept people apart, the balls-ups, the betrayals and the honest mistakes. The drawback is that there is no accounting with history.[3] Everything is new. Even the activist cadres barely consider the roots of today's collective dissidence, which should be known.

This book may help to explain the continuity between the most intransigent revolutionaries of the nineteenth century and the most exciting fighters of the twentieth century. While the great revolutionaries of the 1890s were those who were attached to mass parties, and were therefore likely to be best known, the most creative figures of the 1930s, the 1950s or the 1970s were just as likely to belong to smaller movements. Thus it is the often-submerged strands of left-wing politics that should nourish the new anti-capitalist movement today.

This book is a history of the political left through a certain moment in time. The easiest way to explain its context is to imagine a dialogue. The conversation could take place in any year from the 1930s to the 1980s. The place could be anywhere outside the Eastern bloc: Britain, perhaps France, America or Egypt. A young man or woman is selling a political magazine, and a prospective buyer walks past:

'You are a socialist?'

'Yes, of a kind … you see, our party is not in parliament. We think the capitalist state will always serve the interests of the rich.'

'Ah, so you must be a Communist. I've heard of them.'

'No. We think that the Communists just want to create another bureaucracy, another class society.'

'Well, then, *who the blazes are you*?'

The confusion in the minds of the imaginary listener would reflect both the marginality of the dissident group and also the complexity of the global situation. From the perspective of our left-wing paper-seller, the world was shaped by two great processes. The first was the rise of a parliamentary left, so that in most countries high 'politics' appeared to be a conflict between a conservative right (representing the interests of the propertied) and a social-democratic left (seeming to reflect some of the desires of the workers' movement). The second was the existence of first one society, Russia, and then several (China, the Eastern bloc) that claimed to stand outside the capitalist system.

Living in a world shaped by these forces, all radicals and revolutionaries were compelled to position themselves accordingly. Yet the two factors weighed differently in people's minds. For most of this period, the parliamentary left offered few attractions to the people who called themselves 'Marxist'. The social-democratic parties had enjoyed their heyday much earlier, in the 1890s and 1900s, when the parties were young and growing, and when they genuinely challenged the market system. The decision taken by socialist parties in almost every country in Europe to support their own ruling classes in the 1914–18 war demonstrated that the official representatives of the left had discarded their internationalist past. Already by 1914, their revolutionary élan was lost.

After 1914–18, in a situation where few Marxists would identify with their own socialist or labour parties, the torch of resistance necessarily passed to the Communist Parties, allied as they were with Russia in revolt. Indeed for the next seventy years, the Western Communist Parties were able to pose as a radical alternative, the true face of the left; but the nature of their challenge was in transition, as the insurrectionary Soviet Union of the early 1920s gave way to a more hierarchical and soon dictatorial society. Influenced by events in Russia, the nature of the Communist Parties also changed. In their day-to-day practice, the parties contested national and local elections. In parliament, they advocated pacts with liberals and even conservatives. Over time, they offered less and less of a challenge to the system.[4] Slowly the idea of a future workers' revolution was lost even from their private rhetoric.

The true dissidents were forced to develop and extend their anti-capitalist thinking, so that they could oppose a global society that was based on mass exploitation, and also reject the two bureaucratised left-wing 'alternatives' of Stalinism and social democracy. The chronology of this book runs therefore from 1917, through 1929, when Stalin's last domestic rivals were defeated, to 1989 and the fall of the Berlin Wall. The most basic indicator of dissidence was a hostility towards the purges and the show trials. Such anti-Stalinism came not for narrow reasons of personal or party privilege, but from an honest belief in socialism, and from an anger at the crimes being committed in the left's name.

The best of the dissidents tended to consider themselves Marxist. By this, they often meant three things. The first was that they were revolutionaries. In the work of Marx, Engels and their later interpreters, the dissidents found a means to change society, through working-class revolt. Second, the dissidents shared some of Marx's historical and philosophical method, including the claims that society was an objective reality, and that it developed according to certain economic processes. Different societies were distinguished by the hegemony of one class over another. The rise of new forms of technology tended to undermine those classes whose ascendancy had been based on earlier forms of economic and social organisation. Third, the dissidents understood Marxism as a unity. The majority of them accepted that socialist practice had to be linked to a living theory. There was no point just being theoretical – that would lead to passivity. There was no point just being active – how would you know that your practice would bring the revolution closer? Marxism was both programme and analysis, and it required both to be combined.[5]

The two movements that came closest to expressing the kernel of dissident Marxist politics were Trotskyism and the New Left. Both these forces emerged as critiques of Stalinism but the nature of their rejection varied. For the New Left, the failure of the Soviet USSR was primarily moral. The regime had prioritised economic goals over people's lives. It may have been socialist, but it was not humane. The New Left criticisms applied to Western Stalinism, as much as they applied to the tyrannies in the East. Left-wing politics needed to be rescued from Stalinist thinking, in which the party was the highest authority, and all manner of crimes were justified by grand appeals to the court of necessity. Such ideas enabled writers of the stature of George Orwell, E.P. Thompson or Jean-Paul Sartre to fulminate against the Soviet regime – but their argument was vague and its full implications unclear.

For the Trotskyists, the failure of the Soviet regime was political and conjunctural. In most important respects their critique was more impressive. It was rooted in a Marxist historical method; it was more coherent and systematic. Yet it was also one-sided. If the failure of 1917 was bound up with the nature of Stalin's personality and rule, then it followed that other forces might have gained control of the same situation, and used it to different ends. In the East, this led to sterile debates as to whether a 'political' or 'economic' revolution was needed to topple Stalinism. In the West, the limits of this theory were expressed in what Peter Sedgwick termed the socialism of 'The Pretenders'.

> The throne of working-class leadership is, on this view, held by a usurper of some kind, of doubtful authenticity and probable bastard petty-bourgeois stock. If the true heir, equipped with the royal birth-marks of 'clarity', 'scientific Socialism', 'Socialist humanism' or whatever, were to occupy his lawful place, all would be well with the movement.... Pretenders are so pre-occupied with the problem of King-ship (or leadership as they insist on calling it) that they seldom bother to find out the attitudes of their prospective subjects, the working class of this country. Or rather, if they draw upon the opinion of the workers, they do so in such a way as to add to their own particular claims to royalty.[6]

One of the starting points of this book is that creative, activist Marxism was most likely to be found in those writers whose critique of Stalinism was influenced (at least to some extent) by *both* of these dissident traditions. What the Trotskyists provided above all was a historical explanation of how and why Stalinism had been able to triumph. The isolation of the Russian Revolution had reduced the general set of possibilities. The rise of a home-grown Soviet bureaucracy meant that there was a group of people in Russia who could profit from the restoration of quieter times. The dual context of isolation and bureaucratisation ensured that Stalin would necessarily triumph over his rivals. What the New Left provided was a renewed sense of anger at this process, a howl of moral outrage, and a loud insistence that socialism should never again be like that. While the Trotskyists were undoubtedly 'correct' to argue that Marxism was not about making ethical judge-ments, the New Left with its simpler moral outrage offered a direct route into the minds of new activists. Angered and enthused, politicised, there was no limit to where their politics would end.

Sometimes, dissidence was just as much about a time or a place as it was about a theory or a group of people. The revolutionary upheavals in Russia in 1917 represented the first time in history that revolutionary socialists had captured a state. Unlike many of those who would later claim to find their inspiration in Bolshevism, Lenin and his comrades based their political support on a wave of urban insurrectionary fervour. The hopes that 1917 brought with it had a life about them, which the later dissidents would emulate. Revolutionary Barcelona, so well described by George Orwell, was as much revolutionary, and even more so dissident – factories were expropriated against the orders of the Comintern representatives in Spain. In Europe, the twin rebellions of 1956 and 1968 – the first and second New Lefts – were movements of protest aimed both against home-grown tyrannies (Suez, de Gaulle) and the despotism of the East (Hungary, Prague).

There are several reasons for choosing the title *Dissident Marxism*. One is to distinguish this generation from the classical Marxists of 1889 to 1914. In recent years, several writers have sought a pure set of left-wing values, a 'classical Marxism' unsullied by the defeat of the Russian Revolution. The phrase is taken from the Polish revolutionary Isaac Deutscher, who was an inspiration to the New Left of the 1960s. Deutscher bemoaned the

> striking, and to a Marxist often humiliating, contrast between what I call classical Marxism – that is, the body of thought developed by Marx, Engels, their contemporaries and after them by Kautsky, Plekhanov, Lenin, Trotsky, Rosa Luxemburg – and the vulgar Marxism, the pseudo-Marxism of the different varieties of European social-democrats, Stalinists, Khrushchevites, and their like.[7]

For Isaac Deutscher the obverse of classical Marxism was vulgar Marxism, which he termed 'the hypertrophy of practice' in distinction to the intellectual wealth of the founding fathers. Yet for all the undoubted qualities of Lenin, Luxemburg and the best of their contemporaries, the majority of the earlier generation were hampered by an over-literal trust in every dot and comma of Marx's work. In the 1890s, when the movement was growing, it was enough simply to to declare yourself an opponent of capitalism, but in the early 1900s, when capitalism went into deep crisis, the question of how to defeat it was more sharply posed. Such figures as Karl Kautsky had led the socialist parties through years of growth in the 1890s. They took their Marxism seriously but they were incapable of developing their ideas to meet the changed, revolutionary circumstances of 1905–14.[8] A moment pregnant with possibility passed both them and their parties by.

How could you recognise a dissident Marxist? The first and most important point is that they were socialists who were self-consciously influenced by Marx. Thus while Edward Thompson is included in this book, his predecessor George Orwell is omitted.[9] Marxism was the common currency of the mid-century inter-national left. It provided its supporters with a potential clarity and consistency of insight. The second point is to distinguish the dissidents. This term is used to refer to people who did not treat their socialism as an inherited canon of knowledge, but at each moment were willing to think their politics anew. The acid test of dissidence was a willingness to criticise the conduct of the Soviet state. The point has already been made that by far the most likely sources of such dissidence were the ideas of the New Left and Trotskyism combined, but there were other left-wing traditions including African socialism, Titoism, Castroism and even Maoism that could sustain dissidence, for a certain short time. The third point is that although the dissidents were brave and creative, theirs was also a narrow tradition. Many dissidents were found arguing inside or against their own party. The space to allow such independent, creative thinking did not come easily, certainly not in the 1920s and 1930s, nor even in the 1950s or early 1970s. People had to fight with their friends for the chance to be heard.

Some readers may be surprised by the critical tone in which the authors discussed in this book are treated. The dissident Marxists were open to a conception of socialism as a process of complete, democratic change; in Hal Draper's phrase, 'socialism from below'.[10] Such values were rare indeed before 1968. Yet being open to some-thing does not always mean that it is taken up, and the weakness of the revolutionary tradition caused all sorts of problems, which are traced in the following chapters. We might talk of a dissident im-perative, the needs for clarity and democracy and change being constant, but their expression varying. There is no single, dissident text that transcends the literature. Short of the successful creation of a genuine socialist society, this politics will remain incomplete.

Is it useful to describe a dissident Marxist *tradition*? The term is awkward, because it could suggest a deferential attitude towards the past, which was not shared by most writers mentioned in this book. The term is used here more modestly to refer to habits of co-thinking and mutual support. At times, the dissidents themselves confronted the question. For example, in one 1973 essay, E.P. Thompson asked himself, 'Why should one maintain allegiance to the [Marxist] tradition at all?' 'In my own case', he wrote, 'the choice presents no difficulty':

> Marxist historiography was never, in Britain, deformed beyond recovery, even when failing to make a clear intellectual disengagement with Stalinism. We had after all, the living line of Marx's analysis of British history – in *Capital*, in Marx and Engels' correspondence – continually present to us. To work as a Marxist historian in Britain means to work within a tradition founded by Marx, enriched by independent and complementary insights by William Morris, enlarged in recent times in specialist ways by such men and women as V. Gordon Childe, Maurice Dobb, Dona Torr and George Thomson, and to have as colleagues and scholars such scholars as Christopher Hill, Rodney Hilton, Eric Hobsbawm, V.G. Kiernan ... I could find no possible cause for dishonour in claiming a place in this tradition.[11]

Like Thompson in the above passage, this book employs a biographical method. The important insights of the dissidents are placed in context, according to the lives and historical situation of their authors. This method was chosen from a feeling that abstract arguments for socialism – expressed as they can be in terms like 'misery', 'recession', 'impoverishment', 'alienation', 'exploitation', 'consciousness', 'protest', 'demonstration' and 'occupation' – are not nearly so vivid as specific histories, rooted in the experience of people's lives.

The writers and activists surveyed in this book were chosen because they were seen to express key arguments, important moments in the left, or common dilemmas. The first of the biographical chapters begins with the experience of Soviet Russia. Four socialists are used to convey the history of the Russian Revolution, from the enormous optimism of 1917 to the defeat and internal degradation of the movement. Vladimir Mayakovsky was the poet of the revolution, a Bolshevik by the age of 13, a lifelong champion of political and aesthetic experimentation. As the bureaucrats crowded the academy, he despaired. He died in 1930, by his own hand. Alexandra Kollontai was a leader of the Bolsheviks' women's organisation. She contributed to an extraordinary burst of legislation, which made Soviet Russia briefly the most equal society on earth. Yet Kollontai was removed from power, as early as 1922. The Bolshevik commissar for education Anatoly Luna-charsky was the patron of countless diverse movements in culture, youth and university education. He was removed from this post in 1929. Last in this chapter, Victor Serge expressed the activist critique of the October Revolution's defeat.

The German socialist Karl Korsch is chiefly famous for his pamphlet *Marxism and Philosophy*. The chapter here evaluates his contribution to Marxist theory, as well as his attempt to lead an activist life outside the constraints of German communism. The third biographical chapter is devoted to the French–Egyptian sur-realist Georges Henein, one of the first socialists to establish a revolutionary and anti-Stalinist party in Africa. The next con-centrates on Dona Torr and E.P. Thompson, two labour historians, both of whom received their political education within the British Communist Party. Their lives are treated in a dual sense, for their activist contribution, and for the attempt they made to write history 'from below', reading the story of the past through the struggles of the majority.

Paul Baran and Paul Sweezy were two mid-century activists, editors and writers, chiefly famous for describing the advent of 'monopoly capitalism'. Walter Rodney was another historian and activist. His best-known book is *How Europe Underdeveloped Africa*. His dissidence lay in relationship not to the workers' states of Eastern Europe, nor indeed to planned revolutions in the West, but to the revolt of the African masses. Harry Braverman was the author of *Labor and Monopoly Capital*, which studied the social relations of modern capitalism starting from the emergence of a managerial class.

Samir Amin is an Egyptian economist, author of many cele-brated studies of capitalist development and underdevelopment. His books reflect the experience of Maoist theory outside China. They also express an activist strategy that is close to the thinking of the anti-capitalist movement today. David Widgery was an East End of London doctor and committed anti-racist. He helped to establish Rock Against Racism, an extraordinary cultural movement, which also has a strong contemporary resonance. As well as contributing by means of such activity, Widgery was a talented journalist writing for the left-wing and underground press, and his life is studied through the prism of this work.

For all the mistakes they often made, the dissidents were as much a healthy part of the Marxist tradition as the classical Marxists of the 1890s, who are today much better known. Given the conditions of the present, it seems that any revival of Marxism in Europe or North America will have to take place on a more activist terrain, under the leadership of a generation who are able to distinguish the essential from the inessential in revolutionary politics. The point in writing about dissident Marxism is to explore this group fraternally, asking aloud if the anti-capitalist movement might enable such a Marxism to re-emerge.

1

Dissident Marxism 1917–1989

In order to explain the distinctive character of the left in this period, it is appropriate to introduce the main historical forces. This chapter describes the most important processes that shaped the lives of the dissident left, including the trajectory of capitalism in this period, and the main traditions of the dissident and non-dissident left. There is not the space to offer a full history of the short twentieth century, nor even to provide a complete history of dissident Marxism. The history of this tradition was too diverse for it to be summarised in the limited space here. The purpose of this chapter is simply to introduce some key issues, which will be developed more fully in the subsequent chapters.

This chapter begins with a history not of the left, but of the world around it. It would be possible to write a history of socialism which was purely internal in character, but such a history would be misleading. At its best, the dissident left was an activist, combatant tradition. Any history of the left that observes only its own favourites can make no sense of their distinctive position. It would be like a Hollywood film of the Second World War, but a distinct one in which every single actor played a British or American role. If there were no opponents, then why was there a conflict? Before examining any movements of the left – either the dominant traditions of Stalinism and social democracy or the challengers which sprang away from them – it is right to say something about the way in which the world's economic and political system developed in these years. The changing nature of capitalism was the most important factor in making the left what it became.

The other side

At the start of our period, the majority of people lived on the land. Large numbers had already migrated from small towns and the countryside into the major cities. There, they exchanged forms of near-subsistence farming for a new life as paid industrial labourers. Huge proletarian bastions were formed in such cities as Glasgow, Turin, Paris, London, St Petersburg, Chicago and Berlin. The voters from these districts had already chosen socialism. In Germany, for example, the Social Democratic Party (SPD) received by 1914 roughly twice as many votes as each of the conservative parties combined. In global politics, the world was divided into several blocs. The great military powers, including the French, British, Ottoman, Russia, Japanese, Austro-Hungarian and German empires, controlled vast territories, and many diverse peoples. The greatest economic power was Britain, but her influence was slipping. As recently as 1850, around one-half of the world's industrial production had been controlled by the United Kingdom. Sixty-five years later, there was a rough parity between the volume of industrial goods (minerals, metals and chemicals) produced by each of America, Britain and Germany. The economic competition between these mighty states was a major factor pushing the world towards war. In the meantime, other processes were working to change the world. Among them can be counted the development of science and technology, the spread of democracy, the growth of liberation movements among the colonial people and next among women and other 'minorities', the capture of the world's population by the unit of the state, the relative decline of some powers (Austria, Britain), and the rise of others (Russia and the USA).

These seventy-five years witnessed extraordinary progress in human understanding of the world, and in the mastering of technique to apply this knowledge. In the field of biology, breakthroughs included the discovery of penicillin and vaccination. In physics,

Einstein's theory of general relativity was confirmed in 1918. It was followed by the validation of quantum mechanics, and the splitting of the atom. Yet the application of science was manifested not only in the spread of new products, cars, cinema and radio (in the 1930s), television and washing machines (in the 1950s and 1960s). The spread of technology also enabled other people to perfect the technique of killing. Millions died in the two world wars. We should also remember those civilians who were murdered in Armenia in 1915–23, in the Ukraine during collectivisation, in the Holocaust, and those killed by US bombers in Vietnam, Laos and Cambodia during the 1960s and 1970s.

Over the period as a whole, two important ideas seem to have gained currency. One was that every person in the world belonged to a certain state. Another was that the political leadership of these societies should not be fixed by inheritance, but instead should be decided with some reference to the choices of the people living in them. The proliferation of a consensus in favour of political democracy helps to explain why it was that at the start of our period only two states in Africa enjoyed independence (Liberia and Ethiopia), while at the end the majority of states possessed limited political sovereignty. The most important single story of these years was the gaining of democracy by the nations of the Third World: a process which continued through until the defeat of American forces in Vietnam. By the end of our period, some degree of internal equality had also been won, for example by the women's liberation and Black Power movements of the 1960s and 1970s.

Although such secular trends as the proliferation of science, war, feminism and democracy are important, it is also useful to talk about the different periods that people lived through. From one period to another, the strategies of the people in power varied. Successive decades 'felt' different – even if sometimes the exact contrasts were hard to pin down. The most obvious breaks occurred at the levels of the states and state policy. Ruling-class tactics changed from one period to the next. Between 1914 and 1929, for example, the shape of the world was determined by the events of the First World War. The conflict was a total mobilisation of people and capital, in which ten million died. The conduct of the war was economic. The two main rivals, Britain and Germany, attempted to starve each other to death. States were given un-precedented powers to organise their people for war. Strong states with huge economic powers having been established, there was a profound unwillingness after 1918 to return to the pre-war liberal order. Into the 1920s, the end of the war seemed to create a brief economic boom. The new machinery that had been produced was given over to peacetime tasks. In America, the 1920s were seen as prosperous and carefree – the jazz age – an era of conspicuous wealth. Yet in Europe the short boom of 1919–21 was followed by decline. The victorious powers blamed Germany for war and de-manded compensation. Reparations were set at an extraordinary level, $33 billion. In the aftermath of war, Germany owed money to France, France to Britain, Britain to America. The fact that reparations were set so high encouraged non-payment, and the easiest way to do this was through reducing the value of the German mark. A cycle of debt, inflation and crisis was established, whose consequences would only become apparent after 1929.

While most of the world seemed to be set on re-creating the conditions that had caused the great war, one society appeared to have broken out of this harsh cycle. Following the victory of the Bolsheviks in October 1917, Russia declared itself a revolutionary, socialist society. Given what we know of the long demise of the revolution, it is hard now to understood the sheer enthusiasm with which people initially set about creating a new world. For its first six months, the sovereign body in Russia was the *soviet*, in each city an assembly of working-class representatives. The new society granted women the rights to divorce, contraception and abortion. New forms of art prospered, new relationships in life. Indeed the revolution was supposed to spread. A Communist International was established to speed up this process. Russia itself was renamed the 'Union of Soviet Socialist Republics', its very name implying that the idea of socialism should expand beyond mere borders. Banknotes were printed with 'Workers of the World Unite' in all the main languages of the world. Even those societies that were most opposed to the change they saw responded by imitating some of its features. Within a year of women gaining the vote in Russia, they won it also in the USA. American President Woodrow Wilson came out as a convert to the rights of small nations. The USSR was a revolutionary threat to the old order. While it lasted, there could be no simple return to the pre-1914 ways.

A second period began with the Great Depression that followed the Wall Street Crash of 1929. The recession led to the most terrible waste of human life. By the mid-1930s, world trade had fallen by two-thirds. The Depression legitimised a particular form of economics, capitalism with a stronger state. One economy that survived the crash unharmed was the Soviet Union, secure behind a wall of protective tariffs. There the early 1930s was an epoch of growth, as millions of peasants were forced to leave the country-side for the towns. They contributed to the construction of huge iron and steel plants, like Magnitogorsk behind the Urals,[1] one of the largest steel plants in the world. By the mid-1930s, the econo-mies of each of the major powers had become intertwined with the industrial bureaus of each state, as public-sector-driven growth seemed to be the best means to escape global slump. The most extreme form of militarised state capitalism was Nazi Germany. Hitler's party was the main beneficiary of the slump, moving in just three years from the margins of politics to the centre of power. Yet fascism was not merely a new economic form of capitalism; it was also a different form of politics, content to use the utmost brutality against its own people. The challenge of opposing fascism was one of the most urgent tasks that the left faced in this whole period. The dynamic of fascism pointed always towards military competition leading to war. Once one of the world's major powers had developed in that direction, then it was likely that several of the others would follow.

The era of state capitalism culminated in the war of 1939–45. Even the democratic powers copied the economic habits of the dictatorships. Major companies were nationalised. In Britain, a Tory minister of agriculture drafted plans to nationalise every single acre of land! Yet at the same time, the idea also emerged that such extraordinary power should be used not for war, but to defend the conditions of the people. There were two faces to the state capital-ism of the 1930s and 1940s. The desire to prevent another depres-sion led both to the militarised state and to welfare-state capitalism. The same processes of state management caused both the most terrible later slaughter and egalitarian change.

After the war, most states began the process of constructing a welfare society, often funded by the workers through insurance schemes, sometimes paid for through general taxation. In the two decades after 1945, life itself seemed to demonstrate that the alliance between private capital and the state was the most successful way to run a country. In this period social democracy also reasserted itself, as the movement most committed to the public sector. Through the 1950s and 1960s, capitalism enjoyed the longest boom it has known in its entire history. The economic security of the times was matched by the political stability of the Cold War. There were now two superpowers, the United States and the Soviet Union, the two victors of the war. Military competition was pushed to the margins of the system. Both powers sought to assert their strength, not through the direct colonial rule of the nineteenth century, but through creating indirect 'spheres of influence' in Europe, Asia and Africa.

This system was based on conditions that did not, perhaps could not, last. By the late 1960s and early 1970s, the cost of remaining a superpower was too great for either of the major powers to bear. Ironically, it was the USA that buckled first – suffering setbacks and eventual defeat in the Vietnam War. Students and young workers took to the streets. New forms of protest politics emerged, in every country, based on race, gender and sexuality. Yet when the system stabilised itself again, life had changed. The public-sector model had lost its élan. Now, the whole world moved in the direction of privatisation. The most successful economic forms appeared to be the giant multinationals, many of which were now richer than whole states. Welfare-state capitalism was now presented as the cause of poverty. The election of Margaret Thatcher in Britain and Ronald Reagan in the USA highlighted the transition to a new era marked by the ascendancy of globalised, private capitalism.

Nowhere was the new era more destructive than in the old Eastern bloc. Incapable of sustaining economic competition, the rulers of the USSR turned towards a project of reform. Yet the person charged with managing the transition, Mikhail Gorbachev, was unable to control his own project. Members of Russia's oppressed nationalities demanded full independence. Workers were unwilling to bear the cost of transition. Gorbachev attempted to navigate between reform and revolution, but the pressure of the outside world was too great. In 1989, the Berlin Wall fell. Two years later, the Soviet Union was dissolved. The process of transition only secured the position of the elites. The old leaders of the Communist Party and the Communist Youth succeeding in re-inventing themselves as nationalist politicians or businessmen, the owners of local concerns. One witness, Olga Kryshtanovskaya, has described the transformation from the system of state management to the new private capitalist form. 'A ministry would be abolished, and in its ruins a business concern would be created in the form of a joint-stock company (same building, same furniture, same personnel) ... as a rule, the second or third figure in the abolished ministry would become head of the concern.'[2] The transition of Eastern Europe was less violent or dramatic than the equivalent processes of 1917 or 1928–32. Yet the system that emerged was new: an entire historical epoch had reached its end.

Challenges

So far, the events of the twentieth century have been described in an almost 'neutral' fashion. The point of remembering these years, though, is in order to explain the motives of the dissident left. From the perspective of socialist activists, what were the challenges facing the workers' movement between 1917 and 1989? When could we say that a movement had lived up to its duties, and when could we say that it had failed? One task was clearly the need to retain a commitment to the long-standing belief in workers' international fraternity. The urgency of this task was demonstrated (negatively) by the great betrayal of 4 August 1914, when the world's socialist parties failed to unite against the threat of slaughter. More positively, people could look on the example of 1936, when workers from all over the developed world travelled to Spain, to join the international fight against fascism.

As far as the dissident Marxists were concerned, a second test was the need to make sense of developments in Russia, including both the rise and the decline of the revolution there. This task faced socialists in the East, and indeed activists all over the world. If in the 1950s or the 1980s it was correct that the Soviet Union was still socialist, as its defenders claimed, then surely this meant that socialism should be defined as a police state run by a privileged gerontocracy? Such a 'utopia' was not an attractive prospect. Meanwhile, those writers and activists who insisted that Russia had nothing to do with the form of socialism that they sought had themselves to explain how an oppressive society could have emerged from what had been the first successful workers' revolution in the world.

A third challenge required socialists to explain what exactly was taking place in the world economy. In the 1920s, the most important financial processes included the re-establishment of a world economy in the ruins of the war. Initially, it was unclear whether this system would be dominated by private or state capital. Through the 1930s, 1940s and 1950s, the nature of capitalism changed. Roosevelt's New Deal was of course different from Hitler's Nazi Germany, yet the relative success of both societies seemed to prove the virtue of a managed society. The left had to explain whether a mixed economy was 'better' than a private economy. If nationalisation was the answer, then why did the list of societies with the most state ownership include both Stalin's Russia and Mussolini's Italy? Were they really a model for socialists? This question was not merely a theoretical challenge but a practical one as well. Those people who supported nationalisation – or any alternative system – then went forward, and attempted to make it happen.

A fourth task was the need to explain and oppose fascism. At the start of our period the socialists could feel secure that theirs was the only angry party of the dispossessed. Yet by the late 1920s another mass movement had emerged, which claimed to surpass the passion of the left. The ways in which socialists tried to make sense of fascism were complex and often contradictory. In Italy, the socialists and Communists first ignored the threat, as they sought to make sense of their own recent divisions. In Britain, Labour's paper, the *Daily Herald*, initially dismissed Mussolini as a fanatical Communist. By the late 1920s, the German Communist Party had fallen into the opposite error, damning the German Socialists as 'social fascists'. Yet there were also thousands who urged the left to unite against the threat. Outside the mainstream left, such disparate voices as Leon Trotsky, Antonio Gramsci, the *Weltbühne* circle in Germany, August Thalheimer, Ignazio Silone and Wilhelm Reich recognised the threat.[3]

Finally, all socialists in this period had also to explain the old problem – one which they inherited from the Marxists of the pre-1914 era – of how to get from here to there? No socialist utopia would be created blindly. For the Communists of the 1920s, the answer was simple: activists should start by copying the organisational model of Lenin's Bolshevik Party. Likewise the advocates of reformist socialism were clear in their own minds that change would come through parliament. Between the extremes stood a number of interim positions. In the moments of global revolt, including 1956 and 1968, it was even possible to argue that both traditions were flawed, and that some other way should be found.

Between 1917 and 1989 the left was dominated by two powerful traditions, social democracy and Stalinism. Each had emerged from the split in the workers' international which took place at the end of the First World War. Initially, both emerged from revolutionary socialism. Yet the dissident Marxists defined themselves against each of these movements. Such writers as Hal Draper maintained that there was a socialist 'third camp' which was different from both Stalinism and social democracy. Yet one problem facing the dissidents was that most people considered 'the left' to mean socialists and Communists, and not much else. In order to understand why people broke from these traditions, risking terrible political isolation in the process, we must first understand what social democracy and Stalinism were like. One way to do this is to assess their performance against the tests that people set them. It was the failure of both traditions to live up to these challenges that explains why people left the major parties and set up organisations of their own.

Social democracy

For parliamentary socialism the decisive moment came in August 1914. We live on the other side of this chasm, and it is hard to conceive now the extent of the betrayal. Before then, it seemed possible that the socialist movement could act as an offensive instrument of the working class in its fight against capitalism. In

1907 and again in 1912, the socialist parties of the world had pledged that if a major conflict were to break out, they would respond with a general strike against war. This position was then defended in the socialist press and at innumerable anti-war congresses. Yet when the crisis came, the major socialist parties of the world – with a handful of exceptions – voted to support 'their' ruling classes, knowing full well that such a decision would condemn millions of workers to death. The German Socialist Party (SPD) was then the largest left-wing party in the world. Its leaders claimed to have inherited a radical legacy direct from Marx and Engels. When Lenin heard that the German Socialist deputies had voted to support the war, granting military credits to the government, he simply refused to believe the news. Writing from prison, Rosa Luxemburg of the SPD attempted to make sense of the role played by her own party.

> In the Second International German Social Democracy was the determining factor. In every Congress, in the meetings of the International Socialist Bureau, everything waited upon the opinions of the German group.... And what happened in Germany when the great historical crisis came? The deepest fall, the mightiest cataclysm. Nowhere was the organisation of the proletariat so completely subservient to imperialism.... Nowhere was the press so thoroughly gagged, public opinion so completely choked off; nowhere was the political and industrial class struggle of the working class so entirely abandoned as in Germany.[4]

The effects of August 1914 were decisive. From then on, the world's socialist parties set themselves more limited goals. The idea of a different sort of society was postponed into the indefinite future. Afterwards, if the parties evolved, they moved to the right.

Having failed the test of 1914, parliamentary socialism again failed to act as a consistent, strong barrier against the rise of fascism. This process is profoundly ironic, because nothing motivated Mussolini or Hitler so much as a visceral hatred of socialism. When Hitler announced that he would be 'the destroyer of Marxism', he did not mean the small German Communist Party, but rather the huge Socialist Party, with its massive trade unions and cultural associations. Indeed the Nazis paid the SPD the ultimate compliment, modelling their own party on the mass structures of the socialists. The first victims of both dictatorships were the left, who constituted the first targets of street attacks, the first people to find themselves jailed in concentration camps. In Germany, the Socialists submitted tamely, pretending to themselves that 'legality' would 'tame' the Nazis, as indeed it had tamed them. Admittedly in France and Spain socialist parties did form a mass alliance with local Communists – but by then the greatest damage had been done.

After the war, the process of political dilution continued. For most supporters of the reformist parties, socialism came to mean little more than a strong welfare state. In Germany, the SPD declared its rejection of its older 'Marxist' programme in 1959. In Britain, the most distinctive feature of 'old Labour' ideology was its commitment to public ownership, expressed in Clause IV of Labour's constitution, which was printed on the back of every Labour Party membership card. The first Labour leader to call for the removal of this clause was Hugh Gaitskell in the early 1960s. In Spain and Portugal, the key moment came following the fall of military dictatorships whose origins dated back to the inter-war years. In the aftermath, socialist parties were able to present themselves as the most careful champions of a transition to European-style capitalism. Meanwhile, an increasing number of Third World parties, often groups that had begun as independence movements, including the African National Congress (ANC) in South Africa and Congress in India, came to adopt the same politics as the Western parties. As social democracy spread throughout the globe, it was not radicalised.

If anything continued to hold the socialist parties to the left, it was in many countries their rivalry with the Communists. In this sense, 1989 was a watershed also for the parliamentary left. The collapse of the Soviet Union seemed to prove to the socialist parties that the old barriers between parliamentary left and right were meaningless. Afterwards, they struggled to seize the ground of privatisation from the right. Under the shadow of the supposed end of history, such parties as the SPD, Labour in Britain and Australia, ditched the last vestiges of any commitment to a different economic order.

In conclusion, we can say that the response of social democracy to the challenges it faced was expressed primarily by adapting to the existing capitalist system. The failure of social democracy, then, is not merely the betrayal of 1914. The problems continue beyond then. As reformism aged, it accepted ever more keenly the logic of competing businesses and competing nation-states. The purpose of government was increasingly seen by social democrats as being to secure the relative advantage of 'their' national bloc of capital. Initially, the hope may have been that, in defending their own boss class, this process would secure benefits that might trickle down to the workers. By the end of our period, this identification between social democracy and business was so close that, to all intents and purposes, what existed was another set of pro-capitalist parties.

Stalinism

How did the politics of the Soviet Union face up to the test of the short twentieth century? Again, it is useful to see this process through the eyes of the dissidents, the people who would eventually break from Communist politics. The first point to make is that (unlike social democracy) the Stalinist tradition was content to claim the mantle of revolutionary socialism, and continued to assert this legacy even when the USSR had become one of the most conservative societies in the world. People outside Russia believed that it was the classic example of a socialist country, and that the Soviet Union represented the fate of Marxism. Yet the people of the Eastern bloc were forced to live in the disjunction between an ideology of human liberation and a reality which was entirely at odds with the words. In Stalin's Gulags the morning alarm sounded to wake the inmates with the words of 'The Internationale': 'Arise ye starvelings from your slumber, Arise ye prisoners of want.' Ordinary people survived the contradiction by immersing themselves in a counter-world of jokes and cynicism. 'Under capitalism man exploits man. Under communism, it is exactly the reverse.' 'Is it true that Joseph Stalin collects political jokes? No, but he collects people who tell them.' The decline of the revolution was a horrible, embittering experience.

Yet the beginning of this society could not have been more different, as we have seen. In its first years, the Soviet Union was a genuinely revolutionary society. The first problem facing the revolution was its isolation. Both Lenin and Trotsky had always insisted that the revolution must spread, or it would be defeated. The model they had in mind was the Paris Commune of 1871, when insurgents held a city for two months, before being defeated by military forces sent from the outside. No one predicted that the Russian Revolution could be defeated by a counter-revolution that would emerge from within.

The setbacks came thick and fast. Within six months of taking power, the Bolsheviks were forced to conclude a peace treaty with Germany. At this very moment their allies, the Left Social Revolutionaries, left the government, indeed declared war on them. There followed two years of brutal civil strife. The war ended with a further cycle of peasant revolts in Russia. At the end of them, Kronstadt, the red fortress, revolted against its own former leaders. Lenin responded to threats with concessions, but at each stage the revolutionary content of the workers' state was diminished. Communist-led revolts were defeated in Munich, Berlin and Budapest. Meanwhile in Russia, a bureaucracy emerged. By the last years of the 1920s, Stalin had taken power. Within Russia, he was seen as the champion of the new state order. Finally, his ascendancy was marked by the collectivisation of the farms. The peasants were driven off the land, supposedly into collective farms, but most migrated to the cities, to endure starvation wages. In the subsequent famines millions died. In the towns and in the factories, the revolutionary workers of 1917 were finally displaced by a new generation who knew only rumours of the memory of struggle.

The internal defeat of the revolution had consequences for the many activists abroad who looked to Russia for their model of socialism. The parties of the Communist International were instructed to follow the many twists and turns of Soviet foreign policy, waltzing left and right and back to a tune set by Moscow. Many activists were baffled by the whole experience, and simply dropped out of the movement. Even those who continued to accept the necessity of Russian leadership found that the process changed them. In the late 1920s, they were expected to be as ultra-left as possible. In the late 1930s, they were instructed to seek deals with socialists, liberals and patriotic conservatives. The glue that held this mix together was a rigid and undialectical 'Marxism'. The formula went something like this. All workers were either passive and apolitical or Marxists. Communism was the only party of the working class. Likewise Russia was the only country where the workers had taken power. Therefore the role of Communists was to follow the 'proletarian' party line. This summary is of course exaggerated. In many situations, individuals were able to organise around the party, and created a more democratic culture in the struggles outside. Yet the people who began this process were typically deemed 'oppositionists', and many ended up siding with the dissidents described here.

Following the end of the war, the Russian bloc included the states of Eastern Europe, and soon afterwards China. Yet this process of territorial expansion proved hard to manage. Over time, increasing numbers of Communist states sought to distance themselves from the Soviet Union. The first was Yugoslavia, under Marshall Tito at the end of the 1940s. The second was Mao's China, twenty years later. Tensions at a state level were also played out in the Western Communist Parties. Traditionally, the Communist Parties of the world had been organised in an international association, the Communist International or 'Comintern'. After 1945 this body was replaced by a looser association, the 'Cominform'. In retrospect, it appears to be true that the leaders of the Soviet Union felt a decreasing need to threaten the rulers of the West with the prospect of working-class revolt. The Russians possessed the atomic bomb and that was security enough for them.

By the end of our period, the Soviet Union was in some disarray. The high economic growth rates of the 1960s gave way to a new condition of near-permanent stagnation. From 1980, the economy ceased to grow. Meanwhile, the rulers of the Soviet Union found that they could no longer afford to pay the cost of a 5 million-strong standing army. Military defeat in Afghanistan raised the question of whether there was still any point in the USSR fighting a cold economic war against the USA. Mikhail Gorbachev attempted to resolve the crisis through economic and political reform (perestroika and glasnost). The processes of reform proved too tough to control, though, and the Soviet Union collapsed.

Given the several challenges that faced the left between 1917 and 1989, we can now see why it was that so many socialists determined to oppose the Soviet Union, and that Marxism which was championed in its name. If the purpose of the socialist movement was to create an equal, just society based on working-class democracy, then from the late 1920s (if not before) the rulers of Russia were on the other side of the barricades.

There were many different attempts to make sense of what had gone wrong. Some argued that Russia was a degenerated workers' state, others that it was a form of state capitalism, or bureaucratic collectivism, or a society led by a new class. Others employed the label 'totalitarian', which was mainly borrowed from the political scientists and journalists of the West.[5] The relative merit of these tags is discussed in this book in the chapter on Korsch. Behind all these labels were attempts to explain the Soviet Union, to learn from the lessons of the defeat, and to build something different, so that a new generation of socialists could grow up without the cynicism of those who had seen Russia fall.

In terms of the challenges that the activists of the left set themselves, it was only right therefore to describe parliamentary socialism and Soviet-style Communism as two failed Marxist traditions. There clearly existed some space, then, for rival movements that were part of the left, but that rejected in practice that top-down tradition within socialism, which was the common source of both Stalinism and social democracy. The remainder of this chapter will describe some of those trends, including Trotskyism and the New Lefts of 1956 and 1968, their solutions to the various challenges that faced the left, the moment at which they emerged, their logic and their performance since.

Trotskyism

The first of the dissident Marxist traditions dates from Lenin's death, and the subsequent struggle for power between Stalin and Trotsky. Leon Trotsky (1879–1940) had been the public face of the revolution in 1917. A sublimely talented organiser and speaker, Trotsky led the Red Army to victory in the Russian Civil War of 1918–21. Trotsky's greatest contribution to the revolution dated back to the pre-revolutionary period. In the aftermath of the first, 1905, revolution, Trotsky began to formulate an approach that argued that Russian workers could indeed seize power. This theory of 'permanent revolution' began with the most basic claim common to all Russian Marxists, that a revolution in a feudal society could only produce a capitalist state. The difficulty with this theory was that most Russian workers were unwilling to undergo a long struggle only to achieve capitalism and wanted to establish a more equal society straight away. Trotsky argued that this problem could be surmounted, provided that the revolution was extended to other societies, so that the issue would not be the future of Russia, but the future of Europe. In Russia alone you could not achieve socialism, but socialism could happen if the revolt became international. In the run-up to October 1917, Lenin accepted the implications of this argument, and shared with Trotsky the idea that the revolution could only succeed if it spread.

The early to mid-1920s were a period of bureaucratisation in Russia. The power of the state grew tremendously, and popular control over the apparatus diminished. Russia returned to an era of social peace, under the control of Stalin's group. Not surprisingly, Trotsky's star waned. Leon Trotsky tended to perceive the party struggles as a conflict for the soul of the revolution. Against the theory of permanent revolution, Stalin and Bukharin defended the rival approach of 'Socialism in One Country'. Trotsky interpreted the idea that Russia could progress alone towards socialism as a complete rejection of Marx's idea that capitalism was a global system, which had to be defeated on a global terrain.

Having been expelled from Russia at the end of the 1920s, Trotsky then grouped together his followers into a movement. He established a newspaper, *The Bulletin of the Opposition*, and published a series of books to explain his differences with Stalin. One of the most important was *The Revolution Betrayed* (1937),[6] in which Trotsky insisted that revolutionary Russia was a degenerated workers' state – a shadow of its former self.

Initially the idea of the Left Opposition was to build groups within each of the Communist Parties. This idea was dropped following Hitler's accession to power in Germany in 1933. Both socialists and Communists had appeared more keen to fight each other than Hitler. Leon Trotsky concluded that the two monoliths were bankrupt, and an entire new international movement should be built. Yet there were many obstacles in his path. One problem was that the group Trotsky looked to as his allies were the 'centrist' parties of the former Amsterdam International – groups like the SAP in Germany, the POUM in Spain and the Independent Labour Party (ILP) in Britain. These recruited leftward-moving former social democrats. The pressure of events pushed these parties towards Marxism, but as the 1930s went on the pressure eased, and the politics of the groups drifted in all sorts of different directions. In Spain the POUM remained revolutionary, but Trotsky fell out with the leaders of the party, when they supported a Popular Front alliance with liberals, socialists and Stalinists. In Britain, the ILP was a much less impressive body of men. In unfavourable circumstances, Trotsky determined to create a revolutionary party in the image of Lenin's Bolsheviks. Lenin was always an ardent polemicist, he believed in political clarity, and his idea of a revolutionary party emphasised the need for political and ideological unity among the comrades. Through all the rows, his party was often held together by little more than the favourable tide of history. Sadly, Trotsky was not working in such easy times. The rows multiplied, and even such loyal followers as the revolutionary writer and novelist Victor Serge drifted away. Towards the end of the 1930s, Trotsky did declare a Fourth International, but the groups represented by it were small.

Following Leon Trotsky's death in 1940 at the hands of one of Stalin's agents, the Trotskyist movement lost his guiding hand. Over the next fifty years the movement seemed to possess two faces. On the one hand, it possessed an extraordinarily powerful political and moral critique of Stalinism. With this advantage, the Trotskyist movement was able to win (for shorter or longer periods) the support of a series of remarkably talented writers and activists who graced the socialist movement. One example was C.L.R. James, one of the finest black radicals of the twentieth century, whose book *The Black Jacobins* opened up the story of the great slave revolts, and transformed the way in which we think about the emancipation of the slaves.[7] Others have included such figures as Tariq Ali, Brian Behan, Saul Bellow, Robert Brenner, André Breton, James P. Cannon, Tony Cliff, Hal Draper, Terry Eagleton, Paul Foot, Daniel Guérin, Duncan Hallas, Sidney Hook,

Irving Howe, Ernest Mandel and Sheila Rowbotham. On the other hand, what struck outsiders was the movement's fissiparous character. Many of the parties were too small to be viable. Others took over from Trotsky's last years the worst aspects of the Leninist organisational style. Anyone who experienced the organisational chauvinism of a Gerry Healy, or a Juan Posadas, would know the faults only too well. One of the arguments of this book is that the most creative of latter-day Trotskyists emerged often against the tide of 'orthodoxy' in their movement.

The strengths and faults of this politics can be traced back to the extraordinary character of its founder. Trotsky was without doubt optimistic, brave and generous. He expressed these virtues in his political work and the many ways in which he developed Marxist theory. Yet this book follows John Molyneux's approach in arguing that for all the clarity of such theoretical innovations as permanent revolution, there was a residual legacy of an earlier, more deterministic Marxism in Trotsky's politics.[8] In the late 1930s his political writing showed a tendency to treat all disasters as if they were the final catastrophe of capitalism. He made repeated predictions, many of which came true, but none as soon as had been announced. His party attracted ideologues not workers. He also passed on a certain unwillingness to admit errors – a point repeatedly made by Victor Serge. Why could Trotsky not see that he had been wrong to argue for the militarisation of labour in 1920? Or to defend the destruction of the Kronstadt rebels in 1921? Trotsky's response – that the strategy of the Kronstadt rebels had been equally flawed – contained a grain of truth, but was no answer to all of Serge's criticisms.

It would be churlish to harp on these faults. Of all the dissident traditions that emerged in the twentieth century, Trotskyism was the one which retained most of Marx's conviction that socialism could come about only through a workers' revolution. Trotsky's ideas inspired many of the writers discussed in this book.

The first New Left (1956)

So long as the Communists continued to drift to the right, it was always likely that they would produce rival traditions, based on people who believed that there were more revolutionary possibilities open to the left. When the outside world appeared quiet, then it was hard to avoid the conclusion that there was no life outside the Socialist or Communist Parties. Yet there were also moments when the rebellion of thousands of young workers or students threatened to create healthy movements outside the big battalions of the existing left. The first such moment appeared in 1956. Following the British attempt to take Suez, the Soviet invasion of Hungary, and Khrushchev's speech denouncing Stalin, thousands left the European Communist Parties. A New Left was born. In this book, the chapter on Dona Torr and Edward Thompson relates the early history of this movement.

In France and Britain the dominant figures were Jean-Paul Sartre (1905–1980) and Edward Thompson (1924–93). Both were aware of the history of earlier left traditions, and attempted to defend the most important kernel of their insights. Sartre's dissidence dates from the period after 1956. He was already 35 years old when he committed himself to socialism, and over 50 by the time that he broke decisively from Stalinism, following the use of Soviet tanks to crush the Hungarian revolution. Sartre saw his role as being to enrich and develop Marxism, without reducing its power as an explanatory device. The target of his criticism was the Communist use of the dialectic. In Marx's hands, he insisted, this method was a tool to understand change in human history. In the hands of the Communists it became a defence of historical necessity. The fact that a powerful state (Russia) existed proved that its cause was just. Sartre began by rejecting the idea that knowledge was a reflection of reality. He preferred to emphasise the active role played by human consciousness in understanding the world. The dialectic was a relationship between a human subject and an external object. It was a logic of action, as people were born free, were subject to social rules, and attempted to free themselves again. Sartre maintained that there was always a part for people to play in making their world. Western Communism, making its excuses for Stalin's terror, was no more than a shadow of what could be achieved.[9]

Edward Thompson reached a similar conclusion on the basis of a different, more historical method. Thompson had been a leading figure in the old British Communist Party's peace work, a member of its Yorkshire committee, and was a prominent Communist historian. Together with other disillusioned comrades, he produced a newsletter *The Reasoner*, which became *The New Reasoner*, and then merged with the *Universities and Left Review* to form the *New Left Review*.[10] E.P. Thompson's main contribution to the movement was to defend a new form of Marxism, which he (like Sartre) termed 'socialist humanism'. His starting point was the claim that the philosophy of the Communist Party had become ossified, a 'diabolical and hysterical materialism', which detected patterns in human history more powerful than the agency of any human being. Against this barrier, Thompson insisted on the importance of human experience. This was the basic material of history, and through history, human experience was the fount of all knowledge.

We can see how the New Left answered the challenges facing the left. The movement was profoundly internationalist; one of its most important children was the global Campaign for Nuclear Disarmament. The New Left was critical of Russian Communism and Soviet Marxism. On the negative side, we might say that the movement lacked an economic theory. Its moral critique of Stalinism appeared to many people ungrounded and incomplete. On the other hand, it did possess a theory of how socialism could become real. The answer would be found in the activity of human beings in the labour and peace movements. One of the most impressive features of this tradition was precisely its activism. Thompson's private correspondence is full of letters apologising for the delay in delivering a manuscript, or for his inability to begin what had looked to him like an interesting project. There was always a cause to build, always a demonstration to lead.

The second New Left (1968)

The last group to mention here is the second New Left, which emerged out of 1968, the moment when protesting students in Paris sparked the biggest general strike in European history. This latter movement shared with 1956 the sense that both groups of rulers were equally to blame: the USA was stuck in Vietnam; Soviet tanks put an end to the Prague Spring. Many of the people involved in the first movement became involved in the second. Their common legacy expressed itself in a cumulative anger. Where

1956 differed from 1968 was in the extent of the rebellion. The second New Left came much closer to creating *the* revolution. In France, student protests sparked workers' mass strikes. Yet the decline of the movement was not as inspiring as its rise. With the defeat of the young students' and workers' hopes came a new mood of despair, which dominated intellectual life from the late 1970s to the end of our period. At the end of its useful life, the May 1968 generation invented a new academic Marxism, placing questions of culture so high on the agenda that the concerns of ordinary people were left well behind. The meaning of 1968 forms a backdrop to two of the chapters in this book. Harry Braverman was one of a generation who, despite all their talents, could not relate to the new movement. David Widgery, by contrast, incarnated the best features before the decline.

There was one further feature that distinguished 1968 from 1956. The latter revolt gave rise to myriad movements of the oppressed, including Black Power, women's and gay liberation. None of these movements makes any historical sense unless we begin by recognising that they emerged to challenge not just the racism and sexism of capitalist society, but the residual traces of oppression that people encountered even on the left. The clearest examples of the problem come from the history of the American left. When radical women tried to raise the issue of sexism at national conventions of Students for a Democratic Society (SDS), they were shouted down by their male comrades. Black Panther Eldridge Cleaver claimed that raping white women was an act of political resistance. Another leading activist, Stokeley Carmichael, claimed that 'the only position for women in SDS is prone'.[11] Similar sexism in Italy tore the revolutionary left to pieces.

At their best, the traditions of Black Power, gay and women's liberation attempted to reinfuse socialism with a new breadth of vision. Against the Stalinist and social-democratic monoliths, the 1968 activists insisted on the power of people to change the world. Faced with much the same dilemmas as previous generations, they had something useful to say. In both Britain and America, for example, socialist feminists insisted that the labour movement should learn from women's liberation. Why not apply the collective habits of revolutionary feminism to reinvigorate the socialist parties and trade unions? Sadly, by the time this idea caught on, the appeal of both class and gender politics was on the wane. Yet, rather than dwelling on the movement in decline, it would be better to remember the generous face of the movement at its height.

The dissident situation

It should be clear from this short summary that there was no such thing as a single dissident Marxist situation. Instead, a socialist could find him- or herself in such a position by any number of roads. The most obvious route would have been through political opposition to the Soviet state. These were the first dissidents, who best deserved the name. Yet a dissident could just as easily emerge from those writers and political activists arguing in Germany for a United Front of socialists against Hitler in the early 1930s; from post-war American leftists arguing 'Neither Washington nor Moscow'; or from those young French workers who struck in 1968, against the orders of the French Stalinists.

Indeed, one theme of this book is that the moment of dissidence mattered. For several of the figures discussed in this book, the most important moments were the high points of 1917, 1936, 1956 or 1968. Other writers and activists complained that having grown up in traumatic but exciting times, they were then forced to live in a different, more conservative world. One author who described this problem was Harry Braverman. Having been born in 1920, Braverman was won to the revolution in his late teens. He became a leading figure in a party, the Socialist Workers Party, which based its practice on the idea that 1917 was the greatest moment in the entire history of the working-class movement. According to James P. Cannon, leader of the American SWP, writing in 1955:

> The Russian way is the way to our American future, to the future of the whole world. The greatest thinkers of the international movement since Marx and Engels, and the greatest men of action, were the Russian Bolsheviks. The Russian Revolution is still there to prove it, ruling out all argument. The revolution still stands as an example: all the perversions and betrayals of Stalinism cannot change that.[12]

Yet the mid-1950s were a period of boom, a time of full employment, home- and car-ownership. The political certainties which drove men like Cannon seemed increasingly remote to activists of Braverman's generation. In 1958, he wrote an essay entitled 'Marx in the Modern World'. Its subject was the enormous gap between the political situation which socialists had been led to expect, and the reality they faced:

> The capitalist system has persisted and restabilized itself repeatedly, over a much longer period than had been expected ... Marx and the movement he shaped operated on the basis of imminent crisis. If he never gave thought to the kind of living standard inherent in a capitalism that would continue to revolutionize science and industry for another hundred years, that was because he thought he was dealing with a system that was rapidly approaching its Armageddon.[13]

Braverman's most basic premiss was that life itself had disproved Marx's analysis of capitalism as a chaotic system which would produce mass protest. Such an argument could not have been made in 1917, nor during the workers' uprising in revolutionary Spain. It made more sense, though, against a backdrop of Truman, Eisenhower and McCarthy.

In revolutions and in revolutionary rehearsals, including 1936, 1956 and 1968, dissident Marxism began to find its audience. Then the collision between Trotskyism and the New Left proved creative. From these different traditions, a more exciting politics could emerge. It is a creativity that Karl Korsch detected in the workers' councils of his native Germany, and that Dave Widgery found in the radical counterculture of the bohemian 1960s.

As the moment of dissidence mattered, so did its outcome. For many of the activists described in this book, one great dilemma was how best to relate to the existing parties of the left. In order to become a political class, conscious in itself, confident for change, the working-class movement needed ideas and organisation. However, permanent structures provided obstacles as well as opportunities. Such parties were shaped by the downtimes of the 1930s and 1950s. Both social-democratic and Communist parties appointed a layer of functionaries, who retained the collective memory not of the whole working class but of its bureaucratic organisations. Labour and trade-union leaders 'knew' not to trust their members ... because in the previous downtimes these people had not fought. Likewise the apparatchiks of the Western Communist parties 'knew' how important it was to stress that Russia was socialist ... because if nothing else this myth held together a group of activists, when the times were against the whole movement. The problem of bureaucratisation was clearest when the mood was most radical, and the rank and file strong in its opposition to the moderate paths advocated by their leaders. Most of the people discussed in this book grappled (at one time or another) with the problems of political organisation. Dona Torr identified with a Leninist, even Stalinist, organisation. David Widgery worked in a consistent but critical relationship to his own party.

The chapters which follow are necessarily historical. Their subject is the relationship between the Marxist method and the different times through which subsequent generations lived. It does not matter that Marxist theory was borrowed from the work of a man who died as long ago as 1883. What matters here is the ability of subsequent writers and activists to reapply this method to the world in which people actually lived. One theme of this book is that the best Marxist solutions to the problems of the short twentieth century were not created on the basis of one tradition alone. Instead they were found most often in a collision between different traditions, and also in a living dialogue with the moment of their birth.

Mayakovsky, Kollontai, Lunacharsky, Serge: questioning the Soviet path

One of the arguments of this book is that dissident Marxism was a response to the twin monoliths of Stalinism and social democracy. In the period after Stalin came to power in Russia, and after the defeat of the remaining hopes of the October Revolution, millions of people across the world still called themselves Marxists. Yet their loyalty to the Russian state forced them to defend the most terrible crimes, including the murder of the so-called Old Bolsheviks following the Moscow show trials, and the disappearance of millions in the 1930s. The dissidents were those who continued to think for themselves. One reason why they were able to do this was because many of them retained in their hearts some living appreciation of how great the October Revolution had been, before it was undermined by Stalin and his cabal. In order that revolutionaries such as Leon Trotsky, Karl Korsch or Victor Serge could explain their different interpretations of Marx, each first had to be clear in their own explanation of what had happened in Russia, what was happening, and what had gone wrong. While other chapters examine one writer's contribution to a Marxist theory of philosophy or another writer's contribution towards the development of a socialist understanding of history, the focus of this chapter is different. It begins with the lives of three leading Soviet citizens, Vladimir Mayakovsky, Alexandra Kollontai and

Anatoly Lunacharsky, each of whom was devoured by the spirit of defeat in the 1920s and 1930s. It ends with Victor Serge, and his explanation of the revolution's internal decay.

Vladimir Mayakovsky

Vladimir Mayakovsky was one of a generation of poets who having witnessed the 1917 October Revolution, pledged themselves to it. His contemporaries included Aleksandr Blok, Andre Biely, Nikolas Kilouev, Sergey Yesenin, Konstantin Balmont, Valery Bryusov, Vserolod Ivanov, and Sergey Gorodetsky. Few of them loved the revolution spontaneously. What enthused them was rather its contempt for the previous society, and its goal of profound change. Mayakovsky's socialism was equally passionate, but more deep-rooted than that of his friends. Nothing was more consistent than his rage against the old order. As Victor Serge wrote, 'A vehement revolt broods in him.'[1] David Widgery devoted an early article to Mayakovsky's communism, which was, 'like him, broad shouldered and larger than life, impatient, rude and necessary'.[2] Such grand and generous politics could not escape the stifling grasp of Stalinism. As the old tsarist order of state bureaucracy and police action re-established itself, Vladimir Mayakovsky killed himself in April 1930.

Vladimir Mayakovsky's life was caught up in the tide of revolution. Born in 1893, he was just 11 years old when the news came in of Bloody Sunday, and the tsar's murder of a thousand loyal workers. Soon Mayakovsky was attending a clandestine Marxist circle and learned to call himself a socialist. He became his school's chief leaflet distributor. Aged 13, Mayakovsky joined the Bolshevik Party, presenting the local cell with his father's shotgun. At 15 he was arrested. A group of Bolsheviks had attempted to break certain comrades from prison. Mayakovsky remained for eleven months in Boutirky jail. On his release, he found Russia changed. The period between 1906 and 1914 was a bleak time. Tsarism succeeded in re-establishing its hold, and the revolutionaries were forced on to the defensive. According to Serge, 'The defeat of the Revolution of 1905 resounded long in the spirits of the intellectuals. The art of this time was individualistic, mystical, or mystico-sexual.'[3] As for

Mayakovsky, his art was resolutely grounded in the condition of the coming machine age. The enormous expansion of industry seemed to speak to the condition of the future. There was no point writing in the old realist tradition. 'In the name of Futurism, he and his fellow poets and sculptors travelled Russia, reading poems, denouncing the Tsar and unfurling their manifesto. In many towns they were banned on sight and they remained unpublished.'[4]

All over Europe, previous naturalistic conventions were breaking down – in art, poetry and fiction. The new art rejected illustration in favour of abstraction, and praised pure form over literal inspiration. In many countries, the most resolute of modernist poets and visual artists were dubbed 'futurists'. The Italian poet Filippo Marinetti sang the praise of sexism, xenophobia and war. The British futurist–vorticist Wyndham Lewis listed his enemies as 'nature cranks, domesticated policemen and socialist playwrights'.[5] In Italy, futurism developed a cult of speed, of the pilot and the racing driver. According to Widgery, 'Marinetti and Mayakovsky met only once and hated each other's guts.'[6] Their poetry had a similar notion of form, but Mayakovsky's poems had a creative purpose, democracy.

Vladimir Mayakovsky's first masterpiece, *A Cloud in Trousers*, a long poem of love and violence, goes back to 1914. It fused together two stories of passion, the private joys of romantic lovers, with the collective spirit of human solidarity. Victor Serge wrote, 'If Mayakovsky had remained with his beautiful talent, situated in the large, Bohemian capitalist city, his art would not belong today. After October 1917, it would belong to the past. But the Revolution knew how to renew itself'[7] – as indeed did Mayakovsky.

War and revolution radicalised the entire Russian people, including the avant-garde. The centre of the revolt was Petrograd, a city dominated by giant engineering works. Capitalism began late in Russia, but, having arrived, it took the most modern forms. Steve Smith's history of the revolution in that city has uncovered a complex world of plebeian democracy. It was only by late summer that Lenin's Bolsheviks had won a majority, even in the cities. Their ascendancy coincided with a clearing out in the factories. At the giant Putilov works, the director and his aides were murdered by angry workers. Elsewhere foremen and royalists found themselves doused in red lead. Workers campaigned for the eight-hour day, and for the greatest possible forms of direct democracy.[8]

As soon as the October Revolution began, Vladimir Mayakovsky took its side. As Trotsky wrote, 'It was more natural for Mayakovsky than for any other Russian poet, because it was in accordance with his entire development.'[9] The will of the revolt was to break with all tradition. Mayakovsky's rapidly became the choice of a majority. The futurists were the first artists to place themselves beneath the banner of the October Revolution. Mayakovsky found himself writing for a series of radical publications, *Art of the Commune*, *Life* and *New Life*. It was in this period that Mayakovsky's great, triumphant poem *The 150,000,000* was published. The work appeared initially without the name of an author, because Russia had become a nation of 150 million creators:

> We will smash the old world
> wildly
> we will thunder
> a new myth over the world.
> We will trample the fence
> of time beneath our feet.
> We will make a musical scale
> of the rainbow.
>
> Roses and dreams
> Debased by poets
> will unfold
> in a new light
> for the delight of our eyes
> the eyes of big children.
> We will invent new roses
> roses of capitals with petals of squares.[10]

The period from autumn 1917 to spring 1921 was the most difficult, dangerous moment. Hundreds of thousands of people died in the Civil War. At times, White armies were camped even on the outskirts of Red Petrograd. Leading Bolsheviks looked to the historical experience of the Paris Commune to explain their own condition. The struggle ahead of them was a war between the radical population of the cities and the conservatism of the rural areas. They had to win over the people who worked on the land.

The Bolsheviks broke up the landlords' estates, and gave the land to the peasants. More problems followed. What could the cities trade? Rationing and problems of supply reduced the standards of living in the cities to a level of collective starvation. The working-class cadres of Bolshevism died in their thousands at the front. Yet for the early champions of the revolution, this was also its heroic period. Serge's staccato prose describes a time of 'Blockade, famine, Denikin, Yudenich, Kolchak. The Republic bleeds by a thousand wounds. The poet is a workman of propaganda.'[11] Mayakovsky undoubtedly revelled in the moment. 'The work of the poet does not stop at the book; meetings, speeches, front-line limericks, one-day agit-prop playlets, the living radio-voice and the slogan flashing by on trams.'[12]

At this time, Mayakovsky's work was closest to the Russian school of constructivism, the most geometrical of all the abstract styles. This approach possessed a dual radicalism. The art of the constructivists looked and sounded new, but it also related to the very idea of culture in new ways. The sculptors, artists and poets of this school determined to blast art out of its old elitist conventions. Paintings should appear not in gilt frames but on the side of match-boxes. To borrow a phrase from Walter Benjamin, the constructivists were concerned to strip away the 'aura' from a work of art.[13]

Constructivism was not the only art school to thrive in the aftermath of 1917. One major rival was Proletkult, which was sponsored by several leading 'left Bolsheviks', including A.A. Bogdanov and Anatoly Lunacharsky.[14] Proletkultists often preferred realism to abstraction, agitation to innovation. Their school argued that authentic members of the Russian working class should prepare to take over the running of art. This latter demand appealed at times to Mayakovsky, who wrote in 1918: 'And why/ not attack Puskin/ and other generals of the classics?'[15] But the goal itself was flawed. As Lenin, Trotsky and many leading Bolsheviks pointed out, the Russian proletariat was a minority class whose future depended on forming an alliance with the workers of Western Europe. In the actual conditions of Russia 1917–21, the most revolutionary demands were for the state to open up the classics to the Russian people, and to tolerate or even encourage artistic innovation. Until the global isolation of October 1917 changed, and the revolution spread, such creativity would necessarily remain the preserve of a minority. 'Not a single progressive idea has begun with a "mass base"', Trotsky wrote, 'otherwise it would not have been a progressive idea. It is only in the last stage that the idea finds its masses.'[16]

In the years after 1921 the revolution entered into a new phase. With the ending of the Civil War, the position of the Bolsheviks was secured. Yet the urban population was exhausted, and the countryside remained hostile to the new regime. The revolution had failed to break beyond the limits of Russia. The Bolsheviks secured their survival by tolerating a limited restoration of market relations. The New Economic Policy (NEP) saw the emergence of a new generation of wealthy traders, the so-called 'Nepmen', who could acquire sufficient wealth to trade in the new stockmarkets of Moscow and St Petersburg. To many it seemed that capitalist relations were being tolerated. The only bulwark against the restoration of a private capitalist system was the vigilance of the Bolshevik Party. Yet even here, a new counter-revolutionary change was under way. Lenin's last work was a struggle against the bureaucratisation of the Soviet state.[17] His final 'testament' linked the decline of the revolution to the rise of Joseph Stalin as manager-in-chief. 'Stalin, having become General Secretary, has concentrated enormous power in his hands, and I am not sure he always knows how to use that power with sufficient caution ... I propose to the comrades to find a way to remove Stalin from that position.' Following several attempts on his life, strokes and a long illness, Lenin died in January 1924.

Mayakovsky felt increasingly separated from the nascent Soviet state. In his obituary poem *Vladimir Ilyich Lenin* (1924), the poet warned against the deification of his dead hero:

> I'm anxious lest rituals,
>   mausoleums,
>   and processions,
> the honeyed incense
>   of homage and publicity
> should
>   obscure
>   Lenin's essential
> simplicity.[18]

The NEP seemed to him to represent the re-creation of the old capitalist times. 'Many/ without you/ got right out of hand/ So many/ different/ rascals and blackguards/ Prowl about our Soviet land/ There's no end /to their numbers/ and aliases.'[19] *New Life* came under criticism, even from the poets of the Writers' Union RAPP. Mayakovsky was prevented from visiting his lover Tatiana in Paris. The avant-garde was denounced. Visiting dignitaries were taken to see the Bolshoi ballet. Paintings and photographs were doctored to remove the image of Stalin's critics, many of whom had played a much more prominent part than his in October 1917. In opposition to constructivism, Proletkult was supported by the most conservative artists – it embodied a simple and familiar naturalist aesthetic, which was less dangerous to the new leaders of the Soviet state.

In 1924, Victor Serge described Mayakovsky's work as 'The drama of a poet who cannot, in spite of his rough desire, escape from the past.'[20] According to Serge's *Memoirs*, this verdict was reported back to the poet, who confronted him angrily: 'Why do you say that my Futurism is no more than Past-ism?' To which Serge replied:

> Because your hyperboles and shouts, and even your boldest images, are all saturated with the past in its most wearisome aspects. And you write 'In men's souls, Vapour and electricity...' Do you really think that's good enough? Surely this is materialism of a peculiarly antiquated variety?

Serge concludes his account of their row: 'He knew how to declaim before crowds; but not how to argue. "Yes I'm materialist! Futurism is materialist!"'[21] With more than a hint of smugness, Serge diagnosed the poet's weakness as the inability to find a proper audience. How could anyone create the collective art appropriate to a new era – when the workers had always been a minority, and the revolution remained isolated? A similar point was made in Leon Trotsky's collection *Literature and Revolution*, 'the dynamic élan of the revolution and its stern courage appeal to Mayakovsky much more closely than do the mass character of its heroism and the collectivism of its affairs and experiences.'[22]

By the end of the 1920s, the revolutionary socialist Vladimir Mayakovsky was entirely separated from this new and hostile society. Here was an artist who flourished when protest was at its height. Yet under Stalin, the revolution was rolled back. The life of the whole nation became subject to censorship, and poetry could not stand alone. By 1930, the mass character, heroism and collectivism of the first months of the revolt belonged only to the past. Mayakovsky shot himself on 14 April 1930. According to one biographer, A.D.P. Briggs, 'The death of Mayakovsky has no single, straightforward explanation. There were at least three or four prime causes, failures in love, in his work and the public reception of it, in his health and in his inability to come to terms with an increasingly hostile political regime and public order.'[23] Mayakovsky's last poem proclaimed,

I abhor
   every kind of deathliness
I adore
   every kind of life.[24]

Alexandra Kollontai

The genius of Vladimir Mayakovsky lay in his ability to create a poetry that matched the enormous hopes raised by the revolution of October 1917. Mayakovsky's contemporary Alexandra Kollontai was engaged in a different form of creative labour. She more than anyone else was associated with the grand task of introducing women's liberation into the central strategies of the Bolshevik revolution. Years before, Friedrich Engels had followed Charles Fourier in arguing that the extent of progress towards women's equality was the most basic test of the general level of equality in society.[25] After 1917, Communists were faced with the challenge of turning these fine words into reality. This task they achieved with surprising success. In poor, backward Russia, torn as it was by the ravages of war, the Bolsheviks succeeded in granting women a panoply of rights (including the rights to free contraception, divorce, abortion, as well as equal pay) that bears comparison with anything achieved in the West, then or since. This process of achieving liberation was associated in many people's minds with the strong personality of Alexandra Kollontai, the world's first modern female cabinet minister, and for two key years the leader of the Bolsheviks' women's section, Zhenotdel. Yet the story is by no means only optimistic. The same processes of retreat that we have already encountered in the life of Mayakovsky also came to overshadow Kollontai's work. Her life also ended in defeat.

Alexandra Mikhailovna Domontovich was born on 1 April 1872, in St Petersburg. In her autobiography, Kollontai describes herself as 'the youngest, the most spoiled' of the children.[26] Her father was a tsarist general; her mother came from a family of Finnish merchants. The young Alexandra showed few signs of rebellion, her one unusual act being to marry a cousin, Vladimir Kollontai, for love, in 1893. Her family disapproved of the choice, for Vladimir was then just an engineer, although from their point of view he soon proved himself a success. One of Kollontai's close friends was a socialist, Elena Stasova, but in her first twenty-four years, Kollontai showed few signs of following this or any other political path.

In 1896, Kollontai was taken to visit the Krengol'mskaya factory in Narva. This experience made her realise the terrible conditions in which most workers lived. Kollontai sought out members of the Union of Struggle for the Working Class. A textile strike in St Petersburg the following year also helped to push her to the left. By 1898, Kollontai was enrolled on an economics course at the University of Zurich. Here she allied with the socialists on campus, including Friedrich Adler and Rosa Luxemburg. Kollontai also worked with the editors of the socialist magazine *Nuachnoye obozreniye* (*Scientific Review*). Following the 1905 revolution, Kollontai campaigned on the women's question and for Finnish independence. Her book *Finland and Socialism* resulted in an arrest warrant, and Kollontai was obliged to spent the period from 1908 to 1917 in exile.[27] Kollontai's life was devoted to women's politics. With this in mind, one biographer Beatrice Farnsworth asks why she allied with the revolutionary socialists and not with the Russian feminists? Farnsworth's answer is that such writers as Anna Filosofova or Nadezhda Stasova 'did not aim to change the conventional family structure'. By contrast, Kollontai's Communist critique of existing family relationships was much more angry and profound.[28]

In January 1909, Alexandra Kollontai joined the German Social Democratic Party. Invitations followed to speak, first on a tour through Germany, then in Britain, Denmark and Sweden. Kollontai addressed the 1910 international conference of women socialists. She also lectured at the Bolshevik Party school in 1911, which was organised by Lunacharsky and Bogdanov. Yet it was only in 1915 that Kollontai actually joined the Bolsheviks. Kollontai was among the first Bolsheviks to accept Lenin's *April Theses*, with their suggestion that a further revolution would be required to follow the first revolt in February. The October uprising was timed to coincide with the second national assembly of the workers' and soldiers' soviets, and resulted in a Bolshevik–Left Social Revolutionary coalition government. Alexandra Kollontai was appointed Commissar for Social Welfare.

Under the influence of prominent socialist-feminists, including Kollontai, the Bolshevik government introduced a series of measures that were designed to make women's equal status a reality. Women were granted the full right to vote, and the authority of family heads was ended. Marriage was changed from a religious to a civil process. Divorce was established, while laws were passed ending any legal distinctions between legitimate and illegitimate children.[29] Equal pay was placed on the Russian statute book, alongside equal employment rights and paid maternity leave. Adultery, incest and homosexuality were dropped from the criminal code. In 1920, revolutionary Russia introduced free abortion on demand. In 1923, a commission on birth control was established, to provide free access to contraception.[30] At this time, women had the vote in no countries other than Norway and Denmark. Free abortion existed nowhere else in the world. This bundle of activity has not been matched in the West to this day.

It is all very well passing laws, but initiatives such as equal pay can easily become meaningless, unless they are accompanied by a vigorous programme to implement them. This task was devolved to the Bolshevik Party's women's section, Zhenotdel, whose leaders included Inessa Armand, Alexandra Kollontai, and Klavdiya Nikolayeva. The first Zhenotdel conference was attended by 1,200 women in November 1918, and included Lenin among its speakers. During the Civil War, many women found themselves working in communal crèches and canteens.[31] The conditions for women seemed as inspiring as they did for poets and the avant-garde. By 1920, some 12 million people were being fed collectively. A network of communal flats was also established.[32] Over 100,000 literacy schools were established. Many Russian women were ready to thank the Bolsheviks for granting them some degree of freedom. 'Party membership of women nearly doubled, to 13.1 per cent in 1927. Female trade union membership rose from 1,449,000 in 1923 to 2,569,000 in 1927, when women were 26.1 per cent of the total membership.'[33]

This was extraordinary, difficult work. Hundreds of thousands were killed in a wretched civil war. Between 1918 and 1920, nearly 8 million Russians died from famine and epidemics. The natural workings of the factories ground to a halt, as Bolshevik workers volunteered to serve with the Red Army at the front. Each month the food ration was reduced, until it supplied barely one-tenth of the calories required. The determination of the Communists to build socialism even in this time appears extraordinary, almost recklessly generous, against such a background of mass squalor – in which they too suffered. Alexandra Kollontai had to argue with such allies as well as many critics. She was also often ill, suffering from typhoid, nephritis and a heart condition. Meanwhile, Beatrice Farnsworth records that several prominent Bolshevik women were initially unwilling to take part in Zhenotdel, feeling that their politics would be diminished by an exclusive interest in 'women's issues'.[34] They wanted to build socialism for everyone, not just themselves.

Alexandra Kollontai's work with Zhenotdel marked the high point of her political life. Not only was she a tireless activist; even the quality of her writing improved, as Kollontai was faced with the direct possibility of making the future real. One collection of short stories has been published in English as *Love of Worker Bees*.[35] An article from this period, 'Communism and the Family', predicted the imminent decline of women's household chores. Technology would serve to free women. Collective provision of laundries, and other 'domestic' services, would reduce the burden on individual women's lives. The weight of childcare would be liberated, 'Communist society will consider the social education of the rising generation as the very basis of its laws and customs.' Marriage would become more free. 'The red flag of the social revolution ... already proclaims to us the approach of the heaven on earth to which humanity has been aspiring for centuries.'[36]

Alexandra Kollontai was always an independent-minded Bolshevik. Such politics were more common then than is frequently supposed today. We forget that as late as 1921, the Bolshevik Party constitution tolerated the presence of permanent factions, minority groups that were allowed to organise in opposition to the party's Central Committee. We also tend to forget that party positions were elected, and that Lenin's authority as the leader of the Bolsheviks had to be earned – constantly – in the battle of hostile opinions.[37] All of these points conflict with the standard Western explanation of what went wrong in Russia, according to which the revolution was betrayed by some inner totalitarian logic,[38] set out in Lenin's pamphlet on party organisation, *What Is To Be Done?*[39]

There were at least three major controversies during which Kollontai found herself at odds with the party majority. The first, which has already been mentioned, was Kollontai's support for Lenin in April 1917. Most Bolsheviks preferred to wait and see what would come from the Provisional Government. Before Lenin's intervention, the practical politics of such figures as Stalin and Zinoviev were barely distinguishable from the positions of the Mensheviks. The second point of minority came when Kollontai opposed the Treaty of Brest–Litovsk, arguing that its terms would surrender the workers of Finland to mass slaughter, as indeed happened. In 1918, Kollontai was the only prominent Bolshevik to think along quite such lines. Yet the practical steps that would have followed from her ideas – Russia should continue to fight against Germany – were desired by a large minority, which included Nicolai Bukharin, a future darling of the Bolshevik right. Such views may not have been popular, but they were most certainly respected. The third point on which Kollontai stood alone was in her support for the Workers' Opposition of 1921–22. This platform attacked bureaucracy, and stood for the purge of middle-class elements from the Bolshevik Party. It argued for increased democracy and a return to proletarian norms. The faction was rapidly isolated and defeated. More and more of Kollontai's speeches were on the theme of tolerance. She told her listeners that the party should always allow a place for criticism by minority tendencies. One June 1920 speech began: 'Comrades, there should be a guarantee that if in fact we are going to criticise, and criticise thoroughly, what is wrong with us, then people who criticise should not be sent off to a nice sunny place to eat peaches. For this does happen, as we know.'[40] As Alix Holt reports, Kollontai 'does not seem to have come through the experience with the same unshaken belief in her own ideas'.[41]

From the early 1920s, Alexandra Kollontai's belief in equality came in for criticism. She was an easy target – a middle-class woman who had left her husband, and whose oppositional beliefs were well known. Her speeches were distorted. The form this attack often took was to take out of context a famous Kollontai speech in which she had said that sex in a socialist future should become an easy and uncomplicated act, like drinking a glass of water. This 'glass of water' speech was then used against her. In Kollontai's words, 'Many of the opponents of my writings tried to impose on me an absolutely false postulate that I was preaching "free love". I would put it the other way. I was always preaching to the women, make yourself free from the enslavement of love of a man.'[42]

As Kollontai fell out of favour, so the early burst of 'feminist' legislation was replaced by a new period in which women's conditions reverted back to something like the tsarist model. The rights to abortion and contraception were taken away. Women, as much as men, were the victims of the reintroduction of internal passports, and the catastrophic fall in working-class living standards that accompanied collectivisation. Zhenotdel was incorporated into the Stalinist state. In 1930 its slogan for International Women's Day was '100 per cent collectivisation'. In 1932 it was finally abolished. Notions of adultery, promiscuity and illegitimacy were introduced into law in 1936, homosexuality again became a criminal offence, and divorce was placed beyond the reach of working-class families. Between 1917 and 1930 there were 301 state resolutions and decrees based around the 'woman question', while between 1930 and 1967 there were just three.[43]

Although it began hopefully, the story of women's rights in the Soviet Union was not ultimately happy. In a period of declining women's rights, Alexandra Kollontai fell out of favour. She was sent as ambassador to Norway in 1922, and was transferred from there to further diplomatic postings in Mexico (1926–27), Norway (1927–30) and Sweden (1930–45). Alix Holt suggests that Kollontai used the latter post to defend an independent Finland from the worst aspects of Stalin's Greater Russian chauvinism. If this was so, then Kollontai enjoyed more freedom of manoeuvre than most of her contemporaries. She had to make the usual compromises in her conduct and in her public language. She undoubtedly experienced great sadness when the news came through of the Moscow Trials. Kollontai, the very first of the Bolshevik dissidents, was ironically the only Old Bolshevik (beyond Stalin himself) to survive the purges. At the age of 73 she retired from public duties, and settled in a two-room Moscow apartment. She died there of a heart attack in March 1952, the day after International Women's Day. Her death went unrecorded in the Soviet press.[44]

Anatoly Lunacharsky

Another revolutionary, Anatoly Lunacharsky was a talented playwright and a great stump orator. One biographer, A.L. Tait, writes that 'From the outset Lunacharsky was accustomed to performing before and winning the approval of an audience.'[45] He earned his place in history for creating a Bolshevik mass culture. In the years of revolutionary optimism, Lunacharsky was charged with supervising Soviet society in the fields of education and art. A man associated with a relatively narrow political past – the 'Left Bolshevik' empirio-monist position – in power Lunacharsky demonstrated a most extraordinary openness towards all forms of Russian art. He also supervised Soviet education in its more daring and creative years. Isaac Deutscher recalls a verdict from the time, according to which Lunacharsky was 'the intellectual among the Bolsheviks, the Bolshevik among the intellectuals'.[46]

Anatoly Lunacharsky was born in 1875; his mother was Aleksandra Yakovlena and her husband Vasilii Lunacharsky. His real father was almost certainly a state official by the name of A.I. Antonov, in whose liberal household the young Lunacharsky grew up. It was by all accounts a surprisingly happy situation. According to his own later version, Lunacharsky 'became a revolutionary so early that I can't remember a time when I wasn't one. My childhood passed under the powerful influence of Aleksandr Ivanovich Antonov, who although he was an Actual State Councillor ... was a radical and made no attempt to conceal his left-wing sympathies.' There was little religion in the household, and Lunacharsky was left free to run wild. Sadly, this idyllic time could not last. Antonov died in 1885, and the beautiful Aleksandra Yakovlena was forced to return to her husband, depressed and morose. Lunacharsky was a short-sighted child, but for some reason his mother denied him glasses. As a consequence he grew up bookish and quiet, a 'soft, indoor type'. It was only in his mid-teens that Anatoly was able to escape her influence. 'I fell in love with older women from an early age. I began to adore life.'[47]

Like several other leading Bolsheviks, Lunacharsky became a revolutionary in his mid-teens. He joined a student revolutionary movement, reading the great classic texts of Russian populism, including Mikhailovski and Chernyshevsky. By his own account our young activist first read Karl Marx's *Capital* in 1888, although it was only in the mid-1890s, as censorship eased, that such early Russian Marxists as Petr Struve or Georgi Plekhanov felt free to publish their work legally in their home country for the first time. Lunacharsky left Russia for Zurich University, and lived in Switzerland and France between 1895 and 1898. He met all the leading Russian exiles, including Georgi Plekhanov, Vladimir Lenin and Vera Zasulich.

At Zurich, Lunacharsky fell under the spell of the philosopher Avenarius. From this period onwards, he set himself the goal of uniting this theoretical school with the ideas of Marx. What this meant in practice was that Lunacharsky – together with his closest political ally, Bogdanov – adopted an idealist philosophy, according to which the purpose of socialism was to transform man in the image of the divine. Variously described as empirio-criticism or empirio-monism, the philosophy resembled anarchism (or later existentialism) in so far as it placed all emphasis on human choice and deliberate acts of will. 'To me the revolution was a stage', Lunacharsky once wrote, 'incredibly tragic, in the world-wide development of the human spirit towards the Universal Soul.'[48] Although

Lenin dedicated one of his famous polemics to the destruction of Bogdanov and his school,[49] it remains true that he thought highly of the younger man. For several years, Lunacharsky was employed as one of a handful of full-time Bolshevik journalists on papers including *Forward* and *The Proletarian*. Asked directly for his opinion, Lenin said of Lunacharsky, 'He is drawn irresistibly towards the future. That is why there is so much joy and laughter in him.'[50]

In the freedom of the 1905 revolution and its aftermath, Lunacharsky had several plays shown in St Petersburg, including *The King's Barber*, a satire on Tsarism. During the period of the two 1917 revolutions, Lunacharsky impressed as one of the public faces of Bolshevism. Lenin remained in hiding, while other Bolsheviks (including Stalin) lacked Lunacharsky's talent as a speaker. Deutscher describes Lunacharsky's 'indomitable militancy' in 1917. His regular audience was in the thousands. Only Trotsky was better known.[51] The times, he wrote, were 'colossal in everything, tragic and significant'.[52]

Following the victory of the October Revolution, Lunacharsky was awarded with the post of Commissar of Education. The Russian acronym for his ministry was 'Narkompros'. He resigned almost immediately, in protest against the damage caused by the Red Guards in their storming of the Kremlin in Moscow. When Lunacharsky received the support of his fellow commissars, however, the resignation was soon rescinded.[53] The great historian of Soviet Russia, Sheila Fitzpatrick, suggests that Lunacharsky made three outstanding contributions to the revolution. First, he encouraged the development of educational theory, promoting the idea that education should be democratised, encouraging those writers and educationalists who wanted to make the relationship between pupil and teacher more equal. Second, he gave a generous welcome to all healthy outpourings of science and culture, and markedly refrained from promoting only pro-Communist authors. Third, he demonstrated that universal education could be achieved in practice, throwing open the boundaries of primary, secondary and tertiary education, so that all Russians, no matter how poor they had been in the past, now had full access to learning.[54]

Anatoly Lunacharsky shouldered almost single-handedly the task of demonstrating to the world that revolutionary Russia possessed one of the world's great cultures. In his obituary to his former friend, Leon Trotsky described the frequent conflicts that arose between the Bolshevik regime and the universities and 'pedagogical circles in general'. Lunacharsky was given the task of reconciling the educators to Soviet power. 'More than one academic druid had to stare open-mouthed at this vandal, who could read half a dozen modern languages and two ancient ones and, in passing, unexpectedly displayed such a many-sided erudition as to suffice without difficulty for ten professors.'[55]

As well as critical studies of Puskin, Gogol, Tolstoy, Gorky and Dostoyevsky, Lunacharsky also wrote for the theatre. By the mid-1980s, copies of some seventy-two separate plays had been found, written by Lunacharsky, most under the pen name Anatoly Anyutin.[56] According to Isaac Deutscher, 'Nothing in man's artistic heritage was alien to him.'[57] Such praise was echoed at the time by Lenin: 'He is an excellent comrade! He has a sort of French brilliance. His light-mindedness comes from his aesthetic inclinations.'[58] Yet Lunacharsky's greatest literary talent was undoubtedly as the author of prose silhouettes. His brief descriptions of great revolutionaries possess a greater immediacy than the photographs that have come down to us. Of the populist Lavrov, Lunacharsky wrote, 'he lived in something like a cave dug out of books'. This was Lunacharsky on Lenin: 'People who come close to his orbit become devoted to him as a political leader but in some odd way they fall in love with him.' Trotsky was 'the greatest orator of our age' – high praise from a man who had heard Jean Jaurès and August Bebel in full flight. Zinoviev was 'a fat young man, pale and sickly', while Martov possessed 'neither the temperament, the boldness nor the breadth of vision needed for a political leader'.[59] Lunacharsky's *Revolutionary Silhouettes* were published in 1919, 1923, in 1924 and then (heavily edited) in 1965. To the author's great credit, and to the undoubted detriment of his later career, Lunacharsky resisted the temptation to add a chapter on Stalin.

The first declaration published by Narkompros recorded Lunacharsky's anti-statism. 'The people themselves, consciously or unconsciously, must evolve their own culture.... The independent action of ... workers', soldiers' and peasants' cultural-educational organisations must achieve full autonomy both in relation to the central government and to the municipal centres.'[60] Yet a policy of real liberalism in the arts was harder to secure than it seemed. For one thing, Lunacharsky had to defend the autonomy of conservative or even avowedly counter-revolutionary art – which he secured, at least until his own demise at the end of the 1920s. There were also barbarians on the left. Lunacharsky's own philosophy brought him into sympathy with the activists of the Proletkult movement, who militated for workers' control over culture. Lunacharsky's sponsoring of exhibitions by such 'decadent', middle-class artists as Chagall and Picasso raised eyebrows among his occasional allies.[61]

As late as 1927, Lunacharsky's 'Theses on the Problems of Marxist criticism' called for a model of artistic understanding, in which the first response would be to praise. Against the crude police-thinking of most Proletkultists – who asked only, Is the artist on our side? – Lunacharsky set out a different conception of the role of art under socialism, according to which all that was life-affirming was welcome, and all cynicism bad. In order to make sense of his ideas, we must also remember that Lunacharsky's career was nearing its end, and he was undoubtedly aware of the dangers ahead. His theses began with the condition of society at large. 'A new life is being built in the country, and literature is learning more and more to reflect this life in its as yet undefined and unstable forms.' The revolution was faced by many challenges, not least the rise of NEP, and defeatism on the part of the left.

> It is these circumstances which make the weapons of art – particularly literature – extremely important at the present time. They cause, however, proletarian and kindred literature to appear, side by side, with hostile literary emanations, and by this I mean not only the conscious and specifically hostile elements, but also the unconsciously hostile elements – hostile in their passivity, pessimism, individualism, prejudices and distortions.

The threat could be found not only among the small minority of people who campaigned for the restoration of tsarist rule or capitalist conditions. The enemy who emerges here is just as much the cynic who would draw away the lifeblood of the revolution: controversy and democratic debate. Conversely, the real ally was anyone who created real art, anyone who could create a living feel of social conditions and their transcendence. 'Glorious is the writer who can express a complex and valuable social idea with such artistic simplicity that he reaches the hearts of millions. Glorious is also the writer who can reach the hearts of these millions with a comparatively simple, elementary concept.'[62] Lunacharsky's generous theory stands not only as a model of Marxist practice at its best but also as a valuable model of how critics should work in times as different from his as our own.

Sadly, the specific conditions of 1917–21 did not last. Anatoly Lunacharsky survived at the head of Narkompros until September 1929, when he was toppled in a palace coup. The new commissar of Narkompros was Andrei Bubonov, formerly an administrator in the Red Army. Stalin and his allies were able to replace Lunacharsky with a more pliant generation of poet-functionaries, largely composed of former Proletkultists. The argument that the proletariat should monopolise Russian art meant in practice that all dissident thinking was finally outlawed. In 1934, Lunacharsky died while serving as ambassador to Spain. The following year his books were purged from Soviet libraries.[63] Lunacharsky succumbed to the purges posthumously. He was not rehabilitated for thirty years or more.

Victor Serge

The final figure to mention in this chapter is the writer Victor Serge, a dissident par excellence. His friend Julian Gorkín described Serge as an 'eternal vagabond in search of the ideal'.[64] Serge was a novelist, historian, revolutionary activist and (most important for us) also one of the earliest and sharpest of Stalin's critics. He was born Victor Lvovich Kibalchich in 1890. His parents were Russian refugees. His father had been a supporter of *Narodnaya Volya* (*People's Will*); his mother a member of the Polish aristocracy. Serge became an activist at an early age; his autobiographical *Memoirs of a Revolutionary* describe him taking anarchist positions from the age of 6 onwards. In their teens, Victor Serge and his circle of friends joined the Jeunes Gardes, the Belgian young socialists, but they were contemptuous of the main currents within the Belgian Socialist Party. They then quickly left, to join instead Émile Chapelier's anarchist colony. From Belgium, Victor Serge made his way to Paris, and took part in the anarchist movement there. Although Serge was a committed, leading anarchist, his *Memoirs* also record a sense of futility that he claims to have experienced at the time. One by one, Serge's comrades were lost to individual doctrines and adventurism, becoming thieves and petty outlaws, defying the police, choosing mysterious notions of honour over life.[65]

Victor Serge edited the newspaper *Anarchie*, using a pen name 'Valerie'. The authorities therefore held him responsible for the crimes of one group of semi-political adventurers, the Bonnot gang. Determined not to plead his innocence, and refusing to denounce his friends, Serge was sentenced to five years' imprisonment.[66] His experience of jail is described in a novel, *Men in Prison*. In 1914, Serge witnessed the conversion of the socialist leaders to chauvinism. Following his eventual release from jail, Serge took the Barcelona express and participated in the failed uprising of August 1917. This period of his life gave Serge the material for another novel, *Birth of Our Power*. From Spain, Serge made his way back to France, where he was detained. Thrilled by the news of the October Revolution, he succeeded in having himself sent to Russia, as a Bolshevik, in exchange for French prisoners of war. Thus Serge arrived in his parents' country for the first time in January 1919, aged 28, already shaped by many years of revolutionary activity.

From the moment of his arrival, Serge was torn by contradictory sentiments. With his long-held anarchist sentiments, he was shocked by the authoritarianism of the Bolsheviks. Yet, on the other hand, he could see that they remained *the* party of the Russian working class. Serge was soon cured of his earlier disdain for organisation. 'At this moment, the party fulfilled within the working class the functions of a brain and of a nervous system. It saw, it felt, it knew, it thought, it willed for and through the masses ... without it, the masses would have been no more than a heap of human dust.'[67] Serge took part in the military defence of Petrograd and worked as a secretary for the Third International. His novel *Conquered City* describes Petrograd at this heroic stage.[68]

Until late 1920, it was possible to predict an alliance between Bolsheviks and anarchists. Yet the break became final with the 1921

Kronstadt uprising. Serge was sympathetic to the sailors, and argued that the real culprits were the Bolshevik negotiators, Kalinin and Kuzmin. Serge finally supported the government against the Kronstadt rebels, but did so without enthusiasm: 'Kronstadt was the beginning of a fresh, liberating revolution for popular democracy.... However, the country was already exhausted.... There were no reserves of any kind, not even reserves of stamina in the hearts of the masses.' Under such conditions, the rebels could only encourage the conservative elements within Russian society. The slogan of 'Soviet democracy' was utopian – it 'lacked leadership, institutions and inspiration; at its back there were only masses of starving and desperate men.'[69]

In 1922, Serge chose to travel abroad, and worked for the next four years for the Communist International in Germany and Austria. He returned to Russia in 1926, to find that the degeneration of the revolution had reached a new stage. Since Lenin's death, there had been a transfer of power to the state bureaucracy. Serge became an active supporter of Trotsky's Left Opposition. In 1927, Trotsky and his followers united with Kamenev and Zinoviev in a desperate alliance against Stalin. In that year, the Opposition published its platform: 'For the last time (but we had no suspicion that this was so) the party returned to its tradition of collective thinking, with its concern to consult the man in the workshop. Typewriters clattered throughout entire nights in apartments where the Kremlin was still unable to intrude.'[70] In October, Trotsky, Kamenev and Zinoviev were removed from the party's Central Committee. Their supporters were expelled from the party.

For the next five years, from 1928 to 1933, Serge was to live in Petrograd in a condition of precarious liberty. His friends were detained or expelled from Russia. It was under these conditions that Serge became a full-time author, finishing three novels, *Men in Prison*, *Birth of Our Power* and *Conquered City*, in quick succession. Another book, *Literature and Revolution*, was sympathetic to argument for Proletkult, but sided finally against the idea, quoting from Trotsky's attack on the genre.[71] Through all this time, only Victor Serge's status as a prominent foreign writer saved him from imprisonment. He was eventually arrested in 1933 and accused of taking part in conspiracy. Three years of internal exile followed.

Serge describes this detention as the most difficult of times. His fellow activists were denied proper food; they found spies in their midst; the authorities did everything in their power to divide the detainees. Here, Serge finished 'Year Two of the Russian Revolution'; another novel, 'The Torment'; an account of the French anarchist movement, 'The Lost Men'; and a book of poems, *Resistance*.[72] The only manuscript copies were confiscated by the secret police. Towards the end of his time in captivity, the state changed its practice from one of detaining potential critics to one of killing them. Serge was only protected by his reputation. Outside Russia, a campaign had been launched for his release.

Finally, in 1936, Serge secured his freedom. He left Russia for Belgium and then France. In the West, he continued to write. One book, *Russia Twenty Years After*, was devoted to explaining the rise of Stalin.[73] As a prominent former supporter of the Russian Left Opposition, Serge was publicly identified with the Trotskyists and worked with them against the slanders of the Moscow Trials. Along with André Breton, Serge helped to establish a French committee of inquiry. However, Serge did not see Trotsky's Fourth International as the organised basis for a renewal of socialism.[74] Serge and Trotsky broke off correspondence, a separation that would only be reversed in 1944, when Natalia Sedova re-established contact after her husband Leon Trotsky's death.

This new period of exile saw Serge thwarted at every turn. Friends died or capitulated; in Russia the Old Bolsheviks were butchered one by one. Serge's book *Hitler Against Stalin* predicted disastrous Soviet defeats at the start of the war, suggesting that peasants would welcome Hitler's invaders. These forecasts were eventually proved accurate, but in the short term the book's notoriety had the effect of forcing its publishers to close. A further novel, *The Long Dusk*, describes the misery of dispossessed political refugees of Serge's generation. In 1940, when the Nazis overran France, Serge was forced to flee again. After eighteen months hiding from France's new rulers, Serge and his son Vlady were finally able to board a ship to Martinique. Other passengers on Serge's boat included his former colleague André Breton, and the anthropologist Claude Lévi-Strauss.[75] Victor Serge was not allowed to disembark in Martinique, nor in the Dominican Republic, nor in

Cuba, and was only welcomed in Mexico. He was forced to leave his wife behind in France. Serge's greatest novel, *The Case of Comrade Tulayev*, was completed at about this time. Yet its author was declining, alone and in poverty.[76]

How, then, did Serge explain the decay of the October Revolution? Richard Greeman makes the important point that Victor Serge was engaged in a *developing* critique of Stalinism. Although Serge was consistent in his defence of democracy, his critique of Stalin became sharper over time.[77]

Victor Serge's distinctive theories can best be explained in contrast to the arguments generated by his long-term friend and ally, Leon Trotsky. The Trotskyist analysis of Russia went back to the political alliances of the late 1920s. Then the major players had been Trotsky, Stalin and Bukharin. Trotsky argued for a left turn. This meant supporting the towns against the countryside, investment in industry and the gradual collectivisation of the land. The right, around Nikolai Bukharin, tended to argue in the opposite direction. Insisting that there would be no upheavals abroad, but that Russia could create socialism in one country, Bukharin called for a peaceful return to the market. This meant increasing the wealth of the peasantry, through the promotion of urban–rural trade. According to the same model, Stalin represented a middle route, the conservatism of the bureaucracy as it vacillated from left to right and back. Stalin could not act decisively against either of his opponents, and neither could the bureaucracy overthrow the two classes, the workers and the peasants, whose interest stood behind the political left and the right, respectively. From this strategic analysis, Trotsky and his supporters came to the conclusion that the chief threat to the revolution came from Bukharin and the right, who were said to support the open restoration of the market and private property. Yet what happened in reality? In 1929, Stalin turned on Bukharin and introduced forced collectivisation. Millions of small peasant homes were broken up, and the land was given over to huge collective farms. According to the Trotskyist explanatory model, it would follow that things had turned out better than they might. Perhaps Stalin should have acted more slowly, with the consent of the peasantry. Yet it seemed that the shift towards collective property was a step leftwards, and for that very reason many former dissidents now capitulated to Stalin's regime.

From 1929 onwards, therefore, the standard Trotskyist analysis placed Stalin at the head of a new form of society in which politics and economics were at odds. State property, nationalisation and collective ownership of the land were taken as evidence of the increasingly socialist economy in Russia, while the rule of the bureaucracy was described as a temporary and barbaric phenomenon. There was no need for a second revolution to overturn the gains of October. Hence Trotsky's classic work, *The Revolution Betrayed*, argued that Russia remained a form of workers' state, albeit a degenerate one.[78]

In a 1936 collection titled *Sixteen Shot: Where is the Russian Revolution Going?* Victor Serge ventured the opinion that Trotsky's description of the Soviet state was too optimistic. Rather than seeing Russia as some form of workers' state, Serge suggested that the dictatorship of the proletariat had been replaced by 'the dictatorship of the bureaucracy over the proletariat'.[79] At this stage, Serge's opinion was still only of the status of an insight, but over the next ten years it would develop. Richard Greeman has drawn attention to an unpublished manuscript which Serge wrote in 1946, arguing that Russia had now become a new form of class society:

> Trotsky, despite the wisdom of these analyses, seems not to have realised that we were all witnessing the formation of a new system of production, of government, and of exploitation of man by man, which was and is neither capitalist nor socialist; a system which needs to be labelled with a new term and which, without going deeply into a debate over terminology, can only be called Totalitarian. The novelty, vigour and cruelty of this system goes far beyond the most pessimistic predictions of the most bitter and lucid members of the Opposition.

Here Serge drew on the work of another dissident Marxist, the German socialist Karl Korsch, whose work is discussed in the next chapter of this book:

> Karl Korsch observes that Trotsky ... did not see at all that another form of counter-revolution, that is of anti-socialism, was developing from the fact that the technology of large-scale production in our days is drawn to planned collectivism, just as in the beginning of the nine-

teenth century and following the progress of mechanisation, our whole society was drawn into capitalism.[80]

Korsch's analysis, which Serge alludes to, rested on the insight that state ownership was not the same as socialism. Russia had become a form of state capitalism, in which the bureaucracy operated as a ruling class. In terms of similar Marxist voices, Serge also had access to the so-called Verkhne Uralsk theses, written in 1930 by a group of Left Oppositionists who, like Korsch, described Russia as state capitalist. This incident is mentioned in Serge's memoirs, and dramatised in his novel *Midnight in the Century*.

Although Greeman locates Serge as heading towards the state capitalist argument, in the direction of later writers including C.L.R. James, Trotsky's former secretary Raya Dunayevskaya and Tony Cliff,[81] he is hesitant to place Serge too neatly within any one category. Serge's Russian writings are hardly consistent. Beyond 'state capitalism', Victor Serge also toyed with other phrases, including 'collectivism' and 'totalitarianism', a phrase he claimed to have invented. In using these words, he was close to other contemporaries whose analyses were tending in rival directions, including the social democrat Rudolf Hilferding and Anton Ciliga, another former member of the Russian Left Opposition.[82] Whichever term he used, however, Serge undoubtedly understood Stalinist Russia in a different way from Leon Trotsky. He saw more clearly than his friend that by 1929 the Russian state played a uniformly counter-revolutionary role.

Victor Serge died in Mexico in 1947. He left two legacies to the workers' movement. The first was his autobiography, which captures the energy and optimism of the revolution as well as any other document of these times. The second was a theory of 1917 in which Stalin was recognised for what he was, the very gravedigger of the revolution.

3

Karl Korsch, Marxism and philosophy

As the Russian Revolution degenerated from within, so the nature of Soviet Marxism changed. From being an open and creative force, allied to the goal of democratic change, it became a closed system with a new goal – the continuation of Stalinist rule. Dissident Marxism could only be articulated in the West, where imprisonment was a more distant threat. One such dissident was the Marxist philosopher Karl Korsch. In order to understand the quality of Korsch's dissident thinking, it is necessary first to grasp the 'Marxism' that he rejected. Korsch first joined the German Social Democratic Party (SPD) in the years immediately prior to the First World War. At the time, the organisation was the foremost section of the Second International, the worldwide federation of socialist organisations. With its formal stress on the need for a revolutionary overthrow of capitalism, the Social Democratic Party was the custodian of orthodox Marxism within the International as a whole. The SPD had over 100,000 members and printed a hundred daily newspapers; it organised a million supporters in trade unions and was the second largest party in the German parliament. The dominant figure within the theoretical life of the SPD was Karl Kautsky, the so-called 'pope of Marxism'. Kautsky was a figure of enormous stature; close to Friedrich Engels, he was given the responsibility of publishing many of Marx's original manuscripts after Engels's death. Respected by all wings of the Socialist International, it was Kautsky who was seen to have defended Marxism against the attacks of the revisionists, notably Edouard Bernstein, who campaigned for the German Social Democratic Party to convert itself into an explicitly reformist organisation.

Although in his debate with Bernstein Karl Kautsky appeared to be the champion of revolutionary Marxism, beneath the surface Kautsky's Marxism was flawed. According to him, Marx had demonstrated that history was a succession of different societies. Within each society production grew until it could grow no further. At that moment there was a revolution and a new form of society came into being. In Kautsky's writing and in the Marxism of the Second International, there was very little role for human agency. Societies grew and declined, almost independent of what people did to organise against them. It followed that the task for revolutionaries was simply to wait until capitalism finally collapsed.

When challenged, the Marxists of the Second International were keen to insist that they did see a relationship between long-term economic factors and short-term human decisions. Georgi Plekhanov devoted his pamphlet *The Role of the Individual in History* to an analysis of this very question. He insisted that human decisions mattered, and that there was a unity between structure and agency. It was only 'in the last analysis', he suggested, that 'everything depends upon the course of social development and on the relation of social forces'. Karl Kautsky claimed to agree with Plekhanov that there was a role for individuals. He was scathing towards those who saw his Marxism as a form of determinism:

> Strangely enough there are still people who believe that Marx taught that historical development proceeds by itself, without any help at all from men. Even among socialists, this astonishing conception of Marxism is not rare.... Of course, Marx never taught this nonsense. It is absurd to present the theory of class struggle as a theory of inactivity.[1]

When it came to abstract theorising, Kautsky did defend ideas of human agency. However, when it came to applying theory to the pressing questions of everyday life, Karl Kautsky's Marxism worked in exactly this reductionist way that he claimed to reject.

Time and again, Kautsky argued as if the whole evolution of society was working in the direction of collective ownership, as if the victory of socialism was *inevitable*. It followed from this premiss that it would be wrong for the SPD to engage in any hasty actions. Thus, when the left wing of the SPD argued that German socialists should copy the revolutionary general strike which had taken place in Russia in 1905, Kautsky responded by arguing that the pace of history could never be rushed. Calling for patience and moderation, and working in alliance with the leaders of the trade unions, and Bernstein and the revisionists, Kautsky presided over the growing bureaucratisation of his party. Such Marxism was decisively tested in 1914, at the outbreak of the First World War. Kautsky, along with all the orthodox leaders of the workers' International, supported his own nation and his own capitalist class in the slaughter. The evolutionary and fatalistic Marxism of the Second International meant that he did not have the politics to oppose the war.[2]

Korsch and the revolutionary 1920s

Karl Korsch was a member of a revolutionary generation that rejected the deterministic Marxism of the 1890s and early 1900s. Active in the years immediately following the Russian Revolution, such Marxists as Korsch, Georg Lukács and Antonio Gramsci were educated by the rise of the anti-war movement. They witnessed the great breakthrough of the Bolshevik Revolution in Russia in 1917, and the forward wave of working-class struggle that continued from 1917 until the final defeat of the German revolution in the winter of 1923. It was clear at the time that the Russian Revolution opened up the future for a whole new way of using Marxism. Although most of his philosophical work was not published in Western Europe until much later, the Russian revolutionary Vladimir Lenin came to the conclusion that the only way to restore the revolutionary content of Marxism was through examining the origins of Karl Marx's philosophical method in Hegelian dialectics. Lenin insisted that there was a unity between the crude philosophy of Second International Marxism and its reformist politics, and he also argued that a study of dialectics must be at the heart of any restored and revolutionary Marxism. As he wrote at the time, 'It is impossible completely to understand Marx's *Capital* and especially its first chapter without having thoroughly studied and understood the whole of Hegel's *Logic*. Consequently half a century later, none of the Marxists understood Marx.'[3]

Within the generation that came to Marxism in the 1920s, Korsch was one of the standard-bearers of Marxist philosophy. At the level of theory, and without access to Lenin's philosophical works, he came to remarkably similar conclusions. In terms of his political practice, Korsch adopted a number of positions, ranging from Fabianism to ultra-leftism, and stood only briefly at the centre of the Marxist tradition. However, his enduring works, notably *Marxism and Philosophy* (1923), insisted that the purpose of Marxism was to enable a workers' movement to seize power. To a later generation of socialists, some of Korsch's formulations may seem abstract, but nobody could question his commitment to the idea that workers can run the world. Within Marxist theory, Korsch's generation of dissident Marxists did develop new insights, hostile to the ossified and fatalistic Marxism of the pre-1914 Second International. However, the degeneration of the Russian Revolution combined with the revival of social democracy to remove the space for such creative Marxism. Gramsci was jailed by Mussolini's Fascist regime, and only released to die. Members of the Frankfurt School drifted into reformism or academia. Lukács was unable to separate himself from Stalinism. Karl Korsch became a 'left Communist', in the style of the Dutch socialist Pannekoek, or the Italian revolutionary Amadeo Bordiga.

For over forty years, therefore, the work of these dissident and non-Stalinist Marxists was obscured. It was only in the 1960s and 1970s that numbers of Marxists began to look again at these writers in any systematic way. By the late 1970s, four of Korsch's books were available in English translations.[4] Since then, however, and in a period of defeats for the working-class movement, interest in Korsch has waned. Other Marxists from his generation, including Walter Benjamin and Bertolt Brecht, remain fashionable, partly because elements of what they wrote could be taken out of context and used by mainstream writers. Karl Korsch, by contrast, was explicitly committed to revolutionary change, and the academics have found it harder to claim his mantle. In the context of this book, which is concerned with the revolutionary kernel of twentieth-century socialism, it is appropriate to look again at the work of this neglected Marxist.

How Korsch became a Marxist

Karl Korsch was born in 1886 in Tostedt, near Hamburg in Germany. His father was a successful bank clerk and later a bank manager. Korsch went to school in Thuringia, and to university in Munich, Berlin, Geneva and Jena. Like Walter Benjamin, his first political experiences came as a member of the 'Free Student Movement', a broad, liberal and idealist organisation committed to the idea of transforming education in the interest of students. In 1910, Korsch obtained a doctorate in law. At about this time he joined the SPD, although he was not yet an active member. Between 1912 and 1914, Korsch continued his studies in London, where he joined the Fabian Society. At this time, the Fabians distinguished themselves from their competitors on the left by their stress on the values of 'ideas', 'will' and 'humanity', which were counterposed to the lifeless, dry-as-dust economics of Marxism. Korsch preferred this mix to the orthodox Marxism of the SPD. The vague and idealistic nature of Korsch's pre-war socialism can be seen in an article he wrote on 'The Fabian Society' (1912), in which he declared his admiration for the Fabian emphasis on 'The very important orientation on the will. The practical will: to ensure that in the inevitable transformation of human economy, human culture, the ideal of humanity is also advanced.'[5]

On the outbreak of war, in August 1914, Karl Korsch returned to Germany. He served in the war, while also openly expressing his opposition to it. For this position, he was demoted from the rank of reserve lieutenant to corporal. Korsch boasted that he never carried a rifle or sabre. Somehow he survived the hostility of his own commanding officers, and was twice decorated with the Iron Cross, for acts of bravery under fire. In 1917, Korsch joined the Independent German Socialist Party (USPD). There is no evidence that Korsch was active in the soldiers' councils, or in the uprising in Berlin in 1919. However, he did take part in the 1918

Commission on the Socialisation of Industry. His experiences from this period were written up in a pamphlet, *What is Socialisation?* (1920), and in a book, *Labour Law for Factory Councils* (1920). The Workers' Councils were the great achievement of the revolutionary wave of 1917–21. In Russia, during the 1917 revolution, the councils were known as *soviets*, and were the means by which workers were able to control their workplace. Meeting in each area and every city, the councils represented a form of workers' democracy, controlled from the bottom up. During the surge of unrest following 1917, workers' councils were formed in almost every country in Europe, from the shipyards of western Scotland to the armaments factories of central Italy. In Germany, the councils were undermined by workers' continuing support for the SPD, which determined that the councils should not play the role they had in Russia. Despite this, councils grew during the revolution and certainly opened up the possibility of workers' power.

Perhaps because Karl Korsch was a witness to the movement and not an active participant, his views on factory councils are difficult to pin down. At first, they read like the work of a Fabian or a guild socialist, supporting these councils within the framework of a capitalist economy. Later, Korsch took a very different view, and came close to identifying these workers' councils as the means to abolish capitalism and the way to achieve socialism. The new tone of his writing can be seen in an important article he wrote, 'The Question of Socialisation – Before and After the Revolution' (1920). In this essay he criticised both the Fabian view that socialism equals more co-operatives, and the traditional SPD view that socialism equals nationalisation and greater state ownership:

> Today, with the hour of socialism at hand, it is evident that none of these forms will, without far-reaching restructuring, be able adequately to realise that speedy 'socialisation' of the totality of economic life which is demanded so forcefully by the mass of the working population.[6]

If workers did not take the whole economy, then socialisation would not last. If they did not take power themselves, then it would not be socialism. What was needed, Korsch argued, was workers' *control*, producers taking over the whole economy from below.

The experience of the councils acted as a bridge, over which

Karl Korsch travelled closer towards the essence of revolutionary Marxism. Yet although Korsch's new enthusiasm for workers' councils was a step forward from his earlier belief in reformed capitalism, his vision remained flawed. His enthusiasm for workers' councils was a proletarian constitution-mongering (he called for a 'proletarian constitution of labour'), in which workers' councils would act merely as a corrective to capitalist management.

Marxism and Philosophy

Following the decision of a majority of the USPD, Karl Korsch joined the German Communist Party (KPD) in 1920. His wife Hedda suggests that Korsch had doubts about joining the KPD and about the need for a centralised working-class party: 'In everything … he was in favour of decentralisation.' More recently, Douglas Kellner has demonstrated that Korsch was a loyal member of the KPD, and a keen supporter of democratic centralism at least until 1925.[7] Whether or not Korsch then felt a fear of organisation, the next six years of his life, when he was a member of a revolutionary party, were certainly his most creative period, the point at which he formulated his own distinctive variety of Marxism. Korsch was quickly brought into the leadership of the KPD. In 1923, he was elected to the state parliament in Thuringia, and in October 1923 he became Minister of Justice in the coalition SPD–KPD government in Thuringia. At the time, the two parties had different ideas of what this coalition represented. For the SPD, this workers' government removed the need for any deepening of the revolution. For the KPD, it was a coalition that would lead to socialism – although how it would make the transition was not fully worked out. Korsch himself was seen by members of the Communist Party as a military figure, a former officer, the man responsible for preparing at least the defence of the Thuringian government, and potentially the insurrection which was expected to break out in October 1923, on the sixth anniversary of the Russian Revolution. As it happened, the call to arms never came. When a local rising did break out in Hamburg, the army successfully put it down.

For most of this time, Karl Korsch was writing quite ordinary Marxist texts, short pamphlets, introductions and reviews outlining the basic concepts of Marxism. Where his originality came was in his treatment of the Marxism of the Second International, as it culminated in the works of the KPD's rival, the SPD. He followed Lenin in arguing that the SPD's Marxism was a crude and reformist deviation from Marx. This criticism was extended. In 1922, Korsch took part in an important Marxist 'work week' in Ilmenau, Thuringia.[8] The organisational nucleus of this working group was to become the Frankfurt School, while the manuscripts of Korsch's lectures were published as *Marxism and Philosophy* (1923). This pamphlet is very much Karl Korsch's enduring success.

One of the first arguments in *Marxism and Philosophy* is that Marxism itself must be understood *historically*. This idea, that scientific socialism has its own history, is one of Korsch's original and enduring insights. He argued that Marxism originated in the writings of Marx and Engels as a rejection of Hegel and his idealist philosophy. From the 1840s onwards, it had developed in different ways. The Marxism of the Second International, Korsch argued, was a degeneration, inferior to Marx's socialism in two main respects. First, not only Eduard Bernstein and the revisionists but also Kautsky, Plekhanov, Rudolf Hilferding, Jean Jaurès and the other leading figures had all neglected the problem of the state. While formally pledging themselves to the revolutionary overthrow of capitalism, the leaders of the official socialist parties had become reformists. In their day-to-day practice they accepted and defended the continuation of the capitalist state:

> [Bernstein's] Revisionism appears as an attempt to express in the form of a coherent theory the reformist character acquired by the economic struggles of the trade unions, and the political struggles of the working class parties.... With all their orthodox obsession with the abstract letter of Marxist theory [even Bernstein's opponents, Kautsky and the orthodox Marxists within the Second International] were unable to preserve its original revolutionary character. Their scientific socialism had inevitably ceased to be a theory of social revolution.[9]

The second source of the degeneration of Marxism, Karl Korsch argues, was a neglect of philosophy. In criticising the Marxism of the Second International, Korsch reminded his readers of Lenin's call to arms, 'We must organise a systematic study of the Hegelian dialectic from a materialist standpoint.' For Karl Korsch, one of the key components of dialectics was its emphasis on *totality*. Karl Marx himself had always stressed the totality of the world; it was his later followers who had cut Marx's theory into slices. Marxism, he argued, was incompatible with the idea of separate branches of knowledge:

> Despite all their theoretical and methodological avowals of historical materialism, [the Marxists of the Second International] in fact divided the theory of social revolution into fragments.... Later Marxists came to regard scientific socialism more and more as a set of purely scientific observations, without any immediate connection to the political or other practices of class struggle.... A unified general theory of social revolution was changed into criticisms of the bourgeois economic order, of the bourgeois state, of the bourgeois state of education, of bourgeois religion, art, science and culture.

Marxism was a form of revolutionary action, in which theoretical discussion and practice had again to be combined. Thus Korsch saw himself as reuniting the theory of Marxism to a revolutionary purpose, meeting (like Rosa Luxemburg and Lenin) the 'practical needs of the new revolutionary stage of proletarian class struggle'.[10]

For Korsch, the unity of theory and practice was to be achieved concretely, by human action. Thus, in *Marxism and Philosophy*, he placed great emphasis on the importance of consciousness. Karl Korsch stressed that ideologies should not be regarded as mere peripheral consequences of economic facts. The 'intellectual reality' of bourgeois society had as much importance as the economic and social structures on which it was founded. Ideas, politics and economics formed together the totality of bourgeois society. It followed that there was a role for 'intellectual action'. If the working class was to 'revolutionise in practice', then there was also a need to 'criticise in theory'.

In arguing in defence of revolutionary Marxism, Karl Korsch emphasised that Marx's message represented the negation of philosophy. This was a claim that Marx and Engels had themselves both made, from 1845 onwards. Thus Marx wrote, in the *Theses on Feuerbach*, 'Philosophers have only interpreted the world; the point is to change it.' Friedrich Engels developed this idea, arguing that as Marxism had made philosophy obsolete in the realm of history, so all that remained for it to do was to speculate in the laws of pure thought. Engels also pointed out that as German capitalism grew in strength, so the capitalist class was less and less interested in philosophy, leaving the working class as the sole heirs of Hegelian philosophy. Korsch defended and deepened this conception of Marxism as *anti-philosophy*, in three ways. His first argument was that bourgeois philosophy had reached its highest point in the writings of Hegel. Marx, by standing Hegel on his head, had broken with philosophy. Korsch's second argument was that Marxism was a criticism of all aspects of the capitalist world, and bourgeois philosophy was included among the ideas that Marx rejected. His third argument was that philosophy merely reflected the world, while Marxism sought its transformation. This stress on practice meant that Marxism was the negation of philosophy. At the end of *Marxism and Philosophy*, Korsch offered up the possibility of a world in which philosophy had ceased to exist:

> Bourgeois consciousness necessarily sees itself as apart from the world and independent of it as pure critical philosophy and impartial science, just as the bourgeois State and bourgeois Law appear to be above society. This consciousness must be philosophically fought by the revolutionary materialistic dialectic, which is the philosophy of the working class. This struggle will only end when the whole of existing society and its economic basis have been totally overthrown in practice, and this consciousness has been totally surpassed and abolished in theory. 'Philosophy cannot be abolished without being realised.'[11]

Philosophy could be overthrown – but only through the successful achievement of a socialist society, through workers' revolution.

Three Essays on Marxism

Following the defeat of the German revolution in October 1923, the KPD briefly shifted to the left under the leadership of Ruth Fischer and Arkadi Maslow. Fischer and Maslow had already been among the leadership of the party in 1923; at that time they had supported calls for a revolution, but from an ultra-left and unrealistic perspective, in which the revolution was always imminent – were it not for the timidity of their own party. After the October crisis had passed, and with the support of Zinoviev and the leadership of the Communist International, they maintained that Germany would soon enter another period of crisis, which meant that there was an urgent need to prepare for an imminent further insurrection. In this ultra-left climate, Karl Korsch became one of the party's leading spokesmen and editor of its theoretical journal *Die Internationale*. He also became a Communist deputy in the German parliament, the Reichstag. However, the KPD was out of step with the international leadership of the Communist movement, which was itself then convinced that the world was entering a new period of stability. In 1924, *Marxism and Philosophy* was condemned at the fifth world congress of the Communist International. This was the first congress of the International since Lenin's death, and the movement was already coming to be distorted by a series of bureaucratic lurches, which would pave the way for Stalinism. There, Zinoviev accused Korsch, and others including Georg Lukács, of 'revisionism' and 'idealism'. Korsch's book was portrayed as the counterpart in philosophy of the ultra-left political leadership of Fischer and Maslow within the KPD. In response to these criticisms, Korsch himself briefly attempted to form an international Communist opposition, with the support of the Italian left socialist Bordiga. Korsch's group organised as a faction, the 'Resolute Lefts' (Entschiedene Linke), within the Communist International and the KPD. Korsch was himself expelled from the KPD in April 1926. His party continued to exist until 1928, which was also the year that Korsch lost his seat in the Reichstag.

Detached from any significant Marxist organisation, Korsch had first of all to find a milieu in which to operate. He took part in a Marxist discussion circle involving himself, his wife, Georg Lukács and Bertolt Brecht, among others. Korsch was especially close to Brecht, and travelled with him in exile. Brecht in turn seems to have relied on Korsch ('the Professor') for advice on matters of Marxist theory. Even Brecht, however, recognised Karl Korsch's habits of abstraction and academic reasoning. Indeed, Brecht gave his friend a curiously backhanded congratulation, on reading Korsch's *Karl Marx*, in 1938. 'Up until [now]', Brecht wrote, 'I think your Marxism was largely a product of the history of ideas. Now it springs from reality.' Brecht's point, that Korsch possessed an abstract and idealistic Marxism, remained true even after 1938.[12]

In 1929, Karl Korsch wrote an important critique of Karl Kautsky's *The Materialist Conception of History*. The next year Korsch wrote a long article, 'The Present State of the Problem of *Marxism and Philosophy*' defending his earlier arguments; the essay is published at the end of the English edition of the book. Here, he extended his earlier idea that Marxism is a historical science, and that Marxism itself should be understood historically. In particular, he argued that the history of Marxism should be seen as the unfolding of three successive stages. From 1843 to 1848, according to Korsch, Marxism as a theory based itself on the open class struggle of the proletariat. This, then, was the moment at which Marxism first approached its height. After the defeat of the revolutions of 1848, however, it was clear that the capitalist system was secured for a generation. In this climate, Marxism could only survive by describing itself as a humanist and positivist science, identifying itself as a form of general *truth*. In the third phase, from 1900, there was a revival of working-class confidence, originally manifested in the growth of Bolshevism and syndicalism. These restored the subjective quality of Marxism, as a philosophy of working-class revolution and paved the way for a more complete and truly revolutionary theory.[13]

The argument that Marxism has its own history must be one of Korsch's most enduring insights. It reminds us that socialism is based on a living tradition. In many ways, the history of Marxism is a story of growth and development. As capitalism has evolved, so Marxists have come to a richer understanding of the dynamics at the heart of the system. On the other hand, the Marxist tradition is also a story of frequent reversal or defeat. The impact of Second International Marxism was to convert revolutionary socialism into a new variety of reformism. Later, the victory of Stalin meant the defeat of the revolution in Russia, and the rise of a new reductionist and reformist Marxism on a worldwide scale. Korsch did not succeed in formulating an adequate history of Marxism, but such a project is certainly valid, and Korsch was the among the first to advocate it.

In 1933, Korsch was forced into exile. He settled in Britain and then America. Throughout the period of his exile, Korsch saw his main task as being to defend the ideas he had already elaborated in the 1920s. Three of his essays from this period, 'Leading Principles of Marxism: A Restatement' (1937), 'Introduction to *Capital*' (1932) and 'Why I Am a Marxist' (1935) are available in an English edition, *Three Essays on Marxism*. The most important of these essays is 'Why I Am a Marxist', which was originally published in the journal *Modern Quarterly*. It was part of a symposium, with Alexander Goldenweiser, George Santayana and H.G. Wells explaining why they were not Marxists, and Korsch and Harold Laski (on behalf of the British Labour Party!) explaining why they were. The great theme of this essay, as of Korsch's work generally, is that Marxism is a world-view which sets out to change the world. Thus Korsch summarises Marxism in four statements:

1. All the propositions of Marxism, including those that are apparently general, are specific.
2. Marxism is not positive but critical.
3. Its subject-matter is not existing capitalist society in its affirmative state, but declining capitalist society as revealed in the demonstrably operative tendencies of its break-up and decay.
4. Its primary purpose is not contemplative enjoyment of the existing world but its active transformation.

Karl Korsch insisted that Marxism was a philosophy of practice. He was dismissive of those who used Marxist ideas simply as a set of tools to understand the world:

> Marxist 'theory' does not strive to achieve objective knowledge of reality out of an independent, theoretical interest. It is driven to acquire this knowledge by the practical necessities of struggle, and can neglect it only by running the heavy risk of failing to achieve its goal, at the price and defeat of the proletarian movement which it represents.

Korsch argued that the only purpose of Marxist theory was to act on the immediate world of late capitalism. It followed that any attempt to understand any other world was flawed. Not just mere theoretical reflection, but any theorising about any other moment in time, was hostile to the revolutionary spirit of Marxism:

> And just because [Marxist theory] never loses sight of its practical purpose, it eschews every attempt to force all experience into the design

of a monistic construction of the universe in order to build a unified system of knowledge.[14]

It is appropriate at this stage to raise one important point which Korsch himself did not deal with satisfactorily. His argument is that Marxism, as a theory of knowledge, is *relativistic*. According to Karl Korsch, Marxists understand everything simply from the vantage point of the working class. If this is correct, however, then why should anyone be a Marxist? Why should a Marxist explanation be better than any other? One answer, which Korsch rejects, is that Marxist explanations are *objective*: they explain the world. In Karl Korsch's Marxism, the starting point is rather the claim that scientific socialism embodies the historic situation of the working class, therefore it must be true. How would such an argument persuade anyone who was not already convinced of revolutionary socialism? Surely one means to do this would be by finding social facts (such as the tendency of capitalism to go through crises) which can be explained by Marxist explanations, but not by other arguments. For Marx himself, as for Luxemburg, Lenin and Trotsky, socialism was both a science to understand the world and a weapon to change it. Karl Korsch rejected this synthesis, preferring to advocate a Marxism that made no claims to scientific status but was above all a means to effect change. Korsch wanted to rebuild a tradition of resolute Marxism, but he separated Marx's revolutionary politics from any concern with objective reality. Becoming arbitrary and subjective, Korsch's Marxism was separated from a mass audience, and in this way his revolutionary vision was hollowed out and lost. Thus Karl Korsch's Marxism offered a limited defence of historical materialism.

State capitalism

As a member of the KPD, Korsch was very much on the side of Bolshevik orthodoxy. His 1924 speech, 'Lenin and the Comintern', was an argument for Leninism, as the only adequate base on which revolutionary politics could be built. Following his expulsion from the KPD, though, Korsch was increasingly critical of events in Russia. In 1926, he spoke in the German Reichstag against the

Russo-German 'friendship treaty', calling for a renewal of Leninist politics, against the current regime. By 1927, Korsch had turned his back on democratic centralism, blaming Lenin for the degeneration of the revolution.[15] One 1932 article, 'The Marxist Ideology in Russia', is noteworthy in that it describes the Soviet Union as 'state capitalist', characterising the governing ideology of Russia as 'a mere ideological justification of what in its actual tendency is a capitalist state and thus, inevitably, a state based on the suppression of the progressive revolutionary movement of the proletarian class'.[16] The article goes on to compare Stalinism and social democracy, with Korsch insisting that both of these ideologies aimed at the stabilisation of capital. His arguments were not filled out with historical details, and remain abstract, but this remains the high point in Korsch's independent analysis of the Russian defeat. After 1932, Korsch increasingly felt that there was little point attacking the Soviet Union. 'Everything that the workers are told about the state-capitalist continuation', he wrote in 1935, 'comes either from the mouths of their old well-known enemies, capitalists, fascists, and social democrats, or it unavoidably remains vague, abstract, incomprehensible, and unsympathetic.' By 1947, Korsch had come to a pessimistic conclusion, telling Brecht that 'Russian imperialism is better for the world than Yankee imperialism and there is hardly a third chance.'[17]

Karl Marx

Karl Korsch's last major work was a biography, *Karl Marx* (1938). The theme running through the book was taken from Engels's famous speech at Marx's graveside: Karl Marx was 'above all else a revolutionary'. This applies to everything Marx wrote, even his mature economic manuscripts. Thus, according to Korsch, 'Marx's approach to Political Economy was from the outset that of a critical and revolutionary student of society rather than that of an economist.' Hence the title of Marx's famous pamphlet, 'A *Critique* of Political Economy'.[18] Although he was undoubtedly correct to signal Marx's break with bourgeois economics, Korsch failed to notice that this insight would go against his earlier argument that Marxism became solidly reformist after 1848. (Indeed this omission was typical of the man's work: Korsch's Marxism was persistently marked by grand philosophical statements which lacked a basis in detailed, living historical fact.)

Korsch's biography of Marx was divided into three sections: first, Korsch described Marx as a social scientist, then as the critic of political economy, last as the founder of a new way of understanding history. The first section, on social science, made the general point that Marx was not a sociologist. He was not interested in drawing up general rules about the nature of all societies. According to Korsch, the distinctive feature of Marx's analysis of society was his stress on the 'specific' character of different societies, 'Marx is aware of the fact that the only positive way of comprehending the general concept, or the "law" of a particular historical form of society, is through its actual historical change.'[19] The second section, on political economy, interpreted Marx's critique of capitalism as a historical model, which opens the possibility of other histories, 'Political Economy ... is transformed from an absolute and timeless science into one which is historically and socially conditioned.'[20] The most powerful parts of this book came in the third section, on Marxism and history. Here, Korsch restated Marx's metaphor of base and superstructure, the idea that human beings are themselves products of the material world. The section ended with an appeal to readers, to understand Marxism not as set of rules to be learned, but as a living tradition and as a guide to action:

> The Marxian concepts ... are not new dogmatic fetters or pre-established points which must be gone through in a particular order in any 'materialistic' investigation. They are an undogmatic guide for scientific research and revolutionary action. The proof of the pudding is in the eating.[21]

From 1936, Korsch lived in the USA, where he held a number of university positions. For a time, he worked together with Karl Lewin, one of the founders of social psychology.[22] After 1938, the major source of Korsch's ideas was a series of articles he wrote in English for various left journals, including *Council Correspondence*, *Partisan Review*, *Modern Quarterly*, *New Essays* and *Living Marxism*. The last two of these were edited by Paul Mattick, an American socialist, an ultra-leftist and an admirer of Pannekoek. The most interesting of Korsch's late articles is probably 'The World Historians', a long essay he wrote on Marxism and the theory of history. As late as 1945, Korsch could still talk of 'the ray of hope that the living thought of Karl Marx still holds for tormented humanity'.[23] From 1945 onwards, however, he grew increasingly pessimistic. In 1950, Korsch gave a lecture series across Europe, the heart of which was later published as 'Ten Theses on Marxism Today'. In these lectures Korsch combined valid criticisms of the role of the state and capitalism in the Soviet Union with a doubt as to the future of Marxism: 'the first step in re-establishing revolutionary theory and practice consists in breaking with that Marxism which claims to monopolise revolutionary initiative as well as theoretical and practical direction'.[24] In exile in the 1950s, Korsch fell into despair, breaking his connection with Marxism. Few of his writings from that period made their way into print. In 1956, Korsch learned that he was suffering from a serious brain disease, and in 1961 he died.

Karl Korsch's undogmatic Marxism

Writers disagree when it comes to evaluating Karl Korsch's contribution to Marxist theory. The most sympathetic, the German Marxist Erich Gerlach, describes Korsch's biography of Marx as 'the Marx study most close to the actual teachings of Marx'. According to Fred Halliday of *New Left Review*, Korsch was 'one of the most interesting and original, if erratic, Marxist theorists in the West during the 1920s and 1930s'. Patrick Goode (Korsch's biographer) also emphasises what he sees as 'the positive side of Korsch's Marxism', which makes it superior to most varieties of academic Marxism. Less flatteringly, Douglas Kellner (another academic biographer) suggests that Korsch combined a theoretical stress on the need for activity with actual passivity, while Perry Anderson describes Korsch as one of the founders of Western Marxism, an academic and pessimistic step backwards from the classical Marxist tradition.[25] Eric Hobsbawm blames Karl Korsch's philosophical failings on his isolation from the mainstream Communist movement, describing Korsch as a premature member of the 1960s' individualist left, 'an ideological St. Simeon on his pillar'.[26] In another cutting phrase, Douglas Kellner describes Karl Korsch as 'the secretary to the movement of world history'. Meanwhile Leszek Kolakowski, the East European dissident, argues that Korsch never made up his mind as to whether Marxism was a science or just the expression of the interests of the working class. Because Korsch never resolved this problem, so Kolakowski argues, his work is a failure. Helena Sheehan discusses Korsch in the context of the debate over the dialectics of nature. She quotes the verdict of Korsch's great friend Brecht: 'Korsch is only a guest in the house of the proletariat. His bags are packed and always ready to leave.'[27]

If Korsch himself had been asked what his lasting contribution to Marxist theory had been, it is likely that he would have pointed to his success in persuading Marxists to discuss again the question of philosophy. Korsch had his own idea of the fight that he should wage, and that was the struggle against what he described as 'Hegel amnesia'. The Marxists of the Second International had forgotten their dialectics; without it they had lapsed into opportunism and reformism. With dialectics restored, Marxism would again represent the unity of theory and practice; it would again be a weapon for the working class as it sought to transform the world. The most striking way in which Karl Korsch actually distinguished himself from the other Marxists of the 1920s and 1930s was, however, in his stress on the 'specific' nature of Marxism. For Korsch, Marxism was first and above all else a revolutionary critique of capitalism. Marxism was not a utopian vision of a future for humanity, it was simply the science of the working class fighting capitalism.

This approach is especially clear in Korsch's biography of Marx, in which the author wrote that such a *specific* interpretation of Marxism, as a critique of late capitalism, is the only way to restore Marxism as a message of hope: 'The principle of historical specification, besides its original significance as an improved method of sociological analysis and research, becomes of first-rate importance as a polemical weapon in the practical struggle waged against the existing conditions of society.'[28] One critic of this approach was Karl Kautsky, in the mid-1920s still a leading theorist of German socialism. Kautsky was very hostile to Korsch's claims to be defending the unity of Marxist theory and practice:

For Korsch, Marxism is nothing but a theory of social revolution. In reality, one of the most outstanding characteristics of Marxism is the conviction that the social revolution is only possible under certain circumstances, and this only in certain times and countries. The Communist sects to which Korsch belongs has quite forgotten this. For them, the social revolution is always possible, everywhere, under all circumstances.[29]

Kautsky's comments do raise a real problem in Korsch's Marxism. If Korsch was right and Marxism should be understood as being 'just' the appropriate theory of the working class under late capitalism, then did that not limit the scope of Marxism?

The purpose of Marx's writing was to defend a certain conception of socialism not only as a means of working-class revolution but also as a way to make sense of the world. There is a unity between Marxism as a weapon and Marxism as a science. Marx's early writings predate the rise of the working class as a mature and global force and are founded on a historical analysis of pre-capitalist, as well as capitalist, societies. In the same way, Marx argues that because the working class under capitalism is the majority and inherits the enormous scientific advances that have taken place under capitalist society, so the proletariat is the first class that in the act of liberating itself can also liberate all society. Unlike previous oppressed classes, the working class is engaged in collective production. In the past, oppressor classes could divide peasants by offering them land; under capitalism, however, the working class can win its liberation only as a united, collective force. The working class is the first class capable of achieving universal human liberation. For this reason, Kautsky was correct to argue that Marxist theory will still be valid (but in a different way) after the working class has taken power and when the working class, as an exploited class under capitalism, has ceased to exist. If Kautsky's Marxism was the theoretical expression of a reformist compromise in the interests of the bureaucratic structures of the SPD, Karl Korsch's Marxism fitted the perspective of an activist at the moment of capitalism's crisis; it tied Marxist theory to the class struggle and to the need for revolution. Yet it presented Marxism as being simply the consciousness of the working class at the moment of revolution, and there was very little sense in Korsch of the historical traditions which the working class inherits, including the experience of class struggle, the ebbs and the flows, from whose memory the organisations of the left can be built.

Karl Korsch's stress on the specificity of Marxism led him to all manner of uneven conclusions. He argued that Marxism had nothing to say about science, and argued that there was no dialectic in nature. This argument was not in itself unusual, but Korsch defended it by making the extraordinary claim that there could be a Marxist understanding of science only in so far as 'nature' was the product of capitalist society. Therefore, as an example of the way that changes of quantity became changes of quality, he gave the case of trees bending towards human light. Karl Korsch's argument does beg the question of what nature is. For other writers, the point of the debate was to consider what shaped a world without class, a world indeed without human beings. In Korsch's version, nature was only of interest in so far as it was *capitalist* nature, which does raise doubts as to whether he had understood the terms of the debate.[30] Karl Korsch also insisted that there was no such thing as a Marxist theory of human nature, because even to suggest, with Engels, that labour played a role in the development of humanity was to revert to 'a secularised form of those older theories which derived the same facts from the command of God'.[31]

Even at its best, Korsch's Marxism was remarkably abstract. Korsch would invoke categories, such as 'theory, 'practice' or 'philosophy', without giving them any concrete meaning. Thus, while accepting the materialist argument that human beings are the product of their conditions, Korsch refused to say which conditions were important and how they worked. Although Korsch formally argued that Marxism only had meaning as the tool to achieve a working-class revolution, his failure to describe workers or the significance of their fight meant that this was a very Hegelian, impractical and *philosophical* justification of Marxism. At its worst, Korsch's Marxism suffered from a glaring omission. There was almost no sense at all in his writings of the unevenness of working-class consciousness. He assumed that it was always the early 1920s; that the majority of workers were always revolutionary. There was very little sign that Korsch understood how to organise the minority of workers who did consider themselves Marxists. Somehow that would simply happen. Likewise, Korsch never argued that any form of organisation could carry the unity between theory and practice. That task would always be left to individuals.

It is useful to compare Karl Korsch with his contemporary, Georg Lukács. Like Korsch, Lukács stressed the need for a dialectical Marxism and the need to link Marxist theory to Marxist practice. Like his friend, Lukács developed as a Marxist writer. He went through an early ultra-left period, before moving towards the heart of dissident Marxism, as he assimilated the lessons of the Russian Revolution. This stage in Lukács's development was expressed in an important book, *History and Class Consciousness*.[32] More than Korsch, Lukács accepted the need to build a revolutionary party, and this explains his decision to join the Hungarian Communist Party following the Russian revolution. As it happened, Lukács's tragedy was to remain in this party, even after it had degenerated. His refusal to break with Stalinism in the 1930s meant that he was compelled to act as the mouthpiece of Russian policy in the arts and philosophy. Lukács did, however, take part in the Hungarian rising of 1956 and joined the short-lived Imre Nagy government, risking more than other prominent Marxists (such as Brecht), who had compromised more decisively with Stalinism. There are at least three ways, therefore, in which Lukács's Marxism is superior to Korsch's. First, Lukács was not satisfied to limit himself to writing about philosophy. In a number of works, he attempted to marry his philosophical insights to detailed historical examples, against which his theories could be tested.[33] Second, Lukács had a far more urgent sense of the difficulties of revolution, and hence the need to build some kind of network or organisation to bridge the gap between the present (as it was known), and the future (as it was desired). This point suggests the third way in which Lukács's Marxism was superior: it came far closer to expressing the unity between ideas and action. Whatever Korsch's merits as a Marxist, Lukács was more successful in bringing his theory and practice together as one.

This chapter has argued that Korsch's Marxism failed. Because there was no sense of objective reality in his writing, so his philosophical categories remained abstract and empty of meaning. Thus he failed to achieve the task he set himself of reuniting theory and practice. For all its strengths, Korsch's Marxism was a recipe for passivity. Yet it would be better to remember Korsch for the goals he set himself than for what he failed to do. Brought up at a time when official Marxism seemed sterile and empty, he attempted to translate the workers' struggles of 1918–23 into revolutionary theory. Marxism is a means to revolution, and is also a vision of how a different society could work. Karl Korsch may have been wrong when he limited Marxism to a critique of existing society, but he was absolutely right to insist that socialism must be revolutionary or it is nothing. Despite its weaknesses, Karl Korsch's work reminds us that there is still a world to be won.

Georges Henein: surrealism and socialism

The victory of the Russian Revolution was an epoch-making event. So indeed was its defeat, and the replacement of the open society of the first few years by a different, Stalinist order. The echoes of the total process were discussed right across the world, by trade unionists and poets, by militants, artists and musicians, by unskilled day-labourers and the most highly skilled of engineers. Many issues were dragged into the dispute. High Stalinism was a total philosophy of life. Any 'good Communist' knew the correct party line on national development (socialism in one country), democracy (bourgeois in the West, transitional in the East), human philosophy (mechanical materialism), history (Stalin's stages theory of progress), culture (Zhdanovism), biology (Lysenkoism), art (socialist realism) and so on. Independent-minded left-wingers challenged each of these innovations as a distortion of Marxism. The best organised of critics were the supporters of Trotsky's Fourth International. The range of anti-Stalinists who followed the orbit of Trotskyism in the 1930s was extraordinary. In the United States Trotskyists worked alongside philosophers (John Dewey, James Burnham and Sidney Hook), historians (Edmund Wilson) and novelists (Saul Bellow), as well as prominent trade unionists (James Cannon). Britain provided musicians (Michael Tippett), journalists (C.L.R. James) and sympathetic Red priests (Conrad Noel).[1] France added smugglers, syndicalists and surrealists (André Breton), while in Mexico one of Trotsky's allies was Diego Rivera, 'the man who painted walls'.

In North Africa, the 'literary Trotskyists' were led by Georges Henein (1914–1973), a poet and writer, a friend of André Gide and André Breton. Henein published a number of books, including *Déraisons d'être*,[2] *Un Temps de petite fille*,[3] *L'Incompatible*,[4] and *Le Seuil interdit*.[5] In 1939, he joined the International Federation of Independent Revolutionary Artists, an anti-Stalinist initiative organised by Breton. Around this time, he helped to establish a network of Egyptian socialists, Art and Freedom, later Bread and Freedom.[6] He was much later an associate editor of the French magazine *Express*.[7] Henein deserves mention here for at least three aspects of his life. The first was the part he played in thinking through the problems of national liberation in the Third World. The second was the connection he made between an art and a politics of freedom. The third was the pamphlet he wrote, *The Prestige of Terror*, in response to the news of the Hiroshima bomb. In his politics, his art and in his life, Henein played a dissident's role.

For our purposes, the most important period of Georges Henein's life came between 1939 and 1946. During these years, he lived in North Africa and contributed to the creation of a socialist movement in Egypt. There are problems in writing the story of this period. Most histories of the Egyptian left have concentrated on the Communist Parties, neglecting the part played by other traditions. The labour historians Ahmad Abdalla, Joel Beinin, Ellis Jay Goldberg and Zachary Lockman make no mention of the Trotskyist groups. Gilles Perrault dismisses them as 'rare birds'. Even Selma Botman, the most sympathetic historian, argues that Henein's group was of no lasting importance:

> Trotskyism for the most part was an insignificant movement, confined to a small intellectual circle of young Egyptians. While there were limited and sporadic efforts to reach a broader base of the Egyptian population, this brand of Marxist thought never gripped even a small segment of the popular classes.[8]

Yet when Art et Liberté (Art and Freedom) was set up in 1939, it was the first explicitly socialist group to be formed in Egypt since the 1920s. Its newspaper, *al-Tatawwur* (*Evolution*), was the first Egyptian socialist paper to be published in Arabic. When Henein's group stood in the December 1944–January 1945 Egyptian elections, they were among the first socialists to take part in open political work for over twenty years. The group went through a series of changes, calling itself Pain et Liberté (Bread and Freedom, 1940), the Socialist Front (1944–45) and then alternately the Egyptian Section of the Revolutionary Communist Party, the Egyptian Section of the Fourth International, and the International Communist Group (1945–46). It was the group's success that made it visible to the secret police, and forced its leading cadres to escape into exile in 1946.

Perhaps the most important aspect of Georges Henein's activism was his commitment to internationalist politics, which was expressed through his Trotskyism. For most of the twentieth century, the dominant strategy within the left in the Third World was to place all priority on the sole question of national liberation. Within the many Communist parties in Africa, Asia and Latin America, the argument has been that national independence is the first goal, and until that has been achieved, all talk of socialism is meaningless. Consequently, the revolutions that have taken place in China, Algeria, Cuba and elsewhere have set themselves the task of uniting the nation under state control. Much like the old bourgeois revolutions that took place in seventeenth- and eighteenth-century Europe and America, the colonial revolutions of the twentieth century achieved the removal of feudalism and the urbanisation of the workforce. Yet even while the workers and peasants of the Third World have challenged imperialism, and have fought for a transformation of society, their leaders have often been prepared to accept more limited change.[9] Georges Henein and his co-thinkers did not recognise any separation between the struggle for national freedom and the fight for socialism. There have been larger and better-known Trotskyist parties in Vietnam, Sri Lanka, South Africa and Bolivia, but Henein's group is worthy of study. It possessed a broad conception of internationalism, in which the goal was to liberate all the workers of the world. Unlike their rivals in Egypt, the Trotskyists demanded a root-and-branch socialism, for their region and the world.

Both Egyptian and French

Georges Henein was born in Cairo on 20 November 1914. His
father was a Copt (an Egyptian Christian), Sadik Henein Pasha,
who became a minister under King Fouad I. His mother was an
Italian, Maria Zanelli. Their circle was made up of foreign merchants living in Cairo. These were multiple outsiders, Christians
and not Muslims, native Egyptians who retained French documents (enabling them to avoid taxation) and spoke the languages of
Europe. It was an established position, but increasingly precarious.
During the nineteenth century the Egyptian economy had been
transformed as the Middle East was sucked into the emerging
world capitalist economy. Peasants became landless rural labourers,
while artisans found that their handicrafts were replaced by cheap,
mass-produced imports from Europe. The cities attracted an army
of dispossessed peasants searching for work in the factories. Egypt
itself was a nominally sovereign kingdom, but it came under the
sway of a succession of imperialist powers, including the British
from the 1890s onwards. European capitalists encouraged the
development of middlemen and agents, many of whom began to
invest in industry and land themselves. Many such native entre-
preneurs were Greek, Armenian, Syrian or Jewish. They kept
themselves culturally distinct from the rest of the population.[10]
They owed their privileged position to the Capitulations which
allowed some of the religious minorities in the Ottoman Empire to
enjoy the protection of Europeans. Such was Henein's background.

We know little of Henein's early life. He was first educated at
home. In 1924, his father was sent as the Egyptian ambassador to
Spain, and Henein followed. Two years later he attended the Lycée
Chateaubriand in Rome. Later, Henein divided his time between
Cairo and Paris. One early published work was titled 'On Un-
realism' and announced that 'nothing is as useless as the real'. By
1935, Henein was a member of the Egyptian literary circle 'the
Essayists'. One of their publications was a 'Dictionary of the habits
of the bourgeois world', to which Henein contributed the following
definitions: 'Anarchy – victory of the spirit over certainty.... Me –
the most important thing in the world.... Work – everything that
one doesn't want to do.' Such 'libertarianism' hardly transcended

the privileged conditions to which Henein was used. Yet at least our poet was eager to learn, and his sympathies were all on the left. In the same year, Henein made contact with the editors of a French publication, *Les Humbles*, whose contributors included Victor Serge. His first work for them was 'Les chants des violents', in praise of working-class revolt.[11]

In Paris, Henein met André Breton and identified with the art of the surrealists. This was a revolutionary form of modernist art, expressed in painting, collage, poetry and novels. Surrealism employed elements of surprise and montage to shock the audience out of habits of passively accepting art, or indeed its situation in the world. The aesthetic of surrealism was avowedly revolutionary. Such art required a political position to accompany it. The leading surrealist Breton read Trotsky's biography of Lenin. Under the influence of Bolshevism, he encouraged his comrades to join the French Communist Party. Yet the Communists were themselves engaged on a long journey from revolutionary to reformist politics, as we have seen. In 1935, they announced the Popular Front, a permanent alliance with Socialists and even the French Radicals (the political ancestors of today's 'Gaullist' centre-right). The surrealists then broke with Stalinism, and for the rest of the decade were loosely allied with Trotsky. The underlying philosophy of the movement was dynamic and elusive, extending as it did to both art and politics. To explain it, we can do no better than to offer some of the definitions given by leading surrealists themselves:

> Surrealism is not a new or easier means of expression, nor even a metaphysics of poetry; it is a total means of complete liberation of the mind and all that resembles it. (French Surrealist Group, 1925)

> The vice called surrealism is the disordered and impassioned use of the image as a drug, or rather the uncontrolled provocation of the image for itself and for what it brings in the domain of representation by way of imperturbable metamorphosis: for each image, every time, forces you to reconsider the whole universe. (Louis Aragon, 1928)

> The simplest surrealist act consists in going down the street, revolver in hand, and shooting into the crowd for as long as one can. (André Breton, 1930)[12]

In 1936, Henein contributed to the surrealist magazine *La Flèche*, based in France. That September, his name was one of a dozen signatories to a surrealist manifesto denouncing the Moscow Trials and supporting Trotsky's right to claim asylum in Norway or France.[13] The following year Henein organised a conference on surrealism in Egypt, together with Émile Simon (author of a book on Marx), Angelo de Riz (an exiled Italian anarchist) and Ramses Younan (Henein's long-time ally). Months before the war began, Henein attempted to establish a network of artistic co-thinkers in Egypt, Art and Freedom. In December 1939, he helped to set up a left magazine, *Don Quixote*. Its general editor Henri Curiel later became a leading Egyptian Communist.[14] In 1940, Art and Freedom transformed itself into a full left-wing party, Bread and Freedom. Its programme called for the transformation of the Middle East along socialist lines. If such politics were ever going to prosper, then there were many alternative forces that had first to be pushed aside. The war had opened up Egyptian society, and several other movements were better placed to grow.

Rivals

The war years transformed the Egyptian economy. Production expanded in many industries, notably textiles, processed food, chemicals, glass, leather, cement and petroleum. The British camps employed up to 300,000 Egyptians at relatively high rates of pay, who then had money to spend on Egyptian products, without Egyptian employers having to pay a penny towards their wages. One effect of this growth was to give confidence to Egyptian workers. The number of industrial labourers increased, according to one estimate, from around 412,000 in 1937 to over 1.5 million in 1946.[15] Trade unions were legalised in 1942, and the textile workers of Shubra al-Khayma in Cairo responded by building independent unions. There were strikes over pay, conditions and trade-union recognition, which became rapidly politicised through the experience of government repression and British wartime restrictions. By late 1945 the level of industrial unrest was steadily increasing. In December, Shubra was under army occupation as wage disputes spiralled into a full-time confrontation with the government. It was clear that the ending of the war would lead rapidly to social crisis. It was not clear how that crisis would end.

The largest political party in Egypt before 1939 was the Wafd. It was a nationalist organisation, dedicated to removing the British and developing Egyptian industry. Having been placed in power in 1942, the Wafd organised and won the subsequent election. The organisation remained influential, and in 1943 it succeeded in having Fuad Serag el Dine Pasha, one of the richest landowners in Egypt, elected as the honorary president of the existing trade unions. However, the Wafd was seen by most Egyptians as too close to the British, and it failed to grow out of the opportunities presented by the war. Assisted by the failure of the Wafd, a number of small groups took part in the post-war events, including the Muslim Brotherhood and the several small Communist groups.

The Muslim Brotherhood was founded in 1929 by Hassan al-Banna; in the 1940s it claimed between half a million and a million members.[16] The Brotherhood's participation in the nationalist movement was marked by an ambivalent attitude towards the state, which paralysed it whenever it was faced with seizing power. Each time the nationalist movement moved closer to actual confrontation with the state, the Brotherhood moved closer to the palace or the government. During the 1946 crisis Hassan al-Banna, who was one of the leaders of the Brotherhood, co-operated with the government. Then, in the middle of the police strike of April 1948, the Brotherhood published the government's ultimatum to the policemen ordering them back to work. Later that year, the Muslim Brotherhood lurched into terrorism.[17] It attacked foreign shops and businesses, especially Jewish enterprises. In 1952, the Muslim Brotherhood supported the Free Officers' coup; several members of the Free Officers, notably Sadat, were also members of the Brotherhood, but the vacillations of the Muslim Brotherhood meant that the organisation failed to have any significant impact on the leadership or the policies of the Free Officers. The Brotherhood was eventually manoeuvred out of any positions of power and dissolved.

The first Egyptian Communist Party had been set up in 1920. However, it was quickly smashed by repression.[18] This set a pattern for the future. As soon as any left-wing group took part in public activity, it would bring down on its head the wrath of the Egyptian state. In the early 1930s, a series of small Communist Parties were set up, with the backing of the International. All were immediately closed down. Yet by the 1940s the hold of the state had begun to weaken. Communist ideas attracted hundreds of young people, including some Egyptian workers, although the leadership of the various groups typically came from among the sons and daughters of Cairo's resident foreign bourgeoisie. Henri Curiel, son of a wealthy Jewish banker, set up the Egyptian Movement for National Liberation (EMNL) in 1943. Hillel Schwartz, from a similar background to Curiel, set up Iskra, a propagandist group which attracted a following of intellectuals and students.

The perspectives of the Communist groups were determined by the politics of the Popular Front. Liberation was seen as a process that would take place in stages. First the Egyptian bourgeoisie would emancipate itself from British rule, and only then could workers' issues come to the fore. The Communist Party of Great Britain's colonial office, which was expected to supervise work in Egypt, together with the equivalent office within the French Communist Party, offered this advice to the Egyptian groups: 'The people's democracy we want to establish in Egypt is not a form of the dictatorship of the proletariat. We aim to establish a democratic dictatorship of all the classes struggling against imperialism and feudalism.'[19] This emphasis on the political priority of the interests of the Egyptian bourgeoisie does not mean that the Communists absented themselves from the trade unions. Inside the trade unions, however, Communist groups argued that the most immediate issue was not pay or conditions, but the question of national liberation. The limits of this politics became clear following the following the Free Officers' coup of July 1952. The EMNL and the trade-union leadership responded to the coup by calling off planned transport strikes. In 1952, and in subsequent crises, the Communists could not decide whether the new government was proto-fascist or representative of a local 'progressive bourgeoisie'. Leaflets vacillated alternately between support and hostility to the new system. The Communists waited to see which side the officers would support in the Cold War. That August, a strike broke out in the mill town of Kafr al-Dawwar near Alexandria. Despite the fact that the workers had declared their support for the coup, the Free Officers hanged two of the strikers. The EMNL and the trade unions opposed all calls for sympathy action in support of the strike.

Henein and his group

The name of Georges Henein's group, Art et Liberté, would suggest that this was originally a literary salon.[20] Lotfallah Soliman,
one of the earliest members, describes the group as a collection of
bohemians, 'intellectuals, writers, artists'.[21] Beyond Soliman and
Henein, other members included Ramsis Younan, Anwar Kamal
and Kamal al-Tilmisani.[22] Although the group was almost unique
among the Egyptian left, in that its leadership was drawn from
Arabic-speaking indigenous Egyptians, the language used was
French, the language of cosmopolitan Egypt.[23] As Botman indicates,
'the audience capable of appreciating the form and being influenced by the content of the group's ideas was extremely limited'.[24]
Art and Freedom organised exhibitions in Cairo, in 1941, 1942,
1944 and 1945. The purpose of these exhibitions was to raise the
profile of Egyptian surrealist art, and they were chiefly remarkable
for the large number of women artists and photographers who took
part. The group also organised public lectures. Art et Liberté
owned its own publishing house, Éditions Masses (The Masses),
operating from 10 rue Eloui in Cairo. A typical pamphlet was *Qui
est monsieur Aragon?* by Jean Damien (a pseudonym for Henein).
This pilloried the French poet Aragon's lapse from surrealism to
conventional verse, which was explained in terms of his political
ties to Stalinism. Aragon's work 'confirms to us the urgent need
for a critical reappraisal, which would halt at last the immense
"Russian retreat" which has lost the majority of the ambitions of
our time'.[25] These words may have contributed to the Egyptian
artistic scene, and Aragon was a popular and well-known figure
especially in France, but they did not contribute to the building of
a mass party, offering a socialist solution to the crisis of Egyptian
society.

The first way in which Art and Freedom did attempt to break
the bonds of polite society was by publishing its newspaper, *al-
Tatawwur*. Between January and September 1940, seven issues were
published, in French and Arabic. The first five were produced in
magazine form, the last two as newspapers. This was very much a
literary review. The magazine described itself as 'the premier review of art and literature in the Arab world'. Articles addressed

questions of imperialism and women's rights, education, philosophy and literature. There were also Arabic translations of Albert Cossery's short stories.[26] The magazine was edited by Anwar Kamal. Its tone is evident in an article published in March 1940: 'This review fights against the reactionary spirit, protects the rights of the individual and insists on the right of women to live in freedom. This review fights for modern art and free thought, and presents to young Egypt the movements of today.'[27]

The paper achieved a passable circulation, and was respected within educated circles, but was useless for propaganda work. Perhaps this was not the fault of the Trotskyists. Given the high level of police activity, any publication would have to be propagandist in character. Alex Acheson, a British soldier stationed in Egypt during the war, describes the group working in conditions of strict secrecy: 'The Egyptians had to work under extremely difficult conditions. There was apparently an "open society", but [one] where revolutionary politics of any kind were illegal, and the penalty was imprisonment (which was often used to break people, physically and psychologically).' Acheson mentions Henein's wife Iqbal Alaily, who had published a book on *The German Genius* to counteract the atrocity propaganda of the Allies. Despite her condemnation of German chauvinism, Iqbal Alaily received the hostile attention of the British police. 'She was told that unless she curtailed her activities and stopped associating with the group, she would finish up in the Tura quarries. For a delicate girl like that it would have been a death sentence.'[28]

From the middle of 1940 onwards, Art and Freedom was superseded by a second and different organisation, Bread and Freedom. The new name represented a change of emphasis. Although the exhibitions continued until 1945, the group was now far more determined to recruit working-class support. Speeches and public meetings addressed economic issues, including poverty and class, and the need to transform the existing parties. Indeed, Bread and Freedom did have some limited success among textile and aviation workers.[29] By 1942, the group may have had around a hundred members. Some of the character of the group at this time is conveyed by Sayed Suleiman Rifai, who was later a prominent member of the Egyptian Communist Party, working under the name

Badr. In the 1940s, he was a mechanic in the Egyptian Air Force. His account of two Trotskyist meetings is romanticised and overblown, but still revealing:

> My first contact, which came about by chance, was with Anwar Kamal's group, Bread and Freedom. Later, I learned that Georges Henein belonged to it. It was a group of intellectuals. A meeting was arranged in the country, near the Pyramids. There turned out to be about a dozen of us. Kamal arrived. I can see him now, with that lock of black hair falling over one eye and a cigar stuck in his face. He greeted us and said, 'We'll sing the anthem'. Just like that, in the middle of the desert, they sang this song that began, 'Onward comrades, to live is to struggle!' I was amazed. Then Kamal made a speech, waving his cigar about. I found it meaningless.
>
> The next time, the meeting was [in] a house. There were three guys I had known in the Air Force, and Kamal again. He gave a talk on historical materialism. I understood nothing. Not a word! What's more, none of the others did, either. I went home utterly discouraged, depressed. I was convinced I was completely useless. There never was a third meeting because Kamal was arrested. The group had to disband. In any case, I lost contact.[30]

In 1942, the state acted against Bread and Freedom. Sixteen of its members were arrested and held for a year. Selma Botman suggests that this was the end of the group: 'while it did live on until 1946, it did so in a very truncated and quiescent form ... the group simply withered away.' In reality, the group survived this first wave of arrests, and was able to continue as a clandestine organisation. The Trotskyists published a newspaper, *el-Megela el-Gedida* (*The New Magazine*), which was closed down by the government in May 1944.[31] The organisation may have grown, indeed it reached the peak of its influence in 1945–46.

Despite the repression, Bread and Freedom carried out international work. It corresponded with Palestinian Trotskyists, and published the Palestinians' letter on Zionism.[32] In 1943, the Israeli Jewish socialist party, Hachomer Hatzaïr, made contact with Bread and Freedom, asking if it would support a two-state solution in Palestine. Hachomer Hatzaïr argued that 'the revolutionary solution [was] to stop the domination of one nation by another', suggesting that the Arabs already had several states to call their own, so it would only be fair if Arab socialists supported Jewish demands for self-determination. The Egyptian group turned down their appeals. What the Trotskyists were looking for was united action around an agreed policy, and neither Hachomer Hatzaïr nor Mapam was keen to listen. Perhaps the most interesting aspect of this dialogue is that it took place at all. The left Zionists were aligned with the official Communist International, while Bread and Freedom was not. The Jewish groups were still keen to make links with the Arab left. After 1945, when there were larger Egyptian Communist parties, and when parties like Mapam could easily have kept up with them, such contacts hardly took place at all.[33]

From its inception, Bread and Freedom was distinguished from the other forces on the left by its internationalist stance. The Communist groups tended to dissolve themselves into the 'patriotic' struggle for Egyptian liberation. In the process, they came up against the Egyptian bourgeoisie's ambitions for territorial expansion, notably in the Sudan. By contrast, the Trotskyists attempted to combine demands for national liberation with a continuing emphasis on class. One manifesto declared, 'We must struggle against British imperialism. We must struggle against budding Egyptian imperialism. We must struggle against imperialism wherever we find it. That is why we call for active solidarity with all the peoples who are fighting for their liberty.'[34] Unlike so much of the left, Bread and Freedom avoided the trap of supporting the Egyptian state's demands for territorial expansion.

1944–46

The Trotskyist group attained the height of its influence during the elections of 1944–5. The party stood Dr Fathy al Ramly for the Cairo constituency of Mahkamet al Sayeda, then held by Ahmed Hussein, the leader of Young Egypt. Afterwards, Bread and Freedom sent back to their comrades in Britain a report on the election, which described the intervention as a success. Alongside Communists who also took part in the elections, this was the first time that any socialist had taken part in open propaganda work in Egypt since the 1920s. According to a letter written by Georges Henein,

Dr. Ramly's initiative led to the immediate formation of a Socialist Front (*al-Gabha al-Ishtirakya*) in support of his candidature. At the beginning the Socialist Front was a grouping of two Stalinist centres plus the whole Trotskyist movement.... But as soon as the electoral campaign took a definitely Socialist shape with a predominant internationalist note, the Stalinists withdrew. Nevertheless, the Socialist Front did very well without the Stalinists, and the gap they left behind was immediately filled by an enthusiastic new element, youth from the University, and advanced workers.

Despite the withdrawal of the Communist Parties, the agitation continued, and a programme of transitional demands was elaborated:

About ten days before the poll, the Government began to take the matter quite seriously. Orders were given and the socialist propaganda brought to a standstill; meetings were disrupted; supporters arrested; demonstrations roughly handled and disbanded.... Dr. Ramly was given the charity of 23 votes (while securing in reality at least 200 votes out of the 1000 expressed in this constituency). Whatever the official result and the Government's treachery, the campaign was excellently conducted and its effects are developing every day.

Surviving members of the group would later remember the enthusiasm with which Georges Henein threw himself into the campaign, as well as the lessons that the Trotskyists drew from their intervention: 'It showed us the necessity of working together with other groups.'[35] Bread and Freedom seem to have grown as a result of this intervention, notably in Alexandria, where the organisation recruited 'many new elements'.[36] Other socialist candidates did well. Mohamed Mustafa, from the truck-drivers' union, and Fadaly Abdel, a textile worker, received 230 and 820 votes, respectively.

In the summer of 1945, it seemed that Bread and Freedom's successful intervention in the Egyptian general election might enable the Trotskyists to win enough other forces to found a mass socialist party. This, at least, is what Georges Henein predicted, in a letter sent in July to Ann Keen of the Revolutionary Communist Party (RCP) in Britain:

The Socialist Front ... has become the Committee for the Foundation of the Socialist Party of Egypt. A popular meeting is going to be organised shortly under its banner, for the celebration of Labour's victory.

The Egyptian workers are simply stirred by the left triumphant swing all over the continent and they are asking themselves, 'Why haven't we got our own Labour Party?'[37]

In October, Henein's correspondence described Bread and Freedom as fighting propaganda work against the Communists. The most important way in which the Egyptian Trotskyists distinguished themselves from the rest of the left was over the question of national liberation. For the Trotskyists, there was a necessary connection between national liberation and socialism. For the Communists, national liberation had to come first:

> The Stalinists are doing their best to bring confusion to its peak. They are openly collaborating with fascists, promoting the same outworn 'national front of liberation' where there is room for anyone and everything. We are going to state our position in a long document on the 'national question' which is due to appear within two weeks.

Georges Henein painted an optimistic picture of a vibrant group, at the height of its success, winning layers of new recruits, and grappling with the real theoretical problems posed by its successful intervention in the general election:

> Already Ramsis Younane has prepared and issued an excellent study in Arabic dealing with the Labour Party, its beginnings, its fight, its perspectives. Loutfallah is working harder than ever and thanks to him and to a group of enthusiastic youngsters it looks as if we are going to have a brilliant season.[38]

From mid-1945, however, state repression intensified. The Egyptian government established a 'Supreme Court of Security'. With this new institution designed to coordinate the campaign of the security forces against the Egyptian revolution, it was the Trotskyists who were singled out as the first group to smash.[39] By December 1945, Henein's reports made it clear that police repression had intensified:

> Forty-five people have been arrested. At their head our friend Anwar Kamal who is being charged with the recent publication of a pamphlet in Arabic.... The editorial board of the Stalinist weekly, *Al-Fagr al-Gadid* [*New Dawn*], has also been arrested. The repression is fluid and the authorities are hitting in all directions.... Now any direct publicity in the Trot. papers will do more harm than good.[40]

While rejecting help from his British comrades, Henein was less cautious about asking his French literary contacts to raise a clamour. On 22 December 1945, he wrote to Henri Calet asking for help to secure the liberty of Anwar Kamal and Salama Moussa. Two months later, Henein could report that one friend, Younane, had been freed (on bail of 10,000 francs). Younane was now hoping to leave Egypt, if the authorities would let him go.[41]

In retrospect, it seems clear that the arrests of December 1945 permanently knocked the confidence out of the members of the group, who now felt unable to publish any public newspaper. All their open political activities were scaled down. Despite this, Bread and Freedom took full part in the protest movement of February 1946. This followed the publication of the Egyptian government's negotiations with the British Army, which were seen as a betrayal of the struggle for independence. University students organised a demonstration to petition the King. They were attacked by the British Army and the Egyptian police force on the Abbas Bridge, and twenty-seven people were killed. The massacre was the signal for a wide-scale radicalisation of the national movement. Several large unions agreed to call a full general strike, but the transport unions pulled out and the strike collapsed.[42] Henein's group joined the demonstrations, bringing out at least five breathless leaflets in the days that followed, urging the students to take their protest into the working-class districts and the factories.

> Students And Workers!! unite as the spectre of reaction is haunting over the Country. You students alone cannot overcome the police, go to the workers and you will find enough power to meet the police, without a swift link with the workers our revolution will lose its popular grounds. Don't appear before the Royal palace but to the Factories, to the Workers, the true representatives of the People.[43]

This explosion of protest was ended in the spring and summer of 1946 by another wave of arrests. On 21 March 1946, the French paper *Le Monde* named those interned without trial, including Yusuf al Mudarrik and his fellow delegates to the 1945 world trade-union congress, and also the well-known socialist Salama Moussa. E. Sablier, writing in the French newspaper, pointed out that a number of Trotskyists had been detained, although like other contemporaries he may have exaggerated their significance:

In a new country like Egypt progressive ideas are still the prerogative of intellectuals. Those among them who devote themselves to the study of Marxism find the opportunism of the official communists today hardly intelligible. Thus they are drawn for the most part towards the undiluted Leninism which is incarnated by the Trotskyists. Moreover, while the solicitude evidenced by Soviet Russia for the Arab peoples is visibly inspired by its own strategic or diplomatic interests, Trotskyist propaganda is based on the interests of defending the proletariat. Furthermore, Trotsky and his revolutionary followers are feared as much, if not more, by the official communists as by the reactionary circles. Thus, by applying the label Trotskyist to the people arrested the Egyptian government is seeking, no doubt, to avoid Soviet remonstrances of the type which Ankara recently experienced during the anti-Communist demonstrations.[44]

Two months later, Ahmed Kamel Moursi Pasha, the Egyptian Minister of Justice, introduced a new law enacting fines of between 50 and 10,000 Egyptian pounds for persons 'receiving subsidies from or maintaining contact with foreign organisations with a propaganda aim'. By the summer of 1946, over one thousand people were held in detention, four papers were banned, and the government had closed down five bookshops and two socialist clubs.[45]

After the February demonstrations, and following the consequent arrests, there seems to have been a lull in the group's activity. Alex Acheson suggests that Loutfallah Soliman developed a sympathy with the German Trotskyist IKD against the International Secretariat, and this may have exacerbated the differences between the group and the rest of the International. If this is true, then it is likely that Soliman was more concerned to defend the IKD's right to be heard than to support their actual analysis of events in Europe. The argument between the IKD and the International centred around the question of whether national liberation or social liberation should be the primary concern for socialists in the occupied territories of Europe in the years between 1940 and 1945. It is not surprising that these arguments had a resonance for socialists opposing the British presence in Egypt, but it would be strange if Soliman had absorbed the full IKD position. By extension, that would have meant support for the idea that Egypt needed national liberation before it could achieve socialism – the antithesis of what he and his friends argued elsewhere.[46]

In a letter, Jock Haston noted that the group was aware of discussions within the British party, but made less effort to make its own discussions more widely known. 'Some of the leading Egyptian comrades have important differences with International policy and with the policy of some of the sections (including the British).' He continued:

> There are, for instance, criticisms of the British policy of attempting to win members from the ranks of the Stalinists; criticisms of the International's policy in regard to democratic centralism, of the organised 'tightness' of the International; views on the fusion discussions in the USA. Now it is no earthly use holding these opinions if you do nothing to make them known within the International.[47]

Within a week of Haston sending this letter, the group did again make contact with its comrades in Britain. Georges Henein contacted the RCP to say that he planned to leave Cairo for Paris, 'where he hopes to publish a book of poems'.[48] Loutfallah was exhausted, 'which makes personal contact with him sometimes difficult'. After Henein left for Paris, the leadership was entrusted into the hands of Ramsis Younane. Around this time, Henein wrote a letter to Nicolas Calas, explaining his frustration with the Fourth International:

> I have come to a growing sympathy with the anarchists whose attitude despite (or because of) its innocence, is fine, consistent and honest.... In truth, what is tearing me away from the strategy of the Fourth International, is its lack of passion, which combines with an over-abundance of plans. With Trotsky, there was passion, nobility, the whiff of gunpowder. I see nothing of these in the voice or the bearing of his successors.[49]

In retrospect, Henein's departure marked the beginning of the decline of the group. There simply were not enough experienced members to keep the party going, at a time when hundreds of thousands of Egyptian workers were taking part in mass strikes. There were huge opportunities to grow and it was the Communist groups that harvested the rewards.

The organisation did not die out all at once. In the spring and summer of 1946, Bread and Freedom, now renamed the International Communist Group, took part in setting up a 'League for the Struggle against Unemployment'. Joint committees were set up in the workers' quarter of Abbasieh in Cairo, among the workers in the military workshops, and among the textile workers living in Shubra al-Khayma. It also seems that Henein wrote to the RCP comrades in Britain in October 1946, although the correspondence has since been lost.[50] In the summer of 1947, the Egyptian Trotskyists issued their 'first manifesto since the re-organisation of the group', which denounced the attempts of the Egyptian bourgeoisie to claim an imperial jurisdiction of its own over the Sudan. In 1952, Anwar Kamal and Lotfallah Soliman issued a manifesto.[51] Apart from these occasional signs, however, there is no sustained evidence of the group's existence after 1946.

As for Georges Henein, in 1947 he helped to establish a literary publication, *La part du Sable*, which owed more to the surrealism of the 1920s than it did to the high political Trotskyism of his immediate past. With his wife Iqbal Alaily, he signed a French surrealist manifesto dated June 1947, arguing that the future belonged to an alliance of anarchism and Trotskyism. 'The personal attitude of Leon Trotsky – astonishingly inspired and most often irreducible in his own views about the moral problem – and his marvellous contribution to *incessant human sedition* have done so much to bring this alliance together and reinforce the pact.' Henein's diary suggests a continuing loyalty to many key ideas of socialism. One entry recorded the death of Victor Serge in 1947. Another reflected on Lenin's philosophical notebooks. 'Hegel corrected Kant, Marx corrected Hegel, and Lenin accepted nothing less than the creation of paradise on earth.'[52] Henein's sympathies continued to belong to the left. Yet their visible practical consequences were reduced, almost to nothing.

Henein versus Trotsky?

We have already seen that Henein was drifting away from orthodox Trotskyism by 1946, complaining that the official movement had adopted plans in place of passion. He seems to have felt that his own politics, however 'correctly' phrased, had been separated from his existence as an artist. Henein felt frustrated with himself and despaired of the world. He was grasping for a higher synthesis of art and politics, which seemed to be located always just out of his reach. It is in this context that we should judge the pamphlet *The Prestige of Terror*, which Henein wrote in the days following the dropping of the atomic bomb. It was published in Cairo in French. 'This is not a thesis', he wrote, but a manifesto. For a thesis would require him to accumulate statistics and references, and would sacrifice 'the moment of revolt and fury' which compelled him to write. His subject was war and the democracies.[53]

'We are invited to salute the eternal destruction of a dragon.' The dragon was fascism; the dragon was war itself. Yet if the allies were St George, then it seemed with each new burst of jousting, they came to resemble more closely their antagonist. The dropping of the bomb was one of the worst days in the career of humanity. 'Soon St George will be nothing more than a hideous variant of that dragon.' Under the guise of a war for democracy, and against racism, old values were re-establishing themselves. 'The cult of the infallibility of the leader, the deliberate creation of false hierarchies, the repression of news and of the means of communication, the frenetic organisation of state lies at all hours of the day, the growing terror of the police with regards to the people' – this was the progress for which the leaders of America, Britain and Russia fought.

Of course, Georges Henein continued, 'there exist just wars'. The danger lay in winning them. He gave an example taken from the Russian war effort. An early Soviet communiqué told the story of a German soldier who said that he would not fight against a workers' state. 'Instead of exalting the popular Russian and German heroes who stretched out the arm to one another in their common liberation struggles, the Russian propaganda services have wasted themselves so quickly in expressing a miserable pathos from which emerged some of the most sinister figures in Russian history.' The Soviets claimed to be fighting for princes like Alexander Nevsky, not for peasant leaders like Pougachov or Stepan Razin. The 1945 Panslav conference gave as its ideal the ethnic wars of the Middle Ages. In such hands, democracy (even Soviet democracy) justified the removal of populations, racism, and ultimately the atomic bomb. 'The penetration of Hitlerian politics into the ranks of the democracies seems to offend almost no-one.'

Georges Henein described a world in which unprecedented crimes were taking place. He bemoaned 'The organised deportation of workers, which no-one suggests will end with the Nazis.' Even progressive political thought that had stood up to such arbitrary repression in the past had contributed 'towards a strange acceptance of that cruel and vain order which has emerged in front of us'. The focus of his pamphlet was on the individual, and their acceptance of the crimes of war. Henein despised the politics of compromise. 'If you join the Communist Party (or any other), without being made aware of its present and future politics, that is "the lesser evil" ... if you vote for a candidate whose hypocritical moralising makes your sick ... that is "the lesser evil".'

What of the argument that Henein's attack was too strong, that by attacking the conduct of the 'democracies' he was in fact making fascism appear respectable? 'I can just hear the murderous sarcasms, "you want to discredit party politics ... compromise action ... throw doubt on the means of deliverance and progress".' Not at all, he replied:

> I pursue nothing. I desire no more than to follow a certain logic of freedom. The phenomenon of fascism, seen from the point of view of its evolution as a party, has only served to encourage ... the development of a moral elephantiasis which affects the most powerful institutions of 'the left' ... the very notion of opposition has been mortally wounded ... in England, America, France, Belgium, the opposition shows solidarity with the great powers, it is not their enemy.

The parties of the left were subservient to the powerful; they accepted the necessity of capitalism; they encouraged the development of a fascistic 'anti-fascist' war.

It will be seen that the most obvious target of Georges Henein's criticisms were the Labour, Socialist and Communist Parties, who claim to stand for something different, but had sold their birthright. It will also be seen that these parties were not mentioned by name. Maybe Henein feared jail. Perhaps Henein wanted to express in the most vivid language the extent of his contempt – and felt that if he descended from the abstract to the concrete, he would get lost in detail, blunting the edge of his rage. Maybe the problem was that he felt his own side had tended to get lost in formulas, and while not culpable (like the Communists) had not done enough to tear the heads off the militaristic left and expose their crimes before a mass audience. Perhaps, finally, the absence of names can be explained in terms of Georges Henein's argument. His interest was not in the betrayals of parties, but in a spirit of conformism, which he detected among the people. The quality of Henein's pamphlet lay in the collision between two modes of socialism: the most highly developed rationalistic Marxism, and a pre-Marxist understanding, in which individual anger and spirit were eulogised. We can quote from the final paragraphs of his argument, where the politics of such surrealist anti-Stalinism are most clear:

> Against this conformism which triumphs in all countries ... we can only pose the forces that it despises most. They are the reverie of Icarus, the spirit of Leonardo, the bursts of energy of the utopian socialists, the generous vision and humour of a Paul Lafargue. Scientific Socialism has been degraded until it is no more than a pompous exercise in memory for the disciples.... Against the odious unity of conformism and terror, against the dictatorship of the middle ... the Mona Lisa of utopia ... raises her smile again and gives back to humanity the promethean spark with which we can find our recovered freedom. It is time to reawaken our dreams.[54]

Conclusion

Between 1940 and 1946, Georges Henein and his co-thinkers introduced the idea into the debates of the Egyptian left that there was no automatic reason why workers should wait. There was no need to put the liberation of the Egyptian bourgeoisie before the liberation of the working class. Indeed the experience of the 1940s shows the possibility of change from below. Far from acting as passive observers, Egyptian workers were at the forefront of the national movement. Egyptian workers in the 1940s sensed that Egyptian capitalists paid the same low wages and used the same methods to smash unions as their foreign colleagues. Their realisation that national unity was a sham terrified the Wafd, the Palace and the British alike. The Egyptian Communist groups determined to prevent class politics from being learned. In so far as they succeeded, they facilitated a defeat which scattered the entire Egyptian left for a generation. Georges Henein and his Trotskyist co-thinkers represented a small and partial alternative. Simply because they existed, they opened up an alternative and internationalist politics, which offered the possibility of genuine revolution, and which remains the best hope for Egyptian workers in the struggles to come.

As for Georges Henein himself, his socialism displayed a tendency to escape out of the mental boxes in which anyone could place it. By siding with Trotskyism at the end of the 1930s, he chose to adopt the most developed revolutionary politics of his day. He then dedicated his next decade to building Trotskyist parties on the ground. Yet the artist was never fully left behind. His greatest 'political' pamphlet, *The Prestige of Terror*, was a rejection of the racism and murder that could be justified to win a democratic war. Henein's manifesto was angry and optimistic; it spoke in the name of the most abstract and almost the necessary hopes. Our time also portrays its conflicts as 'just wars', and again the threat of atomic conflict looms. There is a corridor of experience, of anger and dreaming, that connects Henein's revolutionary manifesto to the politics of our own day.

Dona Torr, E.P. Thompson: socialist history

In the 1940s and 1950s, the Communist Party of Great Britain was the home of an extraordinarily talented group of historians. Eric Hobsbawm, Rodney Hilton, Victor Kiernan, George Rudé, John Saville, Edward (E.P.) Thompson and Christopher Hill transformed the way in which history was written, pioneering the notion that the past should be studied through the experiences of ordinary people. Such an approach came to be known as 'history from below'. Hill's accounts of the English Revolution, Thompson's *William Morris* and his *Making of the English Working Class*, and Hobsbawm's *Age of Capital*, *Age of Empire* and *Age of Extremes* remain some of the most powerful works written from within the Marxist tradition.[1] Previous Marxist histories had tended to speak simply of the succession of new classes and new ways of organising production. According to this model, within each society production grew until it could advance no further. There was then a revolution and a new form of society came into being. Class societies grew and declined, independent of what people did to organise against them. There was a connection between the history from above which dominated within the Communist Party and its political strategy, socialism from above, which meant adapting Marxism to the demands of the nearest Labour MP. History from below was a dual challenge to Stalinism – a rebuke of its theory and an implied critique of the party's political passivity. The school of Marxist history that prospered in 1950s Britain was a marked advance on earlier work.

One of the most influential members of the group was a woman, Dona Torr, but she is today one of the least well known. Since her death, there have been few attempts to understand her place within the socialist tradition. Yet there are reasons for this relative silence. Torr's great work, *Tom Mann and His Times*, came out in 1956, and Torr herself died in January 1957. The generation of historians who understood her life's work were then in the midst of a bitter factional battle. By the time of her death, according to Dorothy Thompson, 'the people who could have written about Dona were outside the party'.[2] While Torr is unknown today, the same cannot be said for her protégé, Edward Thompson. Faced with the news of Khrushchev's 1956 speech distancing the Soviet regime from the crimes of Stalin, Thompson and another historian, John Saville, launched a journal *The Reasoner* to campaign for inner-party democracy. The publication of this magazine was the starting point of the New Left in Britain. His *Making of the English Working Class* became one of the key texts of the 1960s revolt. E.P. Thompson was also a leading figure within the British peace movement, for thirty years from the launch of CND.

This chapter considers the two figures in tandem. The lives of both writers illustrate the difficulties of breaking from Stalinism. Dissidence was more or less possible at different times, and was certainly much easier for Thompson than it was for Torr. Part of the reason Thompson was able to play this role was because others had gone before and eased his path, Torr foremost among them. Both historians contributed to the creation of history from below. Their lives also illustrate some of the political challenges facing the New Left as it emerged.

Dona Torr

Dona Torr was born in 1883, the child of privileged parents. Her father was an Anglican priest and the canon of Chester Cathedral. There have been others of the left whose parents were religious in a similar way, including Olive Schreiner, who was born into a strict

Anglican and later Wesleyan family, and Hugh Dalton, whose father was the canon of St George's Chapel in Windsor. Many of Torr's charges in the history group would come from a parallel Methodist background.[3] One of Dona Torr's brothers became a military attaché to Franco's government in Spain, while her cousin Rosita Forbes was in the 1930s one of the first Western women to explore the Islamic world. Having studied at Heidelberg and University College, London, Torr herself became a journalist. Horrified by the slaughter of 1914–18, she worked for the left-wing paper the *Daily Herald*, which took an anti-war line, and then the Communist *Workers' Life*, which was the forerunner of the *Daily Worker*. In 1920, Torr was an original member of the Communist Party of Great Britain, while in the 1930s she worked for the Communist publishing house Lawrence & Wishart, and married another party member, Walter Holmes.[4]

The Communist Party was formed at a moment when the working-class movement around the world was on the rise. It contained activists with experience going back to before the war. Several of the leading members of the party were sent by the Communist International to assist in the building of Communist Parties throughout the world. Torr was appointed in 1925 to the CP's Colonial Committee, and spent some years overseas. Friends remember her contributing to the Comintern's work in China – if so, then the memory does her no favours, for this was a disastrous episode which culminated in the near-destruction of the young forces of Chinese Communism. Although it is difficult indeed to establish anything concrete about her work for the Comintern, we do know that Torr's work was seen as a success. On her return Torr was friendly with Harry Pollitt, general secretary of the CP, and her appointment as Mann's biographer only makes sense if seen through the support of such allies.[5]

Back in England in the 1920s and 1930s, Dona Torr did not rest on the prestige of her international work, but took a full part in CP branch life. Even when she was busy writing, it never occurred to her that she should take time off from her political duties. Fellow Communists remember her working in her branch, selling the *Daily Worker*, and delivering leaflets from her bicycle during the General Strike. Although in her writing Dona Torr would step beyond the limits of Communist politics, and developed a socialist history that was more alive to the concerns of ordinary workers than the mechanical Marxism that dominated within the party, this is not how she would have seen her own work at the time. Torr was very much part of the CP leadership, and placed herself within the loyal mainstream of the party's politics.

Some of Torr's most important work was in collecting and publishing socialist classics. She was a linguist with an interest in modern and classical languages. She translated and edited Karl Marx and Friedrich Engels's *Selected Correspondence* (1934), wrote supplementary notes for a new edition of Marx's *Capital*, Volume 1 (1938), and also translated Engels's *The Origins of the Family, Private Property and the State* (1940) and Marx's articles *On China* (1951). She edited two volumes of extracts from the Marxist classics, published as *Marxism, Nationality and War* (1940), as well as translating Dimitroff's *Letters from Prison*, the story of the Bulgarian Communist charged by Hitler in 1933 with starting the Reichstag fire.[6] The quality of this material was uneven. *Marxism, Nationality and War* was published by the CP to justify its somersault of 1939, when the party switched overnight – on Russian orders – from support for war to opposition. The method of the book was to juxtapose quotation from Marx, Engels, Lenin and Stalin, suggesting that the dead prose of the latter was every bit as illuminating as the first three. Criticisms could also be made of Dimitroff's *Letters from Prison*, which appeared in time to justify the party's turn towards the Popular Front in 1935. Yet Torr's other translations, and especially her work on Marx and Engels's *Selected Correspondence*, should not be understood in the same light. This was a true piece of scholarship, which made Marx's letters available to English-speakers for the first time.

Dona Torr also contributed to the formation of the Communist Party Historians' Group. At the start of the war she took part in the debates surrounding the publication of Christopher Hill's short book *1640: The English Revolution*. The party leadership originally rejected Hill's book, maintaining that he was wrong to see the Civil War as a bourgeois revolution. Torr was later to tell other historians of her gratitude for Hill's 'pioneer work in this sphere', suggesting also that his victory was responsible for the atmosphere of greater intellectual freedom in which the Historians' Group flourished; 'we all owe it to him in the first place and it was a victory for politics as well as theory.'[7] In 1946, Torr attended the first meeting of the Communist Party Historians' Group. One of a small number of women Communist historians, she was very much the predominant presence in the history group. In 1954, E.P. Thompson brought out his biography, *William Morris*. The foreword described his gratitude to Dona Torr: 'She has repeatedly laid aside her own work in order to answer my enquiries or to read drafts of my material, until I felt that parts of the book were less my own than a collaboration in which her guiding ideas have the main part. It has been a privilege to be associated with a Communist scholar so versatile, so distinguished, and so generous with her gifts.'[8] Torr's work culminated in *Tom Mann and His Times*, a biography of Mann and of the workers' movement in the five hundred years before his birth.[9]

Despite her many independent qualities, Dona Torr was unable to escape the ideas of her time. Her life devoted to building the Communist Party, she could not emancipate herself from the pressures of Stalinism. Victor Kiernan, who had himself opposed Hill in the critical battle over *1640*, remembers Torr hounding another historian, Edmund Dell, in the early 1950s.

> With all her kind-heartedness, she was decidedly strict over questions of Party discipline, in a way perhaps typical of those who came to the Party from a remote starting-point, like Chester Cathedral. When Edmund Dell was dropping out, she presided over a small informal court of historians, and sounded rather unsympathetic, and insisted on the Party rules in full.[10]

With the first volume of *Tom Mann and His Times* complete, but the rest unfinished, Dona Torr died on 8 January 1957. Throughout her last months, the Communist Party was deep in crisis. Many of Torr's young charges, the party historians, resigned from the CP. John Saville and E.P. Thompson began a stencilled newsletter, *The Reasoner*, which was a bridge across which former Communists joined the New Left, which grew outside the CP and often in opposition to the old party. However, Torr herself took no part in the debate. According to Dorothy Thompson, 'She was very ill, and couldn't understand the issues.' After her death Hill, Thompson and the other historians saw themselves as continuing Torr's work.[11]

The unscientific historian

Edward Palmer Thompson was born in 1924. His father, Edward John Thompson, had been an educational missionary in India, became known as a friend of Indian independence, and was a friend of Nehru. Educated at Kingswood and Cambridge, E.P. Thompson joined the British Communist Party as a student. Having undergone military service, Thompson returned to Cambridge, where he finished his degree. There he met his wife Dorothy, who would also become a distinguished labour historian, specialising in Chartism. It is the nature of political activity that those involved in it will experience moments when life itself appears to move at incredible speed. There are also years or even decades when nothing seems to happen of any lasting significance at all. For Edward Thompson the decisive moment was the Second World War. Afterwards, he would return to this period, and find in it a set of lessons, which could guide his hand through later turmoil, of personal, political or historical origin. Although he was later a savage critic of the British Communist Party's 'diabolical and hysterical' Marxism, Thompson never expressed anything but praise for the wartime conduct of his fellow Communists and their milieu:

> I recall a resolute and ingenious civilian army, increasingly hostile to the conventional military virtues, which became – far more than any of my younger friends will begin to credit – an anti-fascist and consciously anti-imperialist army. Its members voted Labour back in 1945: knowing why, as did the civilians back home. Many were infused with socialist ideas and expectations wildly in advance of the tepid rhetoric of today's Labour leaders.... Our expectations may have been shallow, but this was because we were overly utopian and ill-prepared for the betrayals at our backs.[12]

In this passage, one can detect the clearest, most personal expression of Thompson's distinctive socialism: the idea that the people of the wartime anti-fascist alliance constituted *the generation* against which any later socialist politics should be judged. The emotional intensity of these years was also set by the loss of his older brother Frank, another Communist, who died while serving alongside anti-fascist partisans in Bulgaria.

E.P. Thompson was a lifelong champion of the oppressed. So much of his last two decades were spent building the anti-war movement that Thompson's own research dried up. His reader's ticket for the British Library was even allowed to lapse. Yet it would be wrong to suggest that 'history' suffered from Thompson's activism. There were also moments when the experiences gained by a life on the left reinforced the quality of his written work. One example of a book informed by the movement is Thompson's best-known work, *The Making of the English Working Class*. The quality of the book is driven by the materials that Thompson gathered while meeting other activists on the left, as a Communist, as a peace activist, and as a tutor for the Workers' Education Association. Thompson himself called *The Making* his 'West Riding' book, to remember the many old activists whose ideas and old documents helped him to write the history.[13]

One of Thompson's best-known articles, 'The Peculiarities of the English', was written in a polemic aimed against Louis Althusser, the father of French structuralist Marxism.[14] If Althusser was Thompson's long-term target, the immediate focus of his polemic was Perry Anderson, the editor of *New Left Review*, and the nearest available Althusserian. Anderson and his co-worker Tom Nairn had argued that Britain should be seen as a society that had failed to modernise. The explanation was that the British bourgeoisie (unlike its European counterparts) had failed to achieve a proper revolution. According to Anderson, the English Revolution was 'the first, the most mediated, and the least pure bourgeois revolution of any major European country'. Its consequences were felt in the 'permanent partial intergration' of the bourgeoisie and the aristocracy, on the terms of the latter.[15] Instead of becoming a normal capitalist society, England was dominated by its aristocracy, which controlled the state and governed long into the twentieth century.

'The Peculiarities of the English' rejected Althusser and Anderson at every opportunity. Thompson disliked Perry Anderson's claim that transformation was a one-off event. 'I am objecting to a model which concentrates attention upon one dramatic episode, *the* Revolution, to which all that goes before and after must be related; and which insists upon an ideal type of this Revolution against which all others must be judged.' Anderson's history of the left was condemned, for neglecting every movement of interest that had emerged. Anderson's claim that there was a 'British ideology' of empiricism drew more scorn. 'Our authors ... are themselves imprisoned within the myopic vision for which they express such contempt.' And so what if France had modernised differently from Britain? The result had been much the same. 'It happened in one way in France, and another way here.'[16] The general process of capitalist development was only a combination of separate national routes. Differences were neither surprising nor determinate.

Paul Hirst has described this essay as 'an intellectual "police action"' aimed against the importation of continental Marxism into Britain.[17] It can also be seen as part of Thompson's consistent opposition to those socialist historians who were so concerned to build models of the past that they left real people out of their equations. Althusser appeared therefore as an embodiment of Stalinism: the counterpart in historical theory of the craven practice of the Western Communists. This approach was one that Thompson also mocked in verse. 'However many the Emperor slew/ The scientific historian/ While taking note of contradiction/ Affirms that productive forces grew.'[18] So Edward Thompson's history-writing was part of a consistent life's work. It was part of a general concern with socialist humanism and a belief in the New Left, both of which were fuelled by its author's negative experience of the Communist Party. Thompson may have learned his history within the CP, but his belief in history from below led him outside the party, towards a different conception of socialism.

Having rejected the 'diabolical and hysterical materialism' of the Communist Party, Thompson attempted to construct an alternative socialist history, one which combined the best insights of Marxism with a concern for human agency and human experience that was close to the ideals of Marx himself. History-writing and political activism succeeded themselves in an arbitrary sequence decided not by any prior order, but by the requirements of life itself. One of Thompson's last historical polemics was launched in a public debate, held in Oxford in 1979, with Stuart Hall and Richard Johnson. 'We thought, in the late 1950s, watching the flames arise above Budapest, the traditional working-class movement erode around us, while nuclear war seemed imminent that we had to enter different detours in pursuit of the same questions.'[19] By the time of this debate, Margaret Thatcher had been in office for seven months. E.P. Thompson saw the need for a revived peace movement to challenge the threat of nuclear armageddon. 'For the next decade', as Bill Schwarz records, 'Thompson effectively dropped his historical researches to become, again, an activist in the peace movement.'[20] This period of Thompson's life ended prematurely, with his death in 1993.

Against 'good Communism'

The account so far has treated Dona Torr and Edward Thompson as if they were profoundly different types, Torr the party loyalist, Thompson the born critic. Yet the records of the past suggest a more complex relationship, in which Torr's occasional independence eventually found its fullest expression in Thompson's dissident Marxism. This, for example, is how Thompson's widow Dorothy prefers to remember her friend Torr. We can trust in more than memories. One indication of Torr's occasional disquiet can be found in her collection of notebooks, which was deposited with the Communist Party archive in Manchester. Among her papers are seventeen exercise books, with green and orange covers. The contents are made up of jottings, quotations, possibly designed for eventual publication. The dates of the quotations suggest that the notebooks were assembled in the mid-1920s. In other words, Torr was in her early forties when she made these jottings. She had been a Marxist for six years, and was at the height of her influence within the Communist Party and the international movement.

If these were the notes towards an unfinished book, then what would its subject have been? Beyond the passages already mentioned, Dona Torr also culled passages from Malinowski's work on

Australian aborigines and from Westermarck's book, *The Origin and Development of the Moral Ideas*. The notebook on 'Freud Havelock Ellis' contains a long cutting from Sigmund Freud's comments on 'organ-pleasure'. This was Freud's challenge to himself, 'Why are you set on declaring as already belonging to sexuality those indefinite manifestations of childhood out of which what is sexual later develops, and which you yourself admit to be in-definite?' In Torr's Communist circles, Freud was hardly flavour of the month. Yet his ideas were at the height of their popularity among the literary circles of 1920s London. Consequently, Dona Torr was not the only British Marxist to take an interest in Freud's work. John Strachey's brother-in-law translated Freud, and Strachey himself secretly underwent psychoanalysis.[21] Returning to the notebooks, there are also references to the work of the Victorian sexologist Havelock Ellis, 'Excretory organs Vol III 3, 58–62. Glottal region and excretory organs Vol V 47–70; 133–34. Early experiences associated with them Vol V 42, 53, 67, 133, 241. Bisexuality Vol II 310–316. Bisexual cases Vol II 173, 179, 182, 186. Early inverted development Vol II 100, 109, 146. Married inverts Vol II 334.'

If these titles are taken as possible chapters for a book, then the impression is of a 1920s equivalent to Germaine Greer's *The Female Eunuch*, a work on emotion, a study of men's and especially women's passions, written around the core theme of love.[22] A quotation from the novelist Joseph Conrad was underlined thus

> The ship, this ship, our ship, the ship we serve, is the moral symbol of our life…. Of all the creations of man she is the closest partner of his toil and courage. From every point of view it is imperative that you should do well by her. And as always in the case of true love, <u>all you can do for her adds only to the tale of her merits in your heart</u>.[23]

Beside this extract, Torr wrote: 'We value highly what we can benefit greatly.' The passages from Dante and Calvin are similar. In each, the theme is of intense and unselfish love, the sort of love which philosophically minded Christians have sometimes termed *agape*. Indeed, the tone of the collection is striking; it reads more like the work of a pious woman of the nineteenth century than of the labour historian that Torr would become.

Many of the passages chosen are moving, some powerfully so. Torr extracted the following verse from William Blake's autobiographical poem 'William Bond': 'Seek love in the pity of other's woe/ In the gentle relief of another's care/ In the darkness of night and the winter's snow/ In the naked and outcast, seek love there.'[24] The notebooks are made up of quotations; there are few notes in Torr's hand. In the notebook marked 'Pity and Gratitude', Torr makes the following remark: 'Where <u>love's end of Reciprocity</u> is satisfied the lover gladly accepts the pity of the beloved and is eager in gratitude. But a lover unsatisfied most fiercely rejects pity, withholds gratitude, and prefers indifference.'[25] It is hard to make sense of such passages. This could have been a book with links to events in Dona Torr's own life. Yet the book was unfinished, and the connections unmade. There is too great a gap between the source and the few details we know of Torr's private circumstances to use this as a key to unlock the emotions of her life.

Dona Torr's private notebooks have not been published, and could not be in their present state. They are the beginnings of an idea; they are not the idea itself. Yet the impression that emerges is of a woman whose real interests escaped the bounds of the dry and deterministic Marxism with which the Comintern was then associated. There are almost no Marxist writers cited in her collection – just one quotation from the correspondence of Rosa Luxemburg. Torr perhaps wanted to write about love, but the 'Good Communist' of the 1920s was not supposed to concern him- or herself with such bourgeois conceits. The time was not ripe for a politics of personal life.

The first New Left

What can be seen as Dona Torr's covert dissidence stands in contrast to E.P. Thompson's open anti-Stalinist rebellion. Following the events of 1956, Thompson dedicated his life to the struggle for a revitalised and 'humanistic' Marxism, purged of Joseph Stalin's brutal methods, and also of the economic determinism which Thompson saw as having played a key role in the moral degeneration of the Russian Revolution. Such was Thompson's dominating influence within the first New Left of the 1950s that Bill Schwarz has described this movement as 'the precarious translation of the intellectual current represented by the Historians Group into a political force'.[26] If so, then what was the defining content of Thompson's dissident Marxism? The phrase that Thompson used was 'socialist humanism'. In his account, this slogan,

> Arose simultaneously in a hundred places, and on ten thousand lips. It was voiced by poets in Poland, Russia, Hungary, Czechoslovakia; by factory delegates in Budapest; by Communist militants at the eighth plenum of the Polish Party; by a Communist premier (Imre Nagy) who was murdered for his pains. It was on the lips of women and men coming out of gaol and of the relatives and friends of those who never came out.[27]

More context is needed. Following Joseph Stalin's death in 1953, the international Communist movement went into a period of mourning. This lasted roughly until February 1956. Then at a closed session of the twentieth party congress, the new Soviet premier Nikita Khrushchev delivered his famous speech denouncing the crimes and the personality cult of his predecessor.

Visiting foreign delegates were kept away from this session, which meant that few British Communists could report honestly on what had been said. Yet rumours seeped out and a full version of Khrushchev's speech was published in the *Observer* on 10 June 1956. This ushered in a first period of crisis for the British Communist Party, and the pages of the party press began to fill with hostile letters complaining of lies told by the leadership. Worse followed. On 23 October, mass anti-Stalinist demonstrations broke out in Budapest. The *Daily Worker* journalist Peter Fryer initially reported back enthusiastically on what appeared to be a genuine popular revolt. Soon, though, the Soviet leadership decided to crush the uprising. The workers of Budapest had to be presented as misguided innocents. They were the dupes of Hungarian fascists and the Americans. The British Communist Party's branches were now in utter turmoil. An inner-party commission on democracy was established to investigate the lessons of the dispute. Some ten thousand people left the party, Thompson at their head.

Through the winter of 1956–7, E.P. Thompson was the most visible dissident Communist in Britain. His paper *The Reasoner* (later *The New Reasoner*) was the publication of the disaffected CP rank and file. Thompson was also able to draw on the support of friendship ties, built up through joint activity in the Communist Party Historians' Group. As early as 8 April 1956, a 'full and extended' meeting of the Historians' Group passed a resolution criticising the party for its failure to discuss Khrushchev's speech.[28] Although the motion was overturned at the next meeting, the group had by now established itself as an open carrier of dissent.

Why did Thompson leave the British Communist Party? It was a question on which he reflected long, for his answer was only partly derived from the 1956 crisis. Thompson also had to explain what sort of socialist he was, and why the conduct of Stalin, and indeed of the Soviet Union in Hungary, had antagonised him so badly. A series of answers were given in the course of Thompson's polemic against Althusser. We find here the argument that socialist humanism was a critique of Stalinism that emerged from within the ranks of the left, 'the voice of a Communist opposition, of a total critique of Stalinist practice and theory'.[29] We find here also the argument that socialist humanism was the true expression of the best of the pre-1956 left. In that sense, it meant loyalty to a particular generation of people and their insights:

> For the veteran leader of the Derbyshire miners, Bert Wynn, solidarity with our critique meant (as for many others) severing connections within his own heart; for the full-time organiser of the Leeds Communist Party, Jim Roche, formulating the positions of socialist humanism meant getting out his tools and returning to the cutter's bench.[30]

Later on in the course of the same argument, Thompson suggests that socialist humanism was ultimately distinguished from Stalinism by the loyalty it maintained to an older conception of freedom. This is how he responded to Althusser's claim that socialist humanism was a right-wing deviation from Stalinism.

> From any consideration of working-class self-activity, of socialist liberty, how is it possible to be further to the 'right' than the anti-historicism and anti-humanism of Althusser?[31]

So Thompson's real argument was for a conception of socialism which retained a sense of human freedom. We can see, then, how this became a central motif of the New Left. Against the consistent immorality of Soviet rule, a new kind of left-wing moral philosophy was needed in which actions were judged on their own merits. Murder was an unequivocal evil; no socialism could be built through systems of internal repression. After Stalinism, the labour movement could then be built on these terms. Yet from the perspective of previous socialist theory, there were problems with this argument. Indeed one of Thompson's co-thinkers, the young philosopher Alasdair MacIntyre, subjected this approach to critique in the seventh issue of *The New Reasoner*.[32] MacIntyre followed Marx in arguing that no political alternatives to the present could be found in locating a superior, timeless morality, on the basis of which all human history can then be judged. The problem with a approach rooted in ethics is that all our understandings of morality are contingent, and historically based.[33] When the defenders of the bourgeoisie spoke of rights, they meant above all the right to own property. This developed from their conception of humanity as 'economic man'. What shared idea of humanity formed the basis for socialist humanism, and in the defence of which rights should socialists stand? Thompson acknowledged the force of such criticisms, and wrote himself of the 'ambiguities' of socialist humanism. Yet it remained the approach that spoke most clearly to his concerns.

Thompson's belief in socialist humanism was sustained long beyond the moment of 1956. In 1966–7, Thompson came together with Raymond Williams and Stuart Hall to publish what became the *May Day Manifesto, 1968*, which was intended as a socialist challenge to the rightward drift of Labour politics under Harold Wilson. In the 1980s, he was effectively a full-time activist for European Nuclear Disarmament. Thompson warned against the danger of 'exterminism', the natural right-wing way of thinking about the world, which would sacrifice whole peoples for the sake of victory in the Cold War. Martin Shaw terms him a 'nuclear pacifist' – meaning that while Thompson supported the right of small nations to defend themselves against the might of armed superpowers, he was working seriously for a world without war.[34]

History from below

I have already suggested that both Dona Torr and E.P. Thompson contributed to the making of history from below. Thompson's role was greater, but would not have been possible without the earlier part played by historians like Torr. In her writing, Dona Torr was always critical of those Marxist authorities who assumed that an event took place in a certain way because that is what their theory told them to expect. 'She was a Marxist', remembers Dorothy Thompson, 'but the people she really disliked were the Talmudists.'[35] In Torr's writing, history was not subordinate to theory, but instead both were linked and the result was not just more compelling history but also more powerful socialist theory, which treated people as the agents of historical change.

The point at which Dona Torr's dissidence was best expressed was in her last work, *Tom Mann and His Times*. One of the most powerful chapters in this book traces the history of the struggle for 'lost rights', the values of primitive democracy that inspired the early opponents of capitalism, from the Levellers and the Diggers onwards. Torr was not nostalgic; she insisted that the demand for equality did not spring from the recollection of any previously equal condition, but rather from the contrast between the egalitarian rhetoric of capitalism and its brutal reality. The book then returned to the story of Tom Mann, from his early life and membership of the Social Democratic Federation, discussing his first pamphlet published to demand the eight-hour day, through the protests of the unemployed in the mid-1880s, through to the New Unionism, of 1889, when gas workers, dockers and others were able to build the first trade unions for unskilled workers. Mann was described as a leader of the dock strike, and *Tom Mann and His Times* ends in September 1889 with the victory of that campaign.

E.P. Thompson meanwhile expressed his dissidence in *The Making of the English Working Class*, undoubtedly one of the great works of social history. An account of the English workers' movement in the decades between the French Revolution and Chartism, Thompson's book addressed a key moment in the transformation to capitalism. In Karl Marx's original scheme of economic development, this period was just as important as the 1640s. Although by

1780 a capitalist class was already clearly in the ascendant, this was still a merchant capitalist class. It could generate profits in the sphere of consumption, from trade, but not yet in the sphere of production. Only industrial capitalism could secure the indefinite creation of profit in this way. Thus for Marx, industrial capitalism was a higher form of capitalism, perhaps the highest form of all. E.P. Thompson examined the impact of the Industrial Revolution through the experiences of artisans, weavers and others dispossessed by the change from an agricultural to an urban society. The preface argued in defence of seeking out those voices that had been neglected in more conventional histories of these times:

> I am seeking to rescue the poor stockinger, the Luddite cropper, the 'obsolete' hand-loom weaver, the 'utopian' artisan, and even the deluded follower of Joanna Southcott from the enormous condescension of posterity. Their crafts and traditions may have been dying. Their hostility to the new industrialism may have been backward-looking. Their communitarian ideals may have been fantasises. Their insurrectionary conspiracies may have been foolhardy. But they lived through these times of acute social disturbance, and we did not. Their aspirations were valid in terms of their own experience; and, if they were casualties of history they remain, condemned in their own lives, as casualties.[36]

The key concept here is 'experience'. If someone lived and had experiences, then the story of their life is valuable, whether the causes they spoke up for were won or lost. Another passage defines exactly what Thompson had in mind by 'class':

> By class I understand a historical phenomenon, unifying a number of disparate and seemingly unconnected events, both in the raw material of experience and in consciousness. I do not see class as a structure, nor even as a 'category', but as something which in fact happens (and can be shown to have happened) in human relationships.... Class happens when some men, as a result of common experiences (inherited or shared), feel and articulate the identity of their interests as between themselves, and as against other men whose interests are different from (and usually opposed to) theirs.... Consciousness of class arises in the same way in different times and places, but never in just the same way.[37]

In this passage, the power of 'experience' has been magnified. Now experience has become the fundamental historical reality, the prime matter, of greater importance than class or structure, agency, role, ideas, or indeed any of the other generalisations that historians employ to make sense of the past. Elsewhere Thompson used the metaphor of love to explain class and class struggle. Before seeking to establish the nature of the relationship, we must first see that there are two people, and that they are in love! This was the point of his term, to argue that any sociological debate about the meaning of class could only be resolved on the terrain of history, by looking at the real, live experiences of people as they have lived now and in the past.

So what actually *is* experience? Experience is felt in the passing of time. Beyond that, it is hard to say anything definite at all. The term is both pregnant with meaning and also vague. Indeed its imprecision seems to mirror the vagueness of Thompson's socialist 'humanism'. Yet as Thompson's biographer Bryan Palmer suggests, 'Whatever the difficulties in defining such conceptual terms with precision, their utilisation in *The Making* allowed entry to whole areas of neglected importance in the lives of workers, areas that could never again be ignored in negotiating the slippery slopes that connect being and consciousness.'[38] In his work, E.P. Thompson demonstrated that it was pointless to write a narrative of social change in which all the action was completed by impersonal forces, such as the spread of production and the clash of classes. No account of change could be convincing unless it described the new conditions as they shaped the lives of men and women in history. The publication of *The Making of the English Working Class* was a clear advance for Marxist theory.

A full break from the past?

This chapter has already indicated some limitations to the dissidence of both Torr and Thompson. In the former's practice, there are examples of that very party chauvinism against which the dissidents rebelled. In her history writing, the traces appear only occasionally, but they are there. Always determined to see the world from the perspective of the 'common people', Dona Torr described her interest as the Common *English* people, and like other Communist Party historians her work suffered from occasional dark spots of nationalism. Torr stressed the English character of Tom Mann, which was actually to reduce this class fighter, an internationalist who had built socialist parties and trade unions on at least three continents. Torr described Marx's *Capital* as a 'a history of England ... much that lay behind its inspiration came from the first visit of Engels to England in 1842'. Certainly, *Capital* did include a history of the development of capitalism, and that process did take place in a systematic way first in England. Yet *Capital* was many other things as well. Torr also wrote that by 1900 the working class had 'made good its claim to be called *the people*'. In 1900, though, the political tradition that cloaked itself most successfully in a language of Englishness and the people was a right-wing tradition of nationalism and xenophobia with different goals from those of the workers' movement. Thompson occasionally suffered from a similar blight. Parts of his critique of Althusser were written as if the author believed in a pure notion of Englishness which existed beyond analysis, and which could be dragged out to defeat the scourge of continental theory.

There is another important criticism that can be made of both Dona Torr and E.P. Thompson. Eager to reject the mechanical Marxism which then dominated within the Communist parties, they failed to map out a more subtle and compelling but still recognisably materialist method that might explain where socialist history could look next. By the time of Edward Thompson's *The Making of the English Working Class*, this problem had become acute. It was one thing to stress the importance of human intervention in shaping history, but what were the barriers to the smooth running of human will? Eager to avoid the previous sterile fixation with economics, Torr, Thompson and their generation replaced it with an overly 'cultural' Marxism. In the hands of Thompson's followers, class relationships have all but disappeared. Yet it would be wrong to condemn the earlier dissidents for the diffuse conclusions which later generations drew from their work. Both Torr and Thompson committed themselves to the task of renewing Marxist theory. E.P. Thompson in particular drew the practical consequences of this revolt – dedicating his life to the struggle to create a world without poverty or war.

6

Paul Baran, Paul Sweezy and monopoly capital

Paul Baran and Paul Sweezy are associated with two important moments in the recent history of the North American left. The first was the appearance of *Monthly Review*, which began in May 1949 and quickly acquired a reputation as the foremost journal of the left in the USA. The second was the 1966 publication of their joint book, *Monopoly Capital*, which represented the ideas of the journal, expressed in concentrated form. Like all the writers described in this book, the *Monthly Review* generation developed their politics in opposition to totalitarianism, of Eastern or Western origin. What initially marked Paul Baran and Paul Sweezy was a reform-Communist perspective. They despised the aggressive, colonial mindset of America's leaders, and looked to America's enemies for hope. Their socialism condemned the 'excesses' of the Soviet rulers, yet it also accepted the claim that the Russian dictatorship did somehow represent the legacy of Marx. In the 1950s and 1960s this viewpoint was challenged, and Baran, Sweezy and their co-thinkers switched over from a grudging, critical support of Moscow towards more open praise of socialism in Cuba. Fidel Castro's socialism was young, fresh, and its leaders were untainted by the corruption of the East. These American dissidents hoped to root their socialism in that soil.

Two lives

Paul Baran and Paul Sweezy were both born in 1910, but in different circumstances. Baran's family lived in Russia, in Nikolaev on the Black Sea. Baran's father Abram, a doctor, and his mother Rosaly had previously lived in Vilna. Abram sided with the Mensheviks in 1917, and therefore moved from supporting the February revolution to opposition to October's. Forced to flee their home, the family returned to Vilna, now in Poland, in 1921. The young Paul Baran finished his education in Germany, where he joined the Communist youth group. Returning to Moscow in 1926, Paul Baran was able to witness the defeat of Trotsky's Left Opposition, and the consequent destruction of any residual hopes for democracy in Russia. 'I felt that the Opposition was right in its polemics against the Stalin leadership of the Communist Party', he wrote later; 'that it was right in demanding more freedom and more democracy in the country but I was too young and too little rooted in Russian life to take an active part in that political debate.' Disillusioned, Baran returned to Germany in 1928. Two years later, he joined the Social Democratic Party, believing that the only means to achieve a united front against fascism was through persuading moderate left-wing workers. He then worked at the Institute for Social Research in Frankfurt. In 1934, following Hitler's accession to power, Baran again left Germany for the Soviet Union. There he found that many former colleagues had disappeared. Baran attempted to settle in London, before moving again, this time to the United States.

Eventually, Paul Baran found a secure post at Harvard. During the war, he worked for the Office of Strategic Services, while after 1945 he was employed at the Federal Reserve Bank in New York. His wartime work caused the Washington *Times Herald* to name him as a likely Soviet spy. The paper chose not to understand that leftists could be anti-Soviet. Indeed the accusation of treachery hung around Baran's neck for years. The state denied him a passport to teach abroad, in Oxford. Baran was later subjected to FBI interrogation, and even after the worst of the Cold War paranoia had died down, for years he preferred to write under a pseudonym, 'Historicus', rather than use his own name. In autumn 1949, Paul

Baran returned to academia, joining Stanford University. Baran brought out just one book in his lifetime, *The Political Economy of Growth* (1957). He took therapy as a means of overcoming occasional writers' block.[1] The experience of counselling informed a subsequent pamphlet, *Marxism and Psychoanalysis*.[2] Baran died in 1965. The special obituary issue of *Monthly Review* which covered his death included statements of loss from an extraordinary group of international socialists, including Charles Bettelheim, the theoretician of Western Maoism; Isaac Deutscher, the biographer of Trotsky; the Cuban revolutionary Che Guevara; the British Marxist historian Eric Hobsbawm; the Keynesian economist Joan Robinson; and the Italian Communist Palmiro Togliatti.[3]

In contrast to Paul Baran's international upbringing, Paul Sweezy was the product of a different, all-American home. It was only in his twenties that he moved decisively towards the left. His father was an executive at J.P. Morgan's bank and Sweezy himself was educated at Exeter and Harvard. In 1932–3, he spent a year as a graduate student at the London School of Economics. There he fell under the sway of the political scientist Harold Laski, a leading thinker of the Labour Party left. According to Sweezy, 'I acquired a mission in life ... to do what I would to make Marxism an integral and respected part of the intellectual life of this country, or, to put it in other terms, to take part in establishing a serious and authentic North American brand of Marxism.'[4] It might seem surprising to us today, but such a mission was then compatible with the US academic system. Sweezy's first professional article appeared in the *Review of Economic Studies* in 1933; its author was just 23 years old. Through the 1930s, Sweezy continued to make a name for himself as an advocate of left-wing economics. Under Roosevelt, the state was dedicated to a programme of public works to prevent unemployment, the New Deal. There was a space in society for what we would call today 'Keynesian' economics.[5] John Bellamy Foster tells the story of meeting a mainstream economist at a party in the 1990s, only to be told 'Oh, Paul Sweezy, too bad he died so young.'[6] Paul Sweezy died in 2004, at the age of 93.

Following the end of the Second World War, Paul Sweezy became a founding editor of *Monthly Review*, together with Leo Huberman. The first issue of the magazine included Albert

Einstein's famous article 'Why Socialism?'[7] During the McCarthy era, Sweezy was placed under court order to give information on the membership of Henry Wallace's Progressive Party. This he refused to do, and he was jailed in 1953. Sweezy told the US Supreme Court: 'If the very first principle of the American constitutional form of government is political freedom – which I take to include freedoms of speech, press, assembly and association – then I do not see how it can be denied that these investigations are a grave danger to all that Americans have always claimed to cherish.' Sweezy's eventual victory in 1957 was one sign of the decline of McCarthyism.[8] Much of his subsequent life has been dedicated to propaganda for socialism, to the journal of *Monthly Review*, and to his many published books. The latter have included *The Theory of Capitalist Development* (1942), *The Present as History* (1953), *Cuba: Anatomy of a Revolution* (1960), *On the Transition to Socialism* (1971), *The Dynamics of US Capitalism* (1972), *The Transition from Feudalism to Capitalism* (1979), *Post-Revolutionary Society* (1981) and *The Irreversible Crisis* (1989), as well as *Monopoly Capitalism*.[9] The real quality of the man has been expressed in his lifelong, activist's interest in struggle. Barbara Ehrenreich described meeting Sweezy for the first time in 1969. She and a few friends working in the health sector addressed Sweezy and another *Monthly Review* stalwart Harry Magdoff. What struck her most was the patience with which these older men listened to a new generation. They believed that the first task of Marxists, faced with a new expression of class struggle, was not to teach but to learn.[10]

The politics of *Monthly Review*

The origins of the *Monthly Review* generation were eclectic. 'Each member of the group', Paul Sweezy has written, 'came to Marxism by a different route and under a different combination of influences.'[11] We have already described Baran's Menshevik father, his time in Communist youth organisations, and his experience of the Frankfurt School, as well as Paul Sweezy's knowledge of Marxism, acquired first through a British parliamentary socialist of the stature of Harold Laski. Into the mix were added Leo Huberman's classical Marxism, a product of the 1930s when the Western Communist

Parties were at their most exciting and best. Eventually Harry Braverman would also join the group, from a background in American Trotskyism, as is described in a subsequent chapter. In more recent times, other intellectuals have also contributed – including Harry Magdoff, John Bellamy Foster and Ellen Meiksins Wood, among many others.

The group was broad-based, but life itself intruded to shape the journal. The brief twelve months or so after the end of the Second World War was a time of intense optimism. The returning soldiers determined to remake society in a fashion that would justify their sacrifices in the war. All over the world socialist parties achieved more votes than they ever had previously. Mass Communist parties were established in Western Europe, claiming 2 million members in Italy. National liberation movements also grew in confidence. History seemed to be repeating itself. The First World War had ended in revolution, and the second likewise turned people's values to the left.

Everything changed with the start of the Cold War. In spring 1947, President Truman announced the willingness of the USA to intervene against a revolution then under way in Greece. His move was interpreted as the 'Truman doctrine', the idea that America was permanently empowered to intervene abroad against 'Communism'. In June 1948, a massive programme of military aid was announced, targeted at sympathetic regimes in central and Western Europe, Marshall Aid. Churchill dedicated speeches to the horrors behind 'the Iron Curtain'. All four occupying powers lost interest in denazifying Germany, but turned their interest instead to scouring the land for Hitler's rocket scientists, or former Nazi agents who might be 'turned' and used in the conflict ahead. In the East, a new period of disappearances began. Soviet culture was purified of dissonant voices, while Stalin himself began one final anti-Semitic purge. The West also geared itself up for witch-hunts. Hollywood produced films with titles like *I Married a Communist* or *The Red Menace*. Their literary equivalent was Arthur Koestler's *Darkness at Noon* or Victor Gollancz's *The God that Failed*. Andrew Davies estimates that six and a half million Americans were investigated by the state for suspected Communism between 1947 and 1952.[12]

The editors of *Monthly Review* may have hoped to ride a crest of growing left-wing sympathy. Instead, they had to explain this different, rightward time to their readers. The easiest way to respond was to look to older explanatory models. McCarthy's anti-Communist hearings seemed to have their roots in previous purges. One of Paul Baran's first articles for the magazine, published in 1952, was titled 'Fascism in America'.[13] Another essay was dedicated to the cowardice of the intellectuals, who refused to speak out against American terror: 'The more reactionary the ruling class, the more obvious it becomes that the social order over which it presides has turned into an impediment to human liberation, the more its ideology is taken over by anti-intellectualism, irrationalism and superstition.'[14]

In a situation where all politics was dominated by the global conflict between America and the USSR, there were very few options open to socialists. One possibility was to accept the USA as the carrier of global democracy. Many demoralised socialists chose this path, becoming (to different extents) the public advocates of the American system. James Burnham was the classic case, moving quickly from Trotskyism to US nationalism and even white racism.[15] A much smaller group reversed the equation, continuing to speak out against American military power, but keeping quiet on Soviet expansion. Paul Robeson, an internationally acclaimed star of music and theatre, was just one of thousands who suffered as a result of choosing this path. He was isolated from musical audiences, his passport was confiscated, he was boycotted by employers, and his life was shortened. The third and smallest group spoke against all tyranny, of 'right' or 'left'. The 'third camp' maintained that socialism could only come about as a system of direct democracy, not by means of American or Russian tanks. Where did *Monthly Review* fit in? Paul Sweezy described his co-worker Paul Baran's attitude in the following terms:

> It is obvious from the fact that he was expelled in 1935 and refused admission that he was persona non grata there during the Stalin era; and in private he was outspokenly critical of many aspects of the regime ... [but] though he deplored the excesses of Stalinism, he was firmly convinced of the rightness and necessity of Stalin's policies of industrialization and collectivization of agriculture.... He saw the class struggle

in our time as one gigantic worldwide confrontation, and he had no doubt that the Russian revolution was the greatest victory for the side he was on; to criticize publicly the regime which emerged from it might bring aid and comfort to its enemies who were also his enemies, and that he was determined not to do.[16]

The contributors to *Monthly Review* were genuine socialists; they knew and understood the democratic component of Marx's writings. So no matter how enthusiastically they opposed Russia's enemies, they could not be true friends of a bureaucratic system in whose constructions millions had died. Yet theirs was a difficult line to hold, a politics of double negatives rather than one of open affirmation. All the time, Baran and Sweezy were looking for a cause that could be adopted, not tentatively but wholeheartedly, by them. The Cuban Revolution of 1959 therefore appeared like a ray of hope from the skies. Leo Huberman and Paul Sweezy visited for the first time in 1960. 'We fell completely under the spell of this young and fresh revolution, and became almost immediately convinced that the dialectic of its internal and international development must inevitably turn it in a socialist direction.' Paul Baran was sceptical for longer. 'But he too was carried off his feet in the island's heady revolutionary atmosphere.' One photograph shows Paul Baran, Paul Sweezy and Leo Huberman meeting Fidel Castro in Havana.[17]

There were two points at which the 1959 revolution seemed to improve on the theory of past generations. The first was in its insistence that the heads of this revolution were obliged by their role as leaders to be morally better than the rulers of the past. They should be modest, they must refuse anything which might end in corruption. Even those Western socialists who were critical of the regime stressed the 'ascetic revolutionary purity' of its leaders, which secured the extraordinary popularity of Castro's regime. Pete Binns and Mike Gonzalez, British critics of Cuban-style socialism, make the point well:

> [Castro and his fellow leaders] did *not* abandon their fatigues for pin-stripe suits, their jeeps for chauffeured limousines, and nor was this simple affectation: it was largely genuine. What is more they backed this up with laws. They enacted draconian measures such as the death penalty for the misappropriation of public funds *against bureaucrats*,

while at the same time making the biggest efforts Cuba had ever known to eradicate illiteracy, to massively extend preventive health measures and so on. The enormous confidence in the regime that these measures created made sure that a large reserve of loyalty – above all on the part of the workers and the peasants – was built up for when the state itself began to take on a more active role in the direction of the economy.[18]

From a critical perspective, we could insist that even at its peak Cuban socialism was still socialism from above. Yet such an insight does not explain the enormous enthusiasm that the editors of *Monthly Review* showed in this new system. For them, the most important point was rather to contrast Castro with the ageing, militaristic rulers of the USA.

The second point at which the Cuban revolution seemed to distinguish itself from all models was in its support for guerrilla revolt, as opposed to urban, working-class insurrection. Here we encounter the figure of Che Guevara, the man most associated with this strategy. Guevara dedicated his life to the argument that imperialism could be successfully resisted, if only revolutionaries took to the hills, and led the peasant masses into struggle. The tactic succeeded in Cuba, but failed in Bolivia, where Che died.[19] In 1970, Robin Blackburn, then a supporter of the regime, put the case for guerrilla struggle:

> The most shocking feature of the *foco* theory to those who believe in the traditional schemas of revolution is in its apparent voluntarism, best summed up in the oft-quoted declaration of Che that 'it is not always necessary to wait until all the conditions for revolution are fulfilled – the *foco* can create them.' For a long time many revolutionary parties have believed that revolutions are the result only of objectively given social contradictions, which suddenly explode in a general crisis (slump, war). The history of this century has repeatedly refuted this view.... Modern revolutions do not *happen*, they are *made*; and correct revolutionary strategy can help to precipitate as well as to consummate the revolutionary situation.[20]

Activists today might instinctively recognise this argument as bad counsel. We can afford to be more cautious about the limits of rural insurrection. We live in a world where the working class has become a majority, unlike forty years ago, when peasant life was still by far the dominant experience in Latin American, Asian and

African society. We might also be more sceptical about the idea of an insurrection which is always just waiting to begin. If there are no structural limitations imposed by capitalist society on what is possible, then everything Marx wrote to understand capitalism was wasted, and any reader might as well forget this book and begin the revolution now, for it can be done. On the other hand, from the perspective of the late 1950s, such an idea *seemed* to be a revolutionary breakthrough of the first order. Against a background of American hegemony, the Cold War, popular conservatism, the Cuban insurrection 'proved' that socialism was immanent and achievable, everything was just a matter of revolutionary will.

Monopoly capitalism

At this point, we should summarise the argument of *Monopoly Capital*. It was an enormously ambitious book, which attempted to explain the totality of the world economy, and therefore also site the resistance of socialists. The title was borrowed from Lenin's characterisation of imperialism as the monopoly stage of capitalism.[21] Drawing on his argument, plus Marx, Keynes, Kalecki and Schumpeter, the authors argued that at the end of the nineteenth century capitalism had entered into a new period, in which smaller firms were increasingly replaced by huge units of concentrated capital. These huge firms exerted a dominance over markets. In this era of monopoly capital, capitalism generated surpluses which could be reinvested on a layer of technicians who were not directly employed in production. These engineers, draughtsmen and scientists were trained to control workers, enabling even greater managerial dominance over production. In the authors' words, 'Monopolistic organisation gives capital an advantage in its struggle with labour, hence tends to raise the rate of surplus value and to make possible higher rates of accumulation.'[22] Eventually superexploitation would prove counterproductive, as workers would not have the wealth to purchase goods. Consumption would decline and investment would slow down. Workers entered the equation, but primarily as consumers – a point which many critics would pick up. What had happened to the revolutionary proletariat? The more important point, for Baran and Sweezy, was to look at the contradictions within the running of the capitalist economy. Profits rose faster than the opportunities for investment, driving in turn a secular decline in the rate of investment. Capitalism itself had already become a stagnant system.

How, then, had the post-war boom happened? For Paul Baran and Paul Sweezy the growth years of 1950–70 were exceptional. The temporary boom had been based on extraordinary factors, which could not last. One was a second wave of automobilization, which had boosted the glass, rubber, steel and oil-based industries. Another factor had been the military conduct of the Cold War. American arms spending had risen incredibly fast, especially through the Korean and Vietnam wars, providing an extra bubble of investment which would not endure. Finally, the expansion of 'sales effort' had provided a temporary fillip to consumption, which would reduce as personal debt fell. The general picture they painted was one of overcapacity, stagnation and financial instability. It is to the immense credit of the authors that this picture has been more accurate in the thirty-plus years since they wrote. Behind they had the memory of boom; ahead was stagnation.[23]

John Bellamy Foster characterises the book as an intervention in Marxist theory. As such it operated on numerous levels. For one thing, *Monopoly Capital* reminded American Marxists to read Marx. Certainly in the 1960s, there was a tendency for leftists to place their greatest interest in questions of culture – race, gender, sexuality. When the dominant culture was as racist and repressive as the culture of mid-1960s America, we can understand and sympathise with this choice. Yet the practice of leaving economic theory to the classics ('it's fine', you can imagine someone saying, 'Marx has the answer') became over time a different habit, of dropping 'hard' economic arguments, and granting them to the political right. As well as desiring to stimulate a renewed radical interest in economics, including Marxist economics, the authors sought to challenge existing left-wing theory and develop it along new lines. John Bellamy Foster makes the point succinctly:

> Baran and Sweezy's *Monopoly Capital* argued that Marx's 'law of the tendency of the rate of profit to fall' was no longer directly applicable to the monopoly capitalist economy that emerged at the beginning of the twentieth century, and had to be replaced by a 'law of the tendency

of the surplus to rise' – where surplus was defined as the difference between the wages of production workers and total value added. A key contradiction of capitalism in its monopoly stage is therefore that of rising surplus and the associated problems of surplus absorption.[24]

This passage requires unpacking. When Foster talks of the falling rate of profit, he has in mind a famous passage from Karl Marx's *Capital*, Volume 3.[25] In the first volume, Marx had already suggested that capitalism had a habit of going into crisis. The reasons for this can be stated simply: the only source of profit was human labour-power. The competition between capitals tended to reduce the content of labour. Year by year, ever fewer workers were producing the same goods or even more. More was produced than could be consumed. There was a general tendency for capitalism to go into regular spasms of crisis, where the problem of overproduction was solved – brutally – by the destruction of the capital which caused overproduction. In the third volume, Marx went further. Here he argued that the means by which labour was displaced was through the advent of new technology. Despite several countervailing tendencies, which he listed, there was a definite, long-term trend for fixed capital (machinery) to become an ever great cost, and for the organic composition of capital (the ratio between spending on machines and people) to rise. This process is often termed the 'law of the tendency of the rate of profit to fall'. Marx's theory suggested that capitalism was an organic system, and that it was ageing. The regular crises of boom and bust would become much worse as capitalism went on. In addition, it provided a simple and verifiable test. Is it true that the rate of profit has fallen? If so, then we can say that in a fundamental sense *Marx was right*.[26]

When Paul Sweezy and Paul Baran engaged with this argument, and challenged it, they were fully aware of its centrality to Marx's mature economic theory. What they suggested was that a different set of arguments – borrowed from Keynes and such late Keynesian theorists as Michael Kalecki – could provide similar insights, more successfully. There are different ways of explaining this. So far this chapter has been written as if Karl Marx's arguments were self-evidently true. Yet there were certain problems with them, as Paul Baran and Paul Sweezy were well aware.[27] One is the question of the labour theory of value. Marx used this idea as a first generalisation. Yet in the third volume of *Capital* he asked himself how closely value corresponded to *price*. Marx could see that there was competition between firms and even whole branches of industry, and that over time capitalists would tend to invest more in the most profitable businesses. The equations he wrote out to sketch the transformation of values into prices are fiendishly complicated, and in places wrong.[28] So the sheer act of taking Marx's economic arguments seriously requires by its nature a certain revision of Marx. This is no criticism. It is more than a hundred years since mainstream economists gave up on the task of connecting their equations to living reality. It is to their credit that Marxists still take any interest in providing an economic model of society that 'works'. The point is rather that any faithful reading of Marx must to some extent transcend the limits of the source.

It may also be that Baran and Sweezy were unimpressed by the *character* of Marx's argument in *Capital*, Volume 3. For what he described was a world in which the workers' share of the cake was always shrinking. If the rate of profit continued to fall, mercilessly, then the system would become sclerotic. Rising labour productivity could not ultimately bridge the gap between production and consumption. The only option facing the managers was for them to confront labour. From the perspective of the new century, such an argument appears quite plausible. What we have seen in America since the 1970s has been precisely such a world in which average wages have fallen, and real living standards have been maintained only by forcing the average American family to work an extra month a year for what is actually the same wage. From the point of view of the mid-1960s, though, such a view would have seemed extraordinary. All around them, people could see a world in which working conditions were improving, a system (in the West anyway) of mass consumer abundance, in which the working class was being bought off.

We can see, therefore, some of the attractions of Keynesian thinking. This began with observations about consumption, rather than production. The most basic insight associated with John Maynard Keynes is the idea that in a time of recession the easiest (and worst) thing to do is to cut wages. Fewer finished goods will be produced, forcing down the price of raw materials, machines and fixed capital. A vicious circle results, with reduced production and unemployment feeding each other. Drawing on these themes, Paul Baran and Paul Sweezy helped to create a sort of Marxo-Keynesianism, which combined the class categories of the former with the interest in investment, surplus and employment shown by the latter. The result was a new form of Marxist theory.

In their model, the monopoly capitalists faced the problem of massive, unspent surplus cash. Some might be wasted on personal consumption, but this would hardly resolve the problem. We can look again to John Bellamy Foster for a summary:

> Generally, the answer is sought in new investment, but that expansion of capital comes up against consumption limits imposed by the distribution of income: who will buy the increased volume of output? New epoch-making innovations are *historical* rather than economic factors that cannot be counted on to appear when needed or on the scale necessary in terms of surplus absorption.... The system has a powerful tendency towards stagnation, arising from an inability to find outlets for all of the surplus actually and potentially generated at the level of production – a problem partly (but only partly) compensated for by the rise of various countervailing factors, such as the growing sales effort, military spending and financial expansion.

Foster demonstrates the truth of this model with recourse to the American present (1999). The corporations are 'awash in rising profits' but no one knows what to do with them.[29]

So far this account has tended to celebrate the theoretical advances associated with Baran and Sweezy's approach, but by no means all commentators recognised the book as a breakthrough. In 1983, Chris Harman subjected Baran and Sweezy's notion of monopoly capitalism to a sustained critique. He argued that the theory of monopoly capitalism is based on a false chronology of investment, in which high-political decisions were seen to have caused the timing of economic booms and slumps. Yet it would be more accurate to explain the political acts as being shaped by economic events. Another part of their argument was that the greatest monopolies were the most profitable of companies. Yet this claim bears little relation to verifiable fact. Smaller companies are often more profitable than the largest firms. Likewise Baran and Sweezy's notion that huge companies derived their profits from their constant crushing of smaller firms could not be sustained. What would happen if the smaller firms did all go to the wall? Another of their claims was that monopoly capital was doomed because of its success. Paul Baran and Paul Sweezy maintained that declining price competition would create less incentive for accumulation. Having won, monopolies would simply stagnate. Again, this is questionable. For if price competition would decline, what about other forms of economic rivalry? Although (on their chronology) we have been living in monopoly conditions for a hundred years and more, there is no evidence that the general anarchy and competition of the market have withered away. Harman accused Baran and Sweezy of having imported Keynesian concepts into Marxist economics without improving on the original. They maintained that capitalism could not meet human needs and thus would reach a final and objective limit to its development. Yet any economic system will continue unless there is an alternative which can sweep away the old and usher in something new.[30]

Monopoly Capital and Cuba

At first sight, it might appear that there was no obvious connection between the themes of *Monopoly Capital* (surplus and investment) and the political choice of Paul Baran and Paul Sweezy to present the Cuban Revolution as the best hope for humanity. Yet it is striking that many of the writers who have defended the *Monopoly Capital* thesis most vigorously, on economic grounds, were writers from Third World backgrounds, or those who saw the Third World revolution as the key task of the day. Lawrence Lifschulz gives examples,

> In 1968, on his return from a journey through South America, a correspondent for the *Catholic Reporter* noted with some surprise that the two most respected and well-known Americans in Latin America after Abraham Lincoln were Paul Sweezy and Leo Huberman. This impression, as I subsequently discovered, was not merely confined to the western hemisphere. In 1973, sitting in the Workers' Cooperative Coffee House in Calcutta with a group of Bengali writers for the Calcutta weekly, *Frontier*, I was peppered with questions about Sweezy's theory of monopoly capital and Magdoff's views on imperialism. During my

later years as a foreign correspondent in South Asia, the 'Monthly Review Phenomenon' was to recur in far-off places, from Baluchistan in Pakistan to Chittagong in Bangladesh. There was a constant refrain, what did I think of such-and-such an article in *Monthly Review*?[31]

Where did this link come from? One source may have been the insistence, made throughout their work, that capitalism was a combined system. In this total world economy, the greatest divisions were no longer between classes but between nations. It followed that the forces most likely to defeat capitalism were located not in the First but in the Third World. Baran and Sweezy argued in *Monopoly Capital* that 'The revolutionary initiative against capitalism, which in Marx's day belonged to the proletariat in the advanced countries, has passed into the hands of the impoverished masses in the underdeveloped countries, who are struggling to free themselves from imperialist domination and exploitation.' The struggle between nations was itself a form of 'international class struggle' in which the leading imperialist powers (with the support of 'their' workers) did everything in their power to block the subaltern nations (whose workers were likewise allied to 'their' state).[32]

Another place in which these ideas were discussed was Paul Baran's first book, *The Political Economy of Growth*. A major part of this work is given over precisely to such questions as the unequal distribution of global wealth. 'It can be seen that approximately two-thirds of the human race have an average *per capita* income equivalent to some 50 to 60 dollars a year; it needs no explanation that for nearly all areas to which this statistic applies it signified chronic starvation, abysmal squalor, and rampant disease.'[33] Baran argued that the roots of backwardness could be traced back to the eighteenth century. The initial impact of capitalist growth had been to increase the potential resources of all societies. Then, as European capitalism spread, its representatives were forced to choose between two different paths. In some countries they could follow the American path and live as settlers, promoting a way of life based on the conditions in their home societies. Where there were already settled populations, though, the Europeans were forced to live rather as hoarders, stealing as much of the local wealth as they could and delivering it back to Europe. The surplus of the indigenous peoples was taken; their businesses were then subjected to ruinous competition from the most advanced firms in the West. In more recent times, monopoly capitalism took this whole process further. Now the whole resources of the modern state were used up to assist Western monopoly business.[34]

Paul Baran did still believe there was room for hope. 'The Steep Ascent', the final section of his book, was dedicated to the prospects for socialism in the underdeveloped world. 'The rule of monopoly and imperialism' and economic backwardness were 'intimately related'. The close connection between the state and monopoly capital made successful revolutions almost unachievable in America or Europe. What they offered to the peoples of the Third World was the prospect of successful national revolts rapidly converting themselves into a broader social process. 'The establishment of a socialist planned economy is an essential, indeed indispensable condition for the attainment of economic and social progress in underdeveloped countries.' We must remember that Baran was writing before the Cuban Revolution and at a time when the 'really existing socialist states' were still largely united. His words could be applied to China certainly, and perhaps to Egypt or India, if the language of the regimes was to be taken at face value.[35]

Beyond the 1960s

Monopoly Capital was undoubtedly an extraordinary, creative piece of work. For what Baran and Sweezy set out to explain was the process by which huge businesses were able to gather up in their hands the most extreme and unprecedented powers. It remains true that the modern state is wholly bound up with the success of capitalism, even where that is private business. Meanwhile the global power of the monopoly capitalists, organised as multinationals or even transnational corporations, has only grown. Those aspects of the theory are sound. Yet the suggestion that business and the state had fused was combined in these writers' hands with other arguments, which are perhaps of less use. One is the whole discussion of surplus. As true as it may have been in previous times, it seems strange to argue now that the greatest problem facing the world is one of overproduction, and therefore of wasted surplus. The moment of Edsel cars, wine and butter mountains belongs to the past. Likewise, the picture of permanent capitalist stagnation seems (at least to this reader) to rule out the possibility of future waves of technological advance, as happened in the computer boom of the 1990s. Far from being ended, competition continues. Indeed, if competition continues then so does the pressure of capital against labour.

There is also the problem of how to conceive the relationship between capital and the state. Some parts of this contract have undoubtedly altered in the past thirty-five years, not least the attrition of welfare. To argue, with Baran and Sweezy, that the state has become so closely merged with business that world history is only now a story of nations and states seems to miss certain key dynamics. To the workers of the South it offers a picture in which their state might prosper, through rapid socialist advance. In Cuba, the regime retains, even now, some of the allure of its past. Yet the model has not always travelled well. In other countries the radical generals in their army fatigues have played a much less progressive role. More to the point, to insist that all of us remain prisoners of our nationality means that there is no role given to the oppressed of the West, who must remained forever submerged beneath the weight of monopoly capital. And if the workers of Britain or America are to remain forever subaltern, then what chance do the movements of the South have? If the revolutions of the future remain isolated, then the CIAs of the future will always win. In their practical life as activists and journalists in the movement, Baran and Sweezy never once neglected the possibility that mass protest movements might emerge even at the heart of the capitalist system. Yet in their theoretical work, they under-theorized this possibility, looking instead to the margins of world capitalism to find their favoured sources of revolt. The authors of *Monopoly Capital* understood rightly that imperialism needs to be challenged abroad, but if it is ever to be defeated it must also be challenged at home.

7

Walter Rodney, African socialist

The dissidents who figure in this book fought in two ways. First, they raised the banner of workers' resistance against class oppression. Second, they campaigned within the movement for a maximum degree of democracy. We have already seen that Stalinism did not exist merely in the Eastern bloc. In a different 'Western' form, Stalinism shaped the strategies of the European Communist Parties. In the global 'South', it coexisted with a form of developmental politics in which the most important task was to secure national liberation. Only once that goal had been achieved should the question of socialism be raised. From the first 'stage' onwards (the struggle for liberation), social justice was postponed to the future. By the time of the second stage (building the nation), the one-time leaders of rebellion would act as a new governing class. Both in the Communist world and in the global South, 'the party' was given full authority to decide how people's lives should be organised. Even after liberation, workers and peasants were still subordinate to the state.

Walter Rodney's politics reached their height in this context of dual revolution. From the early 1950s onwards, the societies that had been governed by European colonialism had already begun to secure their independence. Colonel Nasser defeated a Franco–British–Israeli alliance at Suez in 1956. After that humiliation, the

British decided to give up their empire, state by state. In 1960, Belgium was compelled to cede control of the Congo. The French were humiliated in Algeria. By the 1970s, the process of securing national liberation was largely complete. Exceptions remained, including the Portuguese colonies and the running sore of apartheid South Africa, yet most of Africa was now self-governing, as indeed was most of Latin America, Asia and the Caribbean. The imperialist countries seemed increasingly content to govern these societies by proxy. Many activists felt that the most important task was now to re-radicalise the very movements that had previously secured national independence. Either the masses would fight or they would have to accept the permanent inevitability of a new, and more insidious, domestic exploitation.

Although he was largely active in Latin America, Walter Rodney was committed to the politics of African socialism. Rodney was born in Guyana. Having lived for several years in Jamaica, Guinea and Tanzania, he returned home. The local dictatorship against which Rodney set himself was Forbes Burnham's Peoples National Congress (PNC), a party which had ruled continuously from independence in 1964 onwards. Guyana was shaped by the same processes of neo-colonialism that shaped black Africa. Rodney's struggle was one for popular democracy and against state dictatorship.

Walter Rodney appears in this book as an important example of what dissident politics could achieve not in a Western but in a Third World context. In writing this chapter, I have tried to keep in mind Mahmood Mamdani's warning that 'Eurocentrism mutilates the experience of both the West and the East, mythologising the former and caricaturing the latter.'[1] I have tried to get away from that misleading impression of Marxism, in which all initiative is supposed to reside with the working classes resident in the richest nations. Where did Marx ever suggest *that*? This chapter is based instead on a method suggested fifteen years ago by John Saul. 'Marxism in Africa', he writes, 'is primarily an *African* phenomenon.' Socialism did not have to begin the West, nor did it automatically spread East or South. 'It is the creative tensions within Marxism, the flexibility and subtlety which these produce, that African Marxists at their best have seized hold of…. Moreover they have availed themselves of the fact that that the Marxist tradition is a *contested* one, where the answers are still in hot debate.' Saul continues: 'Far from offering "quasi-magical solutions" to "semi-educated people" Marxism is seen as offering *the best questions*, the most urgent [for] those who seek to construct socialist solutions to underdevelopment.'[2] Socialists in Africa have possessed at least the same potential for dissidence as activists anywhere else.

The young historian

Walter Rodney was born in March 1942 in Georgetown, Guyana. He attended Queens College in Guyana. One school contemporary has described his generation thus:

> There was an alchemy to the situation that still mystifies me after all these years. Leaders quickly emerged and have stayed leaders ever since: Walter Rodney, Ewart Thomas, Gordon Rohlehr, Walter Ramsahoye, Vic Insanally and Collin Moore. At the end of the year they produced a book of sophisticated essays on the topic of the course, *Caribbean Slave Society and Apartheid Compared*.[3]

After college, Rodney moved on to study at the University of the West Indies in Jamaica. His fellow activist Rupert Lewis studied alongside Walter Rodney in Jamaica. He argues that in this period Rodney was primarily an African nationalist. His ideas were the ideas of equal justice for the entire people. Yet such nationalist politics, pursued to their end, had a tendency to tip over into socialism. Rodney's politics identified the working class with 'the people'. He refused to recognise the idea that ethnic divisions should be more important than the fundamental truth of popular resistance against colonialism. He understood the need for solidarity between different ethnic groups, 'Africans' and 'Indians' in the liberation struggle. Such politics were indeed crucial to his later work in Guyana.[4]

In 1963, Rodney graduated in History from the University of the West Indies, and enrolled for a Ph.D. at the School of Oriental and African Studies in London. His thesis was a study of the Upper Guinea Coast between 1545 and 1800. It is a striking example of the best of African history. Rodney's history is both compelling and polemical. It contradicts the old claim that Africans supported slavery. The narrative begins before the arrival of the colonial powers. There were already many different peoples living on the West African coast, between what we would now call The Gambia and Cape Mount. These peoples were involved in salt manufacture and traded rice. As far as Rodney could detect, their societies did not in any way support the institution of unfree labour. Meanwhile the Portuguese settled at first to trade. The super-profits that could be found in human trafficking came to dominate their societies. By 1582, the combined population of the largest settlements, Fogo and Santiago, was 1,608 whites, 400 freed men and women, and 13,700 slaves. The entire economic, political and judicial organising of society was based on the principle that as many people as possible should be press-ganged, as fast and as securely as it could be managed. Eventually, it became profitable for African slavers to hold on to their victims, knowing that men and women caught for sale could be traded later. The implications of his argument for the present were clear: Africa needed to emancipate itself from European influence. In Rodney's phrase, 'Some of the wounds inflicted in that time are still festering.'[5]

In 1966, Walter Rodney began a two-year teaching assignment at the University of Tanzania in Dar-es-Salaam, which was then and for at least the next fifteen years a centre of radical scholarship. Ali Mazrui recalls the extraordinary number of non-Tanzanian leftists who came to Dar-es-Salaam to meet and share ideas. They included the Ugandan activists Dan Nabudere and Yash Tandon, such British radicals as John Saul and Lionel Cliffe, as well as Mahmood Mamdani, 'a superb orator and eloquent theoretician' and a champion of anti-capitalist (as opposed to 'merely' anti-imperialist) thought.[6] Having spent an exhilarating two years in Tanzania, in 1968 Rodney returned to the University of the West Indies as a lecturer in African and Caribbean history, teaching at the Mona campus in Jamaica.

By this time, Rodney had already secured a global reputation as a scholar who took the side of the oppressed. Yet he was not content with restricting himself to academic studies while he taught at the university in Jamaica. Instead, Walter Rodney began the work of organising trade unions for poor workers and peasants.

This was not an accidental choice. Liberation movements were sweeping Africa, Asia and Latin America. The USA was experiencing opposition to the Vietnam War at home and abroad; and new social movements were growing in strength across Europe, in the wake of Paris and May 1968. West Indian society and culture were in ferment. The new Caribbean sounds of ska, rock steady and reggae were growing in popularity. Rastafarianism was on the rise. In a context of rebellion, Rodney was viewed as a troublemaker. Shortly after his return to the West Indies, he left the Mona campus to attend a black writers' conference in Canada. The Jamaican government took the opportunity to deny the Guyanese academic re-entry. Rodney was forced to return instead to Tanzania. His effective expulsion set off an explosion of protests. Students barred the university gates, shut down classes and marched on the Jamaican parliament, fighting police road blocks and tear gas at several points.[7]

African socialism: three generations

In a memorial speech to his younger comrade, the pioneer Trinidadian Marxist C.L.R. James made the point that Rodney belonged to a second generation of African socialists. 'To be born in 1942 was to have behind you a whole body of work dealing in the best way with the emerging situation in the Caribbean and the colonial world.' Walter Rodney only emerged after most of the great moments of African liberation had already occurred.

> [First] Nkrumah succeeded in securing independence in the Gold Coast and establishing Ghana; then a little later Julius Nyerere did so for Tanganyika, which united with Zanzibar to become Tanzania.... That is why when [Rodney] completed his studies, he was able to build on these foundations. The work that had been necessary to motivate him to study Africa and the Caribbean had been done already.[8]

Rodney's friend Leonard Tim Hector accepts the point.

> Walter and those of us of Walter's generation had been given a foundation to build on. That foundation was laid by C.L.R. James himself, by the great W.E.B. Du Bois, by the most significant Marcus Garvey, by George Padmore, the Father of African Emancipation, and by Frantz

Fanon, the philosopher of post-colonialism, the theorist of the pitfalls of national independence. We had to build on that foundation, in theory and practice, or 'betray the mission' as Fanon had put it.[9]

It is worth identifying the contribution that each of these writers had made. The names previously cited originate from all parts of the Black Atlantic,[10] including North America and Britain as well as the Caribbean and Africa itself. The first group belong to a preparatory stage. By 1900, Africa was under direct foreign rule. The colonial states did all they could to prevent the emergence of any potential source of opposition. Education was closed, black people were denied access to skills and to resources. The most important early figures in 'African socialism' were thus mainly active outside Africa. Only later could the strategies that they discussed have an impact on Africa itself. W.E.B. Du Bois and Marcus Garvey were active in the early-twentieth-century USA. George Padmore and C.L.R. James were pan-Africanists and socialists living in Britain and America.

Before 1914, Du Bois helped to found the American black civil rights organisation, the National Association for the Advancement of Colored People (NAACP). He was later a leading pan-Africanist and then a fellow-traveller of the Communist Party. He was also a powerful historian of the black liberation movement. His *Black Reconstruction* considered the alliance between blacks, poor whites and Northern manufacturers who briefly united in order to transform the Southern states in the aftermath of the American Civil War. Du Bois argued that the rise and fall of this radical 'reconstruction' movement had set the tone for the entire century to come. 'The abolition of American slavery started the transportation of capital from white to black countries where slavery prevailed, with the same tremendous and awful consequences upon the laboring classes which we see about us today.'[11] The competition between First and Third Worlds, manifest in colonialism, was a product of the incomplete replacement of slavery by free labour. One hundred years of racism can be explained in terms of the defeat suffered in the 1870s by workers and the rural poor.

Marcus Garvey's Universal Negro Improvement Association grew in the years following the First World War, becoming a mass movement with several million supporters across North America,

Britain and the Caribbean. Garvey's strategy told black Americans to return to Africa. In different conditions such a message might have reinforced the existing feeling of passivity in black life. In the actual circumstances of the time, though, the opposite was the case. Africa became a symbol for a general project of liberation. The men and women who listened to Marcus Garvey themselves had little desire to 'return'. Despite Garvey's formal message, they heard in his speeches the sound of confidence and authentic black pride. Garvey injected a new note of optimism into black cultural life. The 1920s also witnessed the Harlem Renaissance, the development of jazz music, black film and art.

A third figure, George Padmore, also came of age during the preparatory stage of the colonial revolts. Through the 1930s, Padmore consistently agitated for black independence. For several years, he was close to the politics of the Communist International. Later, Padmore was close to C.L.R. James. Following Benito Mussolini's invasion of Abyssinia, they worked together on the pro-Ethiopian paper *International African Opinion*. In 1945, along with Jomo Kenyatta and Kwame Nkrumah, Padmore was successful in establishing a Pan-African Federation. The fifth Pan-African Congress was held in Manchester that year. Besides Kenyatta and Nkrumah, many other future African leaders took part.

C.L.R. James also belongs to the black diaspora. Born in 1901, James left Trinidad in 1932, going on to spend his next two decades in Britain and America. He became a prominent journalist, activist and strategist in the two worlds of socialism and pan-Africanism. Between 1936 and 1939, he produced a brilliant series of works, including a novel, *Minty Alley* (1936), which captures the relations between the Jamaican petty bourgeoisie and poor.[12] Next, in 1937, James brought out *World Revolution, 1917–1936: The Rise and Fall of the Communist International*. Here James publicly sided with Trotskyism, arguing that Stalin had betrayed the grand aims of the Russian Revolution.[13] In 1938, James published his superb history of *The Black Jacobins*. James's subject was the revolt of the slaves in the French colony of San Domingo, today's Haiti. Largely a portrait of the uprising's leader, Toussaint L'Ouverture, the book is a history of revolt, repression and final popular victory. Toussaint and his supporters were unwilling revolutionaries. Simply in order to secure the maintenance of their freedom, they were compelled to defeat huge British, French and Spanish armies. Their triumph led to the abolition of the slave trade.[14]

C.L.R. James was not 'merely' a writer; he was also an activist who shaped the strategic context in which Walter Rodney's politics was formed. In 1958, James returned to Trinidad, where he became a leading intellectual figure in the national independence movement. He was appointed secretary of the West Indian Federal Labor Party. James edited *The Nation*, the paper of Eric Williams's post-colonial movement in Trinidad. Yet the new state failed to live up to its early, socialistic promise. Like many of the leaders of the first wave of independent states, Williams began with a commitment to equality, but lacked any strong sense of how to achieve it. James broke with Eric Williams in disgust. James helped to found the Workers and Farmers Party, to protest against the degeneration of the national movement, but his group was badly defeated in the 1966 elections. Over the next twenty years, James toured England, the USA and the Caribbean. He was active again in the African liberation movement and helped to write the programme of the Sixth Pan-African Conference. He also argued for a re-democratisation of the struggle for African liberation.[15]

The last author to mention in this section is Frantz Fanon, a doctor, a writer and a militant in the Algerian uprising which began in 1954 and ended in 1962. In the 1950s, Fanon devoted himself to making propaganda for Algerian independence. Given that the colonial power was France, this obliged him to condemn the French left, which largely backed the colonial government against the liberation armies of Ben Bella and the FLN.[16] The experience of civil war brought him into close contact with its victims. Fanon's medical work then caused him to consider the internal, psychological consequences of racism. His book *Black Skin, White Masks* describes how African people could allow themselves to be manipulated by colonialism, and even sometimes collude in its processes.[17] Fanon's real subject was the psychological revolution that would be needed to rid Africa of the long-term consequences of several centuries of Western domination.

Garvey, Du Bois, Padmore, James and Fanon belonged to the first phase of African socialism. They reached maturity before the war. Although their ideas played a role in influencing the tactics of liberation, they emerged too early to play any driving role in the actual leadership of the first African states. Instead, the torch was passed on to a younger generation of leaders, whose outstanding representatives included Patrice Lumumba, Julius Nyerere and Kwame Nkrumah. It is worth describing each in turn.

Patrice Lumumba was the first leader of the Congo (later Zaire, now the Democratic Republic of the Congo) following independence in June 1960. His party, the National Congolese Movement (MNC), was committed to unitary, national politics, a multi-ethnic state, and policies of redistribution to the poor, rural majority. The MNC won the first democratic elections. Lumumba was a popular and charismatic figure. He believed profoundly in national independence from both of the major Cold War blocs. He held that the Congolese people, united, could overcome all obstacles and create a social-democratic society. Yet the previous colonial power, Belgium, was able to undermine Lumumba's authority, working in alliance with the United States. Copper-rich Katanga seceded, and a long civil war followed. The eventual winner was Mobutu Sese Seko, who received Western backing in creating a one-man state. Lumumba was murdered on CIA orders in spring 1961; since then the Congo has suffered forty years of hell.[18]

Julius Nyerere was the first prime minister of Tanganyika, and went on to play a leading role in the politics of that country, both in its first years, and for long after. His party, the Tanganyika African National Union (TANU), included large numbers of whites and Asians, and fought consistently for non-racial democracy. In 1961, Nyerere played a key role in securing the removal of South Africa from the Commonwealth. He went on to supervise the transformation of Tanganyika into a republic. The honeymoon period did not last. Trade unions led strikes against the government's wages scheme. Meanwhile, civil society failed to produce any large parties capable of challenging the TANU for national or even local power. In 1963, Tanganyika was declared a one-party state.

Kwame Nkrumah of Ghana was perhaps the most impressive member of this generation. Born in 1909, he spent the 1930s and 1940s in America and Britain, coming into contact with Marcus Garvey's movement, and the Western left. Following Ghana's independence, Nkrumah played a key role in promoting the idea of pan-African unity. He called a conference of independent African States at Accra in 1958, and tried to promote independence movements in Algeria, the Congo, Guinea and Mali. Nkrumah's autobiography, published in 1957, contains a concise statement of his strategic beliefs:

> Capitalism is too complicated a system for a newly independent nation. Hence the need for a socialist society. But even a system based on social justice and a democratic constitution may need backing up, during the period following independence, by emergency measures of a totalitarian kind. Without discipline, freedom cannot survive…. Independence will not be complete, however, unless it is linked up with the liberation of other territories in Africa. Ghana now joins the independent states of Egypt, Ethiopia, Liberia, Libya, Morocco, the Sudan and Tunisia. Elsewhere the continent is ruled by not less than six European powers.[19]

Yet Ghana's time of plenty was followed by years of lean. The pace of redistribution did not match the breadth of Nkrumah's global alliances. Western governments were still keen to remove their long-time critic. There was a military coup against Nkrumah in 1966. Three years later, civilian rule was restored. The currency was devalued, and the state ruined.

Despite such defeats, it should be remembered that the early 1960s were still a period of African hope. The continent possessed enormous wealth, some 90 per cent of the world's known reserves of cobalt, over 80 per cent of the global reserves of chrome, and a hefty share of platinum and industrial diamonds. When Rodney was a student at school and university, it was still possible to be optimistic. The long-term impact of the CIA-sponsored murder of Patrice Lumumba was not yet evident. Meanwhile, the toppling of Nkrumah belonged to the future. The full extent of the future degradation of the colonial revolution was not obvious. Yet in the period of Rodney's early adulthood some of the problems of the second wave were already clear. For example, the people of the Caribbean had long assumed that once the various islands enjoyed independence from British rule, their future would be found in a West Indies federation. Such a multi-ethnic state was indeed duly established in 1958, but it collapsed four years later amid a chorus of mutual recriminations. Old patterns of ego and interest re-emerged, even in black hands.

Under conditions of defeat, increasing numbers of black writers began to discuss the fatigue of the independence movements. The Kenyan novelist, activist and playwright Ngugi wa Thiong'o, describes the problems well. 'The analysis of the African situation in the 50s and 60s had been seen in terms of black and white.... So when it was the turn of black people to hold the flag, then people were asking "what is wrong, what is wrong, how come that my brother is sitting on me?"'[20] As early as 1960, C.L.R. James had begun to argue that even the strategies of Kwame Nkrumah in Ghana were flawed. 'There are some elements of colonialism still lurking in the minds even of independent countries.' James suggested that any successful independence movement faced a potential crisis of leadership, and could remain true to its roots only so long as those roots restrained any back-sliding by the new rulers. Nkrumah's fall was blamed on his failure to remove 'hesitant, faltering or even treacherous associates'. Another conclusion was that democratic institutions were needed, even if they were critical of the government. One of Nkrumah's gravest errors had been the failure to call a 'revolutionary constituent assembly'.[21]

Other writers spoke of the need constantly to bring the leaders of the colonial revolution back into living contact with the mass of the people. For example, the leading figure in the movement for independence for Guinea-Bissau was Amílcar Cabral. Before he was killed in 1973, Cabral wrote the following account of imperialism beyond independence. 'Neo-colonialism is at work on two fronts – in Europe as well as the underdeveloped countries. Its current framework in the underdeveloped countries is the policy of aid, and one of the essential aims of this policy is to create a false bourgeoisie to put a brake on the revolution.'[22] Cabral's idea of popular resistance was similar to that which had motivated the second wave of African socialists (Lumumba, Nkrumah). His novelty lay chiefly in the demand for the *renewal* of the independence movement,

> My own view is that there are no real conflicts between the peoples of Africa. There are only conflicts between their elites. When the peoples take power into their own hands, as they will with the march of events

in this continent, there will remain no great obstacles to effective African solidarity.[23]

By the 1970s, the conditions were brewing for a third wave of African socialists to emerge, in such countries as Nigeria, Guinea, Mozambique,[24] Zimbabwe and elsewhere. In Guyana, Walter Rodney was an outstanding representative of this new generation.

Academic and activist

Between 1968 and 1974, while still based at the University of Tanzania, Walter Rodney travelled throughout Africa, and in Europe and Asia. He became best known for his book *How Europe Underdeveloped Africa*. This study was the manifesto of a generation. It spoke to different aspects of the African experience. It insisted that the world should be seen through the eyes of the oppressed themselves, 'The purpose ... is to try to reach those who wish to explore further the nature of their exploitation, rather than to satisfy the standards set by our oppressors and their spokesmen in the academic world.' There were many villains in the book, and one or two heroes. In one important passage, Rodney described the role played by Queen Nzinga, the head of the African state of Matamba, which was founded around 1630 to coordinate resistance against the Portuguese slavers in Angola. Queen Nzinga also fought against the slave wars in Africa. Rodney's discussion of figures like Nzinga dispels the myth that Africans did little to contest their enslavement.[25] The key concept in the book was underdevelopment, which meant more than the absence of development, 'because all people have developed in one way or another and to a greater or lesser extent'. Instead it was the reproduction of unequal relationships on a national terrain; 'Underdevelopment makes sense only as a means for comparing levels of development.' The force responsible for African poverty was colonialism, overt or concealed:

> The operation of the imperialist system bears major responsibility for African economic retardation by draining African wealth and by making it impossible to develop more rapidly the resources of the continent ... One has to deal with those who manipulate the system and those who are either agents or unwitting accomplices of the said system. The

capitalists of Western Europe were the ones who actively extended their exploitation from inside Europe to cover the whole of Africa.

Successful independence could only be achieved under socialism: 'Africa can only develop if there is a radical break with the inter-national capitalist system which had been the principal agency of underdevelopment of Africa over the last five centuries.'[26]

One 1968 pamphlet, *West Africa and the Slave Trade*, returned to the themes of Rodney's doctorate. Given that his ideas were published this time for a popular audience, Walter Rodney could be more strident in expressing his anger, 'Africans had absolutely no control over the European side or the American side of the slave trade. Only the European capitalists had such world-wide power, and they used Africans for their own purposes.'[27] Another book, *Groundings with My Brothers*, has a slightly different frame of reference. This time it is America that receives most attention. *Groundings* is concerned to defend Malcolm X and other activists associated with Black Power, and to consider their relevance to activists elsewhere. It is the theoretical counterpart to the 1970 Black Power revolt in Trinidad, which threatened to destroy the regime of Eric Williams.[28]

Walter Rodney: black Marxist?

There are many different models of the activist as writer. Some people use written history merely as a means to advance their own career as an academic or as an author. Others are attracted to the past because the story of the majority fills them with hope, and they wish to share their enthusiasm. Leonard Hector suggests that Walter Rodney was closer to the Marxist C.L.R. James than to Eric Williams, the author of *Capitalism and Slavery*[29] and the one-time leader of the Trinidadian state,

> Rodney brought to historical writing the passion of the participant who set about to change the world, not in dream, but in action, and was seeing and searching in history for new foundations for new action. Without that passion historical writing becomes either chronology or dry as dust dissection of events, without a sense of movement. History moves. Rodney understood that. Williams didn't.[30]

The comparison with C.L.R. James is useful, not least because it was considered by Rodney himself. Speaking at the University of Michigan in 1972, Rodney attempted to grapple with the 'quality and significance' of James's theoretical contribution to the African revolution. Why would a man of the diaspora, whose political thinking was shaped by events in Britain, America and the West Indies, choose to think so seriously about events in Africa? Rodney's answer contains a strong hint of autobiographical meaning: 'There are fundamental political realities which draw the conscious Black man in the New World towards the African continent.' Among such realities, Rodney counted the need for common organisation, so that unity could be brought to bear against a common enemy. 'It is logical enough, too, that one must maximize strong points, so the freeing of the African continent itself became the priority for politically active West Indians, who knew the limitations of their own societies and knew that the weakness of Africa contributed to indignity and low status abroad.' What of James's anti-Stalinism? As far as the older man was concerned, the process of rejecting Stalinism had enabled him to grasp a more important conception of socialism, as the conscious self-awakening of the creative spirit of the majority. Some of James's insights were lost on Walter Rodney, even though the younger man did recognise that 'monstrosities' had been carried out in Stalin's name. 'The African Revolution cannot afford to draw on Marxist theory in its dogmatic Stalinist or even Trotskyist form. But conversely, it should be equally clear that Africans can benefit from mankind's ideological heritage.' Rodney then glided over James's criticisms of Nkrumah, suggesting that the problems with the Ghanaian revolution could be put down to bureaucracy, corruption and the old leader's preference for 'a coterie of sycophants'. In response, we can ask: was this all? At the end of his article Walter Rodney concluded with a few general words about the relationship between African liberation and Marxism:

> It is significant that a question as seemingly abstract as that of the value of Marxism to the African Revolution has recently been revived among African students on the continent and activists in the Black movement in America. It is a recognition that, as oppressed people, we cannot overlook any weapon which could contribute to our liberation. One of

the many positive facets of the career of *Mzee* C.L.R. James is precisely the awareness that African freedom will not be won without building in the positive elements in the history of Mankind.[31]

It would be unfair to read too much into the evident distance that Walter Rodney placed in this passage between himself and Marxism. In the rest of his work, Rodney expressed a lasting interest in socialist terms and theory. Such ideas did not come to him directly, but second hand, because they were part of the common sense of most radicals at the time. Yet Rodney consistently argued that the world was a totality, that social battles fought in one context would have meaning elsewhere. In addition, he spoke frequently of contradiction, seeing that the rule of different people expressed the interests of different classes in society. His world was occupied by great forces, including the neo-colonial powers and the black masses whose resistance would take the form of insurrection.

If we liken Rodney to the classical Marxists of the 1890s – Kautsky, Plekhanov and their ilk – then there are grounds both to compare and to contrast. There were certain areas in which the radicals of the 1890s held the upper hand; their theories were more complex and more useful. They learned from Marx a greater sense of the economic dynamics of capitalism, which enabled a more impressive explanation of the ways in which Africa under slavery or in the twentieth century fitted into a total system of capitalist rule. To state the case for the earlier period most briefly, the primitive accumulation of capital from the sixteenth century onwards made possible the later development of industry.[32] In addition, the classical Marxists had more of a sense of the class divisions that could emerge even within oppressed groups. In the context of Rodney's life, such an analysis might have enabled our activist to see that the new African bourgeoisie was not a marginal or foreign force, but something that was capable of carrying out its own distorted notion of a national transformation process, with the intellectuals and a new state class at its head. As we shall see, Rodney himself began to recognise this lacuna in his thinking, and began to consider the problem of indigenous support for neo-colonialism, but only in the late 1970s, which was effectively too late.

Conversely, there were also many areas in which Walter Rodney's socialism was far in advance of Kautsky and his group. One point where Rodney was ahead was in his realisation that social justice was not divisible; it had to apply equally to the people of the developing world. Although many of the Second International Marxists did oppose European colonialism, certainly in the 1880s and 1890s, there were many others whose anti-imperialism was so abstract that it had no real content, and a few who even supported their 'own' imperial state. Eduard Bernstein's book *Evolutionary Socialism* argued that German socialists should have 'nothing to fear from the colonial policy of the German empire'.[33] A second point at which Rodney was well in advance of the more 'classical' Marxists was in his absolute commitment to the fighting, insurgent spirit of Marx himself. Above all else, Marxism is a science of working-class revolt. Rodney expressed such politics in his life.

People's power

In 1974, Walter Rodney made the decision to return home. His goal was to contribute towards the liberation of Guyana from the PNC dictatorship, headed by Forbes Burnham. While still in Tanzania, Walter applied for a position at the University of Guyana, and was offered a professorship in History, which he accepted. However, when Forbes Burnham heard about this, he ordered the University to rescind its decision. Rodney returned to Guyana with his wife Pat and three children, unsure of any source of income. Burnham's conduct only makes sense if we understand that the regime was weak, and increasingly fearful of opposition. Arnold Rampersaud of the People's Progressive Party (PPP) was already in prison. As well as Rodney, a number of other academics at Guyana University were victimised. Joshua Ramsammy was shot, Clive Thomas was kidnapped, and Mohammed Insanally had his contract terminated on government orders.[34]

On his arrival in Guyana in 1974, Walter quickly became active on the left. He spoke at public meetings and organised education programmes. Friends encouraged him to join the main opposition party, the PPP, led by Dr Cheddi Jagan. Yet Rodney resisted this option, for several reasons. One was the popular feeling that the

PPP was a party that represented the Indian Guyanese. The PNC was able to maintain itself in power largely by exploiting the ethnic fears of the other main group, the African Guyanese. Rodney was convinced that social justice could be achieved only by cutting across ethnic lines.

In 1978, Forbes Burnham called a referendum on a new constitution. According to such critics as Walter Rodney, Burnham's intention was to secure the presidency for life. Yet one of the clauses of the new constitution did provide for an elected parliament, which had the power (in cases of extraordinary corruption) to remove the minister appointed by the president – provided that the president did not dissolve parliament first, which, as the constitution went on to say, he would be perfectly entitled to do. Although Rodney was still unemployed, he was well known in the country and was able to play a prominent part in the campaign for a No vote. Although the referendum passed, Rodney achieved a level of public recognition for his campaign, and friends urged him to establish a multiracial opposition movement.

In 1978, the Working Peoples Alliance (WPA) was formed. Walter Rodney's charismatic style helped the alliance to win support. His booklet *People's Power: No Dictator* derived from one of his many public speeches. It is an extraordinary statement of cold-blooded anger against the dictatorial habits of Forbes Burnham.

> A dictator is one who wields absolute power. The dictator elevates himself above all other citizens.... In more modern versions of dictatorship, the absolute ruler has to facilitate an elaborate cult of the personality to prove that he is more intelligent, more potent and generally superior to any human being.... The dictator is responsible to no-one, no organisation, no social institution.... A dictator is representative of some class other than the majority of the exploited workers and peasants.... The fact that a dictator is ruthless does not make him efficient. A dictatorial system destroys initiative. It does not allow the genius of the people to flourish and it frustrates even that class from which the dictator emerges.[35]

At each end of Walter Rodney's thinking, then, we find two concepts juxtaposed. The negative force to which he gave most attention in his writing was 'imperialism', which created underdevelopment, neo-colonialism and black subordination to empire, in the local form of Forbes Burnham. The positive force was 'the people', whose energy would be unleashed at some stage in the future. The task facing the intellectual was to re-immerse him- or herself constantly in the mass. Placed against this test, Rodney undoubtedly played an exemplary role. According to Wole Soyinka, Rodney 'was no captive intellectual playing to the gallery of local or national radicalism. He was clearly one of the most solidly ideologically *situated* intellectuals ever to look colonialism and its contemporary heir – black opportunism and exploitation – in the eye.'[36] But did he fully understand 'the people'?

In one of his last speeches, Rodney described the majority in the most moving terms. 'I do not believe that it is remotely possible in this country that the enemies of the people can extinguish and put out that humanity which resides in us.'[37] The battle of the future would be waged between 'the people' or 'humanity' and Burnham's machine. Yet the dictator was also human; Burnham and his cronies were as much of 'the people' as anyone else. Rodney pulled back from using those political categories that might have enabled him to distinguish between Burnham and the real 'people', the workers and the rural poor. He started to use a class analysis, but then drew back from the full implications of such a system. Rodney would not develop his sketchy class analysis to explain the conflicts within his own society. The real problem was that in Rodney's thinking 'the people' were all united. They were united now against Burnham, and would again be so, after the tyrant's demise. At the end of *People's Power*, Walter Rodney described what a post-Burnham society might look like. 'The WPA has called for a government of national unity ... it is proof of the maturity of our workers that they fully understand the need for patriotic compromises with other classes.'[38] What has national unity ever meant but that class oppression should remain in place?

The late 1970s were a creative moment in Walter Rodney's life. He wrote short stories for children and began the research for his extraordinary book, *A History of the Guyanese Working People, 1805– 1905*, which would appear posthumously. This history was informed by Rodney's belief that working people in Guyana had played a proud role in challenging the structures of oppression. Of this book, Moses Seenarine writes,

His analysis of the structural forces of European capitalism and colonialism in Guyana is not top-down, but rather revolves around an analysis of the agency of individuals and groups whose interests are served by these forces, as well as those whose exploitative experiences are contradictory to them.[39]

As its title suggests, the book tells the history of the Guyanese workers and peasants. At the front of the story is resistance. The narrative shows the connections between the national struggle and the class war. It also contains a sustained treatment of many subaltern groups whose lives other historians would have ignored. Deliberately, Rodney did not write exclusively about African–Indian relations in Guyana, but distinguished Creoles as a different social group. Rodney observed that a review, *Creole*, served alongside the *Working Man* as one of main pro-independence papers in the 1870s. Another *Creole* newspaper was started by Patrick Dargan in 1905. It attacked the colonial administration over the 1905 agitation and shootings.[40] One further aspect of the book was the emphasis it placed on the condition of women. Rodney showed how at the start of the century some Guyanese women were able to join a local, middle class:

> They sought to earn for themselves, but few survived without turning to an employed male relative, a husband, a 'child-father' or some such. Little wonder that the women were so vociferous and so active during the riots. They were backing their men, and they were also fighting for themselves and for the reproduction of their families – as they had done before in the 1889 when they attacked the Portuguese retailers.[41]

Of the 105 people convicted in the 1905 riots, one in three was female. Not just class and race, but gender as well contributed to the rise of a Guyanese protest movement.

It was the discussion of ethnicity that had the greatest meaning for Rodney. One part of his book suggested that racial boundaries in Guyana were tending to come down. He argued that this process could be seen in many different spheres. Indian immigrants were influenced by Creole African practices, such as funeral customs. Within Creole cultures, there was a tendency for habits to lose their early ethnic associations – for example, all ethnic groups ate rice in the 1890s. Among Africans and Indians, various cultural forms – some of them even of white origin – were tending to become universal, such as cricket and the institution of the rum shop. Yet there were limits to this process:

> The existing aspects of cultural convergence were insufficiently developed to contribute decisively to solidarity among the working people of the two major race groups. The obverse of this race–class conjuncture is that the development of class forces and class consciousness was inadequate to sustain unity of the working people across the barriers created by legal distinctions, racial exclusiveness, and the separate trajectories of important aspects of culture.[42]

We must remember that at this time Guyanese politics were still dominated by the overwhelming enmity between two different parties, who drew their support predominantly on ethnic lines. To suggest that cultural convergence would reduce these ethnic barriers was to argue that solidarity was possible. To maintain that ethnic convergence belonged to the future was to suggest that the prospects facing socialists were in the short-term bleak.

Explain, explain, explain

Even if his opportunities to secure paid employment as a lecturer had been curtailed, Walter Rodney was still committed to pushing back the boundaries of academic knowledge. According to his friend Leonard Hector, 'Walter Rodney and I had agreed in 1979 to do a joint work – indeed a critique.' They were going to take on the formidable figure of Sir Arthur Lewis, one of the first historians to study the history of the failed attempt to achieve West Indian statehood in 1958–62. Sir Arthur Lewis had written, in a little known essay, 'How did these highly intelligent men, all devoted to federation, come to make so many errors in so short a period?' The answer could only be found – Hector and Rodney agreed – in a study of the general class relations which enabled a new governing elite to emerge:

> Sir Arthur had posed a fundamental question.... The whole intellectual history of the world from Socrates to Walter Rodney himself was in question here. We would have to examine the new political class which emerged since 1789 in the French Revolution with Robespierre [and continued] through Lincoln down to Stalin and McNamara, the first

leader of the modern military industrial complex. All this we would have to do in order to understand Adams, Manley and Williams. This new class which nowhere speaks in its own name but hides itself under the banner of labour and, until recently, socialism. This new class which saw itself as holding the balance between Capital and Labour, but which was forever subordinating Labour to Capital.... Together we would work on how these historical tendencies represented themselves in Adams, Manley and Williams. Burnham represented the ultimate deterioration of the political type.... It would be the story of Caribbean disintegration.[43]

This passage hints at an important moment in Walter Rodney's thought. At the time of his death, Rodney was beginning to address the class origins of the African state bourgeoisie. We might say that he was grasping towards a Marxist theory of the failure of African socialism. With his qualities as a historian, we can guess that Rodney might have completed some great, explanatory work. He failed. Yet even in Hector's brief account we can detect the emergence of a key insight, the comparison between the bureaucratisation of the French and African revolutions. A yet more immediate comparison would be between the people around Joseph Stalin and the people around Forbes Burnham and Eric Williams. What the African leaders took from Russia was not merely a defence of their own bureaucratic privileges, nor indeed a belief in 'the party' as the force to which all other social forces should bend. A further debt was the belief that Russia had secured its true independence through a process of industrialisation that began in the late 1920s. Different members of the new African bourgeoisie understood the history of this process to a greater or lesser extent. Yet such figures as Williams were sincere (at least in the beginning) when they claimed to be copying a Russian model, by investing in industry, and promoting the national economy at the expense of foreign, capitalist investment.

Would Rodney have accepted this point? If he had, it would have obliged him to reconsider two deeply held beliefs. One was that the African bourgeoisie was a weak and foreign implant. The implication of the argument above is that its roots were to be found more deeply. The second of Rodney's beliefs that perhaps required challenging was the idea that having toppled their dictators, the African masses should then unite in a national alliance that would proceed to rebuild the economy, by means of investment in industry and national autarky. We can hardly blame Rodney for sharing this model – it was the common idea of socialism promoted by the socialist states of Russia, China, Cuba and beyond. If Williams and the rest had initially been sincere in arguing for such state socialism, though, then what could Rodney offer, if his strategy for development was the same? Such criticisms are not intended to reduce the stature of Walter Rodney. Instead, they point to a set of dilemmas which no one of the left escaped satisfactorily at this time.[44]

State killing

Meanwhile, Burnham's Guyana continued to fragment. Food, water, electricity and medicines were in short supply. The regime felt threatened and responded with violence. Two WPA activists, Edward Dublin and Othene Koama, were killed. In spring 1980 Rodney and several comrades were tried on political charges. The proceedings did not go well for the government and the case was suspended for a two-month period. At the same time, Forbes Burnham's government indicted a further seventeen people associated with the WPA on a charge of treason. A representative of Amnesty International present in the court during the preliminary examination on these charges declared that Amnesty would adopt the case as a subject of its inquiry into political repression in Guyana.[45]

To many observers it seemed that Guyanese society was heading towards a period of decisive conflict. Either the government would succeed in restoring order or the protest movement would force its way into power. Unfortunately, the outcome was popular defeat. Burnham organised Rodney's murder. In his funeral speech, C.L.R. James criticised Walter Rodney for failing to study the art of insurrection, a skill whose successful accomplishment required technique. James believed that Rodney tried to force the tempo of change, when he would have done better to wait:

> Walter was faced with … a very difficult situation. But I think that he was driven to act without the powers at the disposal that were his. And I do not think that Burnham could have struck and destroyed these forces without the forces responding and giving something in return.

That tremendous upheaval of the population in the French Revolution, in the British Revolution, in the Russian Revolution, in the revolution in Iran, everywhere, that is what you have to depend on, and Walter did not wait for that. He tried to force it. There was a danger that Burnham would strike, but I do not believe that, with the people there, Burnham could have put them in jail, and so on. On the contrary, maybe any attempt of his to act immediately might have unloosed the upheaval, because it was there.[46]

Here James alludes to the events of Rodney's death. At the end of the 1970s, the Guyanese state was in utter crisis. Between 1970 and 1979, the production of key export goods such as bauxite had fallen by half. The public debt rose to 2.4 billion dollars.[47] Burnham was forced to ask the IMF for a loan. In the meantime, the country's politics were shaped by two great failures. The left had not succeeded in generating the popular movement that was needed to launch a successful popular rising, but the right was also stymied in its attempts to stop the left though judicial repression. Determined to act first, Burnham rejected the strategy of legal action in favour of more dangerous, underhand tactics. The government placed a spy in the WPA, who won Rodney's confidence by furnishing communications. This agent, Gregory Smith, then planted a bomb in a radio transmitter: it was this device that killed Walter Rodney. His death was just one of several state-sanctioned killings. According to the *New York Review of Books*, 'The Associated Press report on the incident stressed the fact that Rodney was the third senior member of the WPA to have been killed in seven months, the others having been killed by the police.'[48]

Walter Rodney died in an explosion in Georgetown on the evening of 13 June 1980. He was just 38 years old. Future generations can learn from his immense courage in adversity, from the extraordinary quality of his historical research, and from his life-long commitment to the cause of freedom for all. One argument of this chapter has been that aspects of class and populist analyses coexisted unevenly in his thinking. What no one could doubt, though, is that Rodney was a dissident. He saw the party of independence turn against its former supporters. He tried to understand this process, and bring it to an end. Even when he failed, Walter Rodney's mistakes demonstrate an enormous creativity. From a revolutionary of his stature there is much to learn.

Harry Braverman: work and resistance

Every day in our capitalist society the majority of people are subject to paid employment. For most of us, work takes up more time than anything else we do; our work is in this sense the most important aspect to our lives. Almost everyone works, has worked or will work, but how much creativity or pleasure do we find in our labour? For most people, for most of the time, work is repetitive and mundane. Much of it is spent counting down to Friday and the weekend. Often the best moments at work are those that subvert the labour that we do. People remember friends they make at work, talking to people on breaks or out of supervision, the day the manager was ill or on holiday, but the labour itself is rarely pleasurable. Indeed, the tedium of work is probably the single most extraordinary fact about our society. If Craig Raine's mythical Martian were ever to send their postcard home,[1] one of the first things they would notice is that billions of people voluntarily agree to spend their waking hours in effort, drudgery and toil. Part of the reason why work is tolerated is that the alternative – to be without work – is even worse. Unemployment is an even more degrading experience, boring, humiliating and debilitating. Unemployed workers are poorer, more isolated, more prone to depression than their working counterparts. To be unemployed is to be reminded permanently of the potentially liberating character of work. Work should be purposeful, collective social labour; although it usually is not, to point to its debased character is no comfort to those who are without. Thus there is a contradiction. On the one hand, social labour is *potentially* a major avenue to human self-development; on the other hand, work is actually experienced, in our sort of society, in boredom or pain.[2]

The most powerful book ever written about work is Harry Braverman's *Labor and Monopoly Capital*. It is a sustained historical account of the different managerial initiatives that have shaped people's experience of work since the end of the nineteenth century. The book connects the history of other people's labour to its author's own experiences throughout a life spent as an engineer and then an office worker. Published in 1974, *Labor and Monopoly Capital* reshaped the whole field of industrial sociology, and opened up for an instant the possibility of a single history of work, which would supersede the different studies in the field. In the words of Craig Littler, a sociologist working in this field, 'Braverman's major contribution was to smash through the academic barriers and offer the potential for the birth of a new, integrated approach to the study and history of work.'[3] However, *Labor and Monopoly Capital* should not be understood primarily as an academic event. It was a book for workers, written in a clear, accessible style. It was also written by a revolutionary, for Harry Braverman had been a member of the American Socialist Workers Party and then the Socialist Union. Shaped by the strengths and weaknesses of its author's own political background, *Labor and Monopoly Capital* is the most powerful indictment of managerial initiatives, but it also under-estimates the ability of workers to resist, or to defend a political economy of their own. Harry Braverman's book reflects the ambiguous legacy of the American 'third camp' tradition.

From coppersmith to office work

The introduction to *Labor and Monopoly Capital* includes a brief autobiographical section, in which Braverman describes his working life. Born into a poor New York family in December 1920, Braverman became a socialist in his teens. Forced to drop out of Brooklyn College after just one year, he apprenticed at the Brooklyn Naval

Yards from 1937 to 1941. Together with his partner Miriam, Harry Braverman then moved to Youngstown Ohio, finding work as a steel fitter and an engineer. Later, Braverman became an office worker and then an editor for a socialist publisher. Indeed one of the strengths of his book is precisely its connection to real work. While many sociologists have conveyed the detail of how other people's lives were organised, Braverman wrote with the immediacy of someone whose life had been shaped by the processes he described:

> I began my working life by serving a four-year apprenticeship in the coppersmith's trade, and worked at this trade for a total of seven years.... The extremely limited nature of employment in my trade, and its rapid decline with the substitution of new processes and materials for the traditional modes of copper working, made it difficult for me to continue work as a coppersmith when I moved to other parts of the country or from job to job. But because the trade of working copper provided a foundation in the elements of a number of other crafts, I was always able to find employment in other trades, such as pipefitting, sheet-metal work, and layout, and I did work of these sorts for another seven years...

In later years, Braverman gained first-hand experience of some of the most typical office processes of our times, again at the moment when they were beginning to undergo rapid changes. 'Some years in socialist journalism led eventually to my employment in book publishing as an editor, and this in turn led to more than a dozen years as an operating executive in two publishing houses.'[4] Harry Braverman also mentioned that as an editor he was responsible for introducing computer-based administration systems, and thus had experience of white-collar administration, if from the managers' side.

The 'socialist journalism' which Braverman refers to in the biography above was his work on the *American Socialist*, a Trotskyist newspaper. Braverman helped found the paper in 1954, and worked on it as co-editor until it closed. After its demise, he worked as an editor at Grove Press, and later as the managing director of Monthly Review Press. The *American Socialist* was linked in turn to a political party that Braverman helped to found, the Socialist Union. This was set up in 1954, following a large split from the American Socialist Workers Party (SWP). The American SWP was at the time the largest party in the official Trotskyist International. Its early leaders, including James P. Cannon and Max Shachtman, were of a calibre unrivalled among European Trotskyism. Each had held leading positions in the Communist Party. Cannon had been the organiser of the International Class War Prisoners' Association, while Shachtman was a former member of the Central Committee of the American CP. The American Socialist Workers Party was the only one of the Trotskyist parties to approach mass size in Trotsky's lifetime, and consequently held a position of unparalleled authority after his death in 1940. At the time, the SWP was still a living party, with a real understanding of working-class politics. Yet after 1940, the SWP took on a new role, in which it had to decide what tactics the international movement should adopt. In this new situation, the party's politics changed.

The SWP used its authority in a purely defensive way, to protect every last word of Trotsky's inheritance. This defensiveness meant that the SWP followed Trotsky's pre-war catastrophism, compelling it to predict after 1945 that the USA must be on the verge of imminent economic collapse. In reality, America was in its greatest boom. The SWP also held on to Trotsky's prediction that the Stalinist regime could not survive the war. When the war ended with the Soviet state still intact, James Cannon came to the conclusion that the war could not have ended. Writing in November 1945, he insisted that nothing had changed.

> Trotsky predicted that the fate of the Soviet Union would be decided in the war. That remains our firm conviction. Only we disagree with some people who carelessly think the war is over. The war has only passed through one stage and is now in the process of regroupment and reorganisation for the second. The war is not over, and the revolution which we said would issue from the war in Europe is not taken off the agenda.[5]

This was an 'orthodox' conclusion, in the sense that it preserved the letter of Trotsky's argument. Yet, in doing so, it also represented the triumph of faith over reason, the conviction that Trotsky must be correct in all particulars, even if life itself would show that his detailed predictions had been proved wrong. Indeed life did show that Cannon was wrong, as several of his collaborators later recalled:

The turning point in our party's recent history was the party's 1946 convention and its aftermath.... We believed that the class struggle would move steadily forward, and with an oncoming depression, which we were predicting, would be transformed into a great social crisis that in turn would lead to the American revolution in which the Trotskyists would play the leading role.... Unfortunately, this idyllic picture was to be quickly dispelled.... The cold war broke out between American imperialism and the Kremlin, and reaction began to mount the offensive against labour and radical movements at home.[6]

One particular problem for the US party was how to explain the character of the new states which emerged out of Russian conquests in Eastern Europe at the end of the war. The SWP took the position that if Russia was a degenerated workers' state, then each of Russia's satellites must also be some form of workers' state. Why, though, were these countries socialist? There had been no workers' revolution; indeed in Eastern Europe the Soviet tanks had moved in just as the workers' movement was crushed. The solution for the SWP was to maintain that nationalisation and socialism were the same thing. While Marx had argued that socialism could only happen as a result of workers' power, the orthodox Trotskyists came to the different conclusion that state ownership alone was enough. Some of the consequences of this decision are evident today. The US SWP degenerated into faddism, choosing for its heroes first Che Guevara, then the Black Panthers, next Gorbachev's USSR. The trajectory of its politics was away from the working class, but many of its members, especially those who joined in the 1930s, retained a real identification with workers' struggles. Its orthodox Trotskyism killed the American SWP, but the party has been a long time dying and is not yet formally defunct.[7]

Outside the SWP there were other currents in America, less determined to preserve the letter of Trotsky's every analysis, and thus better situated to preserve the revolutionary kernel of his ideas. The first was the Workers' Party, set up by Max Shachtman in 1940, which gave birth to C.L.R. James's Johnson–Forest 'state cap' tendency in 1947. Others would include Hal Draper's Independent Socialists Club in the 1960s, and the International Socialists, the more recent sister party of the British Socialist Workers Party. This is not the place to review every split and tendency across the American left, but it is worth noticing that some of the smaller and more dissident parties did not share the American Socialist Workers Party's growing enthusiasm for the Stalinist states. Those socialists that remained hostile to the USSR, such as Hal Draper, were more likely to retain the argument that socialism meant workers' democratic control of society or it meant nothing at all.[8]

Harry Braverman knew Hal Draper, and corresponded with him. However, his organisation, the Socialist Union, split from the SWP in 1953–54 in exactly the opposite direction to the one chosen by Hal Draper. While Draper and the Workers' Party criticised the American SWP for compromising in the face of Stalinism, the Socialist Union attacked the SWP for having failed to attract former Communists. Such people, Braverman argued, were a major source of support for the revolutionary left. Leo Huberman and Paul Sweezy, two former fellow-travellers of the American CP from the era of the Popular Front, were singled out as important potential allies of the Trotskyist movement. In a 1953 article for the SWP's internal bulletin, Harry Braverman (writing under the pseudonym Harry Frankel) argued that the Cold War had divided the world into two irreconcilable camps. In this way, American Communists would be forced into a revolutionary conflict with their own bourgeoisie. He talked of 'a concerted imperialist drive against the USSR which cuts the Kremlin off from the possibility of deals with imperialism'.[9]

Harry Braverman became a spokesman for the minority in the SWP around Bert Cochran. The minority believed that McCarthyism would force the American Communists to turn left; 'The Stalinist movement, regardless of its desires [has] been thrust into opposition to imperialism, it [is] persecuted and hounded as the chief-target of the witch-hunt.' If the SWP was unable to understand the tensions within the Communist Party, then they believed this was the sign of its sectarianism, which prevented the Trotskyists from becoming a real force on the US left. After the 1953 split, Braverman left the SWP and joined Cochran's group, the Socialist Union. Louis Proyect describes the deliberate decision that Braverman's comrades took to avoid replicating the sectarianism of the American SWP:

The Cochranites had not formed the Socialist Union as another 'Marxist–Leninist' exercise to recruit new members one-by-one on the basis of a fully elaborated programme linked in 'revolutionary continuity' with Karl Marx. Instead, they saw it as a catalyst for regrouping the left around a common broad-based programme that focussed on American issues, rather than establishing who was correct on the Stalin–Trotsky debate, etc. As such, they anticipated similar initiatives that would arise in the 1980s after the implosion of a number of 'Marxist–Leninist' formations.[10]

Harry Braverman worked on the Socialist Union paper, first titled the *Educator* and later the *American Socialist*, until it was closed down in 1958. Later, he allied himself with the magazine *Monthly Review*, whose contributors were drawn from a milieu of Marxists, champions of Third World liberation, and other socialists, as we have seen. It was also at this time that Braverman dropped the pseudonym Frankel.[11] He remained a supporter of *Monthly Review* until his death in 1976, holding to the gut class feeling, but also the blind spots, of the orthodox Trotskyist legacy which had helped to shaped him.

As a result of its author's background, *Labour and Monopoly Capital* was a profoundly political book. It was very much a critique of the dominant trend within academic Marxism. The tendency within the New Left as it moved into the universities in the 1960s was to treat Marxism as a *cultural* method, examining class through the prism of class consciousness, treating questions of class structure as expressions of ideology. There were vigorous debates between Marxist and academic sociologists as to whether the working class was becoming a consumer class, obsessed with goods, depoliticised, and withdrawing from public life. In these debates, the character of the working class was debated at the level of culture. Questions of class domination were obscuring the actual, changing nature of production, which was taken for granted. Workers were reduced to objects, the figures in someone else's intellectual game. Braverman's class instincts compelled him to reject this academic Marxism. His preference was for a Marxism with the workers back in. Thus, as Michael Rose suggests, Braverman's book was 'an event in the development of Marxism', an attempt to replace the cultural emphases of the New Left with a more *economic* Marxism, more closely rooted in the realities of workers' life.[12] Braverman himself was quite explicit on this point, bemoaning the fact that Marxism had been oblivious to the changing nature of the labour process over the previous one hundred years:

> The extraordinary fact is that Marxists have added little to [Marx's] body of work in this respect. Neither the changes in productive processes throughout this century of capitalism and monopoly capitalism, nor the changes in the occupational structure of the working population have been subjected to any comprehensive analysis since Marx's death.... There simply is no continuing body of work in the Marxist tradition dealing with the capitalist mode of production in the manner which Marx treated it in the first volume of Capital.[13]

Some twentieth-century Marxists, including both Vladimir Lenin and the Italian Communist Antonio Gramsci, had taken an interest in such industrial processes as Fordism and American mass production.[14] Yet Braverman's point was essentially correct. Before 1974, the published Marxist descriptions of work had barely advanced from Marx's day.[15]

Although it is appropriate to see Braverman's book as an intervention in debates within Marxism, it would be wrong to treat it as being aimed only at the existing Marxist left. One reason for the immense interest in *Labor and Monopoly Capital* is that it was published in 1974, following ten years of growing workers' struggles. Huge strikes in Belgium, Britain, Germany, Italy, indeed throughout the industrialised world, demonstrated workers' increasing rejection of overwork, job hierarchies and deskilling. The defining moment was the general strike that took place in France, an advanced and fully industrialised country, in May 1968. Educated young workers were challenging the basis of capitalist society. In America, where Braverman lived, 1969 and 1970 saw huge workers' protests, including strikes by Levi Strauss workers, in Mississippi wood mills and among Memphis sanitation workers. Workers at General Electric struck through the winter of 1969–70, and in October 1970, 400,000 General Motors workers took part in an unofficial walk-out.[16] The capitalist division of labour was no longer a hidden aspect of life, something to be taken for granted, but was being openly questioned by millions of people. Thus Braverman's contribution was to re-examine the productive process in a precise and detailed way just as it found itself under attack. Not for the first time, Marxist theory took a step forward, not leading the working class but learning from it.

Labor and Monopoly Capital

Throughout his book Harry Braverman expressed his debt to Marx. He described himself not as someone who had come up with any new theories of his own, but rather as someone who was faithful to Marx's interpretation of capitalism, accepting Marx's description of the factory system 'in every particular'. His novelty, he claimed, was not in abolishing or correcting Marx, but in renewing him. Following Marx, Braverman was fiercely critical of the common-sense approach which treated new technology as something neutral or inevitable. The pessimistic conclusion to be drawn from such a perspective was that if machinery cut jobs, or reduced skills, then it was not in the power of human beings to do anything to prevent it. However, as Braverman pointed out, it is not technology which cuts jobs, but management. Indeed management itself only exists because capitalism is a system of property relations, in which a large majority works, while a tiny minority owns or administers capital. To reinforce the connection between property relations and social relations, Braverman quoted from Marx's polemic against Proudhon:

> Proudhon the economist understands very well that men make cloth, linen or silk materials in definite relations of production. But what he has not understood is that these definite social relations are just as much produced by men as linen, flax, etc. Social relations are closely bound up with productive forces. In acquiring new productive forces men change their mode of production; and in changing their mode of production, in changing their way of earning their living, they change all social relations.[17]

For Harry Braverman, as for Karl Marx, it was primarily the relations of production which distinguished capitalism. The enemy was not machinery or production, but the class divisions which shaped how the machinery was used.

Harry Braverman described capitalism as a system 'dominated and shaped' by the needs of capital.[18] Because of the pressure of competition, management has continually been forced to renew and extend its control over the employed workforce. In this way, managerial control has been an ongoing process, in which capital has constantly renegotiated its dominance over labour. However, to recognise its ongoing nature is not to say that this process has continued always in exactly the same way. For Harry Braverman, it was no coincidence that scientific management emerged at the end of the nineteenth and at the start of the twentieth century. Borrowing from Paul Baran and Paul Sweezey, Harry Braverman described this as the period of monopoly capitalism.[19] What he meant by the use of this term was that the expansion of business in the nineteenth century had enabled the creation of a new category of businesses so huge that they were guaranteed monopoly profits, which the employers had promptly invested on the new social category of managers. Braverman argued that it was only when monopoly profits were enough to finance management studies that systematic management could be introduced.[20]

For Harry Braverman, the characteristic form of managerialism was the system of scientific management, which originated in the work of F.W. Taylor. Thus Taylorism was not merely one managerial method among many, but a defining feature of the capitalist labour process, the obvious managerial sequel to industrialisation. Taylor 'dealt with the fundamentals of the labour process and control over it'. According to Braverman, the later management schools, including Mayo's and Münsterberg's, may have looked innovatory, but they dealt merely with the adjustment of the worker to a labour process which had already been established.[21] For this reason, in order to understand Braverman's argument in his book *Labor and Monopoly Capital*, it is necessary to follow his description of the evolution of Taylor's scientific management system.

F.W. Taylor was brought up in a well-to-do Philadelphia family. He studied for Harvard, and seemed destined for a career in law, but instead chose to enrol on a craft apprenticeship. Helped by his father's acquaintances, he then passed through a series of jobs, becoming in 1880 the gang boss at the Midvale Steel Works. There he developed an absolute hatred of 'soldiering' and other attempts by workers to regulate the pace of their labour. Indeed, one way to read his life is as a single-minded crusade to make workers speed up. He engaged in a battle of will with the workers in the steel mill, which ended with him successfully imposing a system of increased labour discipline. Later, Taylor worked for the Bethlehem Steel Company. There he was able to induce one worker, Schmidt, who was in Taylor's words 'a man of the mentally sluggish type', to move four times the traditional weight for the job, 47½ tons of pig iron, instead of the normal 12 tons per day. This moment Taylor returned to, as he told and re-told the story of how he induced Schmidt and other labourers to work far harder in return for increased pay.

Braverman noted three aspects of the tale. First, that there was very little that was scientific about Taylor's method. Regular breaks were scheduled in, and Schmidt was followed by a man with a stopwatch, telling him how he was doing. There was, however, no real attempt to explain why a man ought to be able to work so hard. Taylor arbitrarily imposed a new norm for the job. 'Since, in the case of pig-iron handling, the only decisions to be made were those having to do with a time sequence, Taylor simply dictated that timing and the results at the end of the day.' Second, Harry Braverman pointed out that Taylor used Schmidt's efforts to establish an impossible work rate for the job. Even after more 'scientific' selection of the best workers, not more than one in eight could match this level. Third, Braverman quoted Taylor's description of Schmidt, as 'a man of the type of the ox'. Although it was impossible in retrospect to establish or disprove the absolute stupidity of Schmidt, Taylor elsewhere reported that Schmidt was building his own house, presumably without anyone to manage his labour. As Braverman remarked, 'A belief in the original stupidity of the worker is necessary for management; otherwise it would have to admit that it is engaged in a wholesale enterprise of prizing and fostering stupidity.' Overall, Braverman interpreted the Schmidt episode as an example of Taylor's longer-term ambition, to separate the planning of work from the workers: 'The merit of this tale is its clarity in illustrating the pivot upon which all modern management turns: the control over work through the control over the decisions that are made in the course of work.'[22]

Over a lifetime spent working as a manager, Frederick Taylor drew up different methods to achieve his goals. He used shop order cards to list precisely what job each worker should do in each shift. Taylor also favoured piece-rate payments, which discriminated against slow work. He developed methods of work-study and task-design, which aimed to control every one of the workers' movements; these methods survive in the modified form of time-and-motion studies. F.W. Taylor published a series of books which popularised scientific management, and was famously invited in 1912 to justify his programme in front of the American House of Representatives. In *Labor and Monopoly Capital*, Braverman summed up the principles which Taylor generated. He saw three of these as distinctive:

> Thus, if the first principle is the gathering together and development of knowledge of the labour process, and the second is the concentration of this knowledge as the exclusive preserve of management – together with its converse, the absence of such knowledge among workers – then the third step is the use of this monopoly of knowledge to control each step of the labour process and its mode of execution.[23]

According to Braverman, the heart of Taylorism could be further summarised in a single phrase, *the separation of conception and execution*. Under Taylorism managers would be the only ones to think about work, while workers would be instructed to get on with it.

As I have already mentioned, Harry Braverman saw Taylorism as the defining system of management under industrial capitalism. He noted that it had already been extended from simple to complex production processes, and to white-collar work as well. Indeed, drawing on his own experience of office work, Braverman gave examples of how this had already taken place. Key-punch operators, for example, worked with computers and data, but did so in the most demeaning way. Data was prepared according to someone else's system, speed was at a premium, and the element of skill was deliberately reduced to a minimum. Braverman quoted one operator in a large farm-equipment office: 'This job is no different from a factory job except that I don't get paid as much.'[24] In the 1980s, even though Braverman's book had come out, the most common argument was that computer work would be creative and emancipatory.[25] It is an impressive testament to his method that Braverman saw in advance how debilitating the new computer technology, and the new management techniques that came with it, would prove to be.

If Braverman's description of work under capitalism could be summarised in a phrase, it would be the tendency under capitalism for work to be *degraded*. The skilled workers who dominated the early years of capitalism were replaced with unskilled workers, condemned to demeaning and unpleasant labour. New skills would emerge; indeed office work was originally a skilled craft profession. Yet each new skill was subject to management authority, and was undermined, because capital required the greatest profit, and was constantly obliged to make work dull and routine as a result. When Marx described alienation, his account had a timeless quality; the word referred to a general condition which marked capitalism. Harry Braverman updated Marx's theory, showing that alienation (or, in his phrase, the degradation of labour) was a process which was constantly created and re-created by capitalist management.

The book's reception

The summary given so far does not do full justice to the qualities of *Labor and Monopoly Capital*. Written with passion, anger and commitment, the book had an extraordinary impact. It discredited the dominant paradigms within industrial sociology, which tended to support management and assumed that technological change was leading to a progressive rise in work satisfaction. The book spawned dozens of imitators, including several which agreed the important outline of Braverman's argument.[26] In America, its reception was glowing. Robert L. Heilbroner reviewed *Labor and Monopoly Capital* in the *New York Review of Books*: 'Until the appearance of Harry Braverman's remarkable book, there has been no broad view of the labour process as a whole.' Paul Baran was even more positive, and described reading Braverman's book as 'an emotional experience, somewhat similar, I suppose, to that which millions of readers of Volume I of *Capital* have been through.'[27] In Britain, the first issue of *Capital and Class* in 1977 was devoted to the Braverman debate. The book was then taken up in dozens of conferences and other public events, spawning a series of further books devoted to the question of whether job degradation was really taking place. Bob Rowthorn described it as 'one of the two most important works of Marxist political economy to have appeared in English in the last decade'. Braverman's accessible book, written for ordinary workers, generated a remarkable interest, and *Labour and Monopoly Capital* sold an extraordinary 120,000 copies in its first twenty-five years.[28]

Braverman's critics have treated him as an authority, an intermediary whose contribution was needed for others to progress beyond him. Even if they rejected aspects of his argument, other writers could go forward only because of Braverman's work. Despite their enthusiasm, however, many writers have been sceptical of his detailed claims. From within the Marxist camp, Al Rainnie has described the book as 'ahistorical'. His claim is that Braverman idealised the character of nineteenth-century craft labour, overstating the independence and control exhibited by workers before the factory system came to dominate.[29] Andrew Friedman maintains that Braverman exaggerated the success of Taylorism, reducing all managerial techniques to a single strategy of aggression. In reality, he argues, managers have been just as likely to divide workers using more subtle ploys of persuasion and through seeking workers' consent. Other writers have insisted that Braverman downplayed the capacity of mechanization to generate new skilled jobs, or that he ignored the role of women or the importance of racism at work.[30] There have been around a dozen books written just about 'Bravermania', the response to *Labour and Monopoly Capital*; rather than going through these arguments at length, this chapter will concentrate on just three important criticisms of Braverman's book. The first is the counter-argument that management takes place basically through consent; the second is the claim that Braverman ignored the impact of women's domestic oppression on their work; the third is the suggestion that Braverman downplayed the possibility of workers' resistance to encroaching managerial control.

Management by consent and coercion

The first point at which Braverman's theory seems vulnerable is in his description of Taylorism as the typical managerial strategy. As any number of academic experts in industrial relations have pointed out, Taylor's full strategy was only rarely adopted as a whole. The history of management initiatives is of a diverse list of different strategies, some of which have been directly influenced by Taylorism, while others, including Mayo's human relations school, have claimed to stand in direct opposition to Taylor's vision of the dumb and stupid worker. One Marxist, Andrew Friedman, has argued that managers have adopted effectively two different strategies to ensure their continued domination over labour. At one extreme, these methods have been overt and despotic, and have involved 'direct control'. At the other extreme, managers have used tactics of encouragement and consensus, what Friedman calls 'responsible autonomy'. Michael Burawoy has suggested that such consensual tactics often succeed. On the basis of his experience as a machine operator, he claims that workers can offer their own subordination. Describing work making diesel engines in South Chicago, he writes: 'We were active accomplices in our own exploitation. That, and not the destruction of subjectivity, was what was so remarkable.' The arguments of Friedman and Burawoy have been influenced by Gramsci's notion that the bourgeoisie rules primarily through consent rather than coercion. As ideology can manufacture consent in politics, so ideology can have the same effect at work.[31]

There are different ways to respond to this argument. Craig Littler makes the point that although pure Taylorism was a failure, the methods of scientific management have had a far wider impact than Friedman and others suggest. In Britain, for example, they were taken up through an intermediary structure, the Bedaux system, which was enormously influential in Britain in the interwar years. By 1939, approximately 250 British firms utilised Bedaux techniques, and as these were the largest and most authoritative of businesses, so Bedaux became 'the most commonly used system of managerial control in British industry'.[32] Other writers, more closely sympathetic to Braverman's argument, have suggested that the disagreements between Braverman and Friedman boil down to the simple question of which strategy dominates. Managers do employ consent, but not always. They typically employ strategies of containment when workers are making gains; often these ploys are counterproductive, and they are rarely used when management can do without.[33] It is also worth noting that although Burawoy and Friedman have been very critical of Braverman's insistence on the historic importance of Taylorism, neither refutes Braverman's linked argument that capitalism is a process out of which workers have increasingly been denied real control over their work. This raises the question of how far consensus at work can go. On closer inspection, Friedman and Burawoy's autonomous workers may turn out to be participating only in their own subordination at work.[34]

Women and work

The second major criticism of *Labour and Monopoly Capital* has come from feminist writers. The book was criticised for functionalism and sexism. Like other Marxist texts, it was accused of reducing the working class to male workers in manufacturing. Jackie West has claimed that Braverman's only explanation for the relative oppression of women workers was that they comprised an ideal reserve army of labour to reduce male wages. West argues that Harry Braverman ignored the role of women as house-keepers, whose domestic subjection explained their subordination at work. Yet Braverman did try to integrate an extended analysis of the changing nature of the family into his account of changes in the labour process. The problem, as Veronica Beechey points out, is not that Braverman ignored women's oppression, but rather that he failed to generate a satisfactory explanation of the changing nature of the family and its effects on work.[35]

Braverman discussed the family in his chapter 'The Universal Market'. His argument was that under capitalism the market has come to dominate every aspect of people's lives. In previous societies, including feudalism, the family had enjoyed functions as an institution of social life, production and consumption. Under capitalism, the family has lost its productive role, and remains only an attenuated location of consumption. Women were taken out of their previous role, in which they had produced use values in the household, and now produce use values at work, under the direct domination of capital. This is where Braverman's analysis of the reserve army of labour came in. He stated that women had been taken out of the family and into this situation without really explaining why it was that women have had a different experience of work compared to men.

Harry Braverman's account is flawed in so far as it exaggerates the transformation in the nature of the family between late feudalism and early capitalism. In both situations, the family has been an unequal institution, absolutely predicated on the domestic subordination of women. The family has certainly changed under capitalism, but very unevenly. In the mid-nineteenth century, many commentators including Marx and Engels predicted that working-class families would break up under the combined pressures of urbanisation and industrial growth. For much of the next fifty years, however, the family was consciously strengthened as an institution, in Europe, America and elsewhere. This process can be traced through the growth of an ideology of 'separate spheres' which insisted that women's rightful place is in the home. More recently, the relative decline of family sizes and housework, the growth of contraception and divorce, and the increasing acceptance of alternative lifestyles, have all served to undermine the family as an institution, although it remains important even now. In this way, the transformation from feudalism to capitalism has represented more of a *potential* revolutionising of the family than any immediate change.[36] It is only in the last thirty years or so that Karl Marx's and Friedrich Engels's predictions of the death of the family have come at all close to fruition.

Such a historical account of the changing fortunes of the family would preserve the heart of Braverman's argument, while shedding some of the form. It would lose his idealisation of the pre-capitalist family, and also his argument that the 'traditional household economy' had recently come to the point of collapse.[37] As a social institution, the family remains important in all sorts of different ways, and it continues to shape our lives. So feminist critics of Braverman are correct to argue that if women have been oppressed at work, then this is largely because of the continuing existence of the family and women's enduring dependency within it.[38] However, even if it is accepted that there are weaknesses in this part of Braverman's argument, it should also be clear from my account that Braverman – unlike most writers of his generation – made a serious and sustained attempt to understand women's oppression. The charge of sexism that is sometimes laid against Braverman is too strong.

Struggle

The third point at which Braverman's account has come under attack is in his neglect of workers' ability to resist management control. In *Labour and Monopoly Capital*, Braverman describes the victory of managers in dividing execution from control. Before, there were powerful and skilled craft workers, who could plan their own work; now there were only unskilled labourers. Craft workers could resist; the unskilled did not have that choice. Certainly, at points, Braverman did pull back from the full, bleak implications of his argument, suggesting for example that scientific management is 'an ideal realised by capital only within definite limits', but these limits were never explained, nor discussed in any detail. Two years after the publication of *Labour and Monopoly Capital*, Braverman responded to this criticism, remarking that he had placed 'self-imposed limits' on his analysis. He also claimed that one reason for his failure to address workers' resistance was that the workers' movement in America, Japan and Europe had been in a state of 'relative quiescence' for most of 'the past half century'. Braverman denied that he was a pessimist, but left the task of investigating workers' consciousness to others.[39] For whatever reason, Harry Braverman's extraordinary and vivid critique of the demeaning effects of management is not matched by an analysis of what workers have done, or could do, to fight back against management control. In the absence of any extended discussion of resistance, the impression given is that managers have all the initiative, workers are inert, and resistance cannot succeed. This, I believe, is the major criticism of Braverman's book. Vividly aware of the destructive and inhuman effect of new management initiatives, *Labour and Monopoly Capital* was less systematic in considering the ability of workers to fight back.

It was perhaps at this moment that the debt to Baran and Sweezy proved problematic for Harry Braverman's Marxism. I have already referred to Paul Sweezy's introduction to *Labor and Monopoly*

Capital. In this short essay, Sweezy acknowledged that his own earlier book with Paul Baran, *Monopoly Capital* (1966), had failed to discuss the labour process. He went on to identify Braverman's work as 'a serious, and in my judgement solidly successful, effort to fill a large part of this gap'. Yet this link to Baran and Sweezy was a theoretical limit. For in Baran and Sweezy's formulation, as we have seen, monopoly capital was victorious. Bosses would reap extraordinary profits, while workers could only suffer. In his introduction to Braverman's book, Paul Sweezy expressed his absolute hatred of the capitalist system, and of the tyranny of capitalist work. Sweezy praised the book, but he did so using a language of abasement and regret, informed at times by an almost religious choice of imagery:

> The sad, horrible, heart-breaking way the vast majority of my counterparts in most of the rest of the world are obliged to spend their working lives is seared into my consciousness in an excruciating and unforgettable way. And when I think of all the talent and energy which daily go into devising ways and means of making their torment worse, all in the name of efficiency and productivity but really for the greater glory of the great god Capital, my wonder at humanity's ability to create such a monstrous system is surpassed only by its amazement at its willingness to tolerate the continuance of an arrangement so obviously destructive of the well-being and happiness of human beings.[40]

These are powerful words, but incomplete. For if the story of capitalism was simply the story of management success, and workers have a role only to be broken, then what hope is there that society can be changed? Gramsci's paper *L'Ordine Nuovo* famously carried as its masthead the slogan 'Optimism of the Will, Pessimism of the Intellect'. Without that optimism, socialism can only be a lament, a sad longing for a moment that cannot be.

Braverman was wrong to imply that only craft workers have resisted the encroachments of capital. Instead the advent of new machinery has often created possibilities for successful resistance by semi-skilled or even unskilled workers. Indeed one of the distinguishing characteristics of large-scale class struggle in the twentieth century has been the extent to which non-craft workers have been able to oppose capital. The history of militant trade unionism over the past hundred years has been a story of new workers coming to the fore. The skilled engineers who were the face of labour in the 1920s have been displaced by more radical groups, including transport workers, car workers, lorry drivers, nurses and teachers. In Paul Thompson's phrase, 'No amount of deskilling or mechanisation can lead to the *complete* domination of capital over labour.'[41]

Why did Harry Braverman fail to discuss workers' resistance? Why does one finish his book with the impression that capital can achieve a permanent victory through techniques of managerial control? Returning to the themes discussed at the start of this chapter, one explanation of Braverman's pessimism can be traced through his continuing loyalty to the orthodox Trotskyist tradition, and especially to its increasing rapprochement with 'really existing socialism' in the Soviet Union. On the one hand, *Labour and Monopoly Capital* accepts that Russia was not a workers' society: 'Whatever view one takes of Soviet industrialisation one cannot consciously interpret its history, even in its earliest and most revolutionary period, as an attempt to organise labour processes in a way fundamentally different from those of capitalism.' On the other hand, Braverman was impressed by the USSR's success in building up a base of heavy industry. Industrialisation and new machinery under national control was seen to create 'progress in technology and production', an unpleasant and contradictory yet still socialist alternative to capitalism.[42] Workers' control and nationalisation were described as if they were the same thing.

Harry Braverman's mature thoughts on Russia can be read in an important but little-known book published in 1963. *The Future of Russia* was a response to changes in the Soviet Union following Khrushchev's 1956 'secret speech' which disclosed the worst of Stalin's crimes. Braverman corresponded with the Polish Marxist Isaac Deutscher on the text of his book, and his own account owes numerous debts to Deutscher's approach. Braverman argued that Russia was undergoing an extremely fast process of liberalisation. At the heart of this process was Russia's economic success:

> The Soviet Union is in an economic race with the United States, and barring a war or some other unforeseen major economic development, the outcome of that race is a foregone conclusion ... the Soviet system has fewer problems and stronger perspectives than the capitalist countries.

Economic growth had ushered in a new era of liberalisation and progress. 'Russia, no longer restrained in the Stalinist straight jacket, is responding to the new conditions created by four decades of industrialisation and modernisation.' Further political changes would come, to match the extraordinary growth in the Russian economy. 'The revolution is still going on.' Stalin was a name from the past; Russia had returned to the vision of its Bolshevik founders. 'Russia is at last on the road to socialism.'[43] Harry Braverman distinguished himself from his contemporaries primarily in his analysis of the Soviet Union – it was this political question which was his major concern from the late 1940s to the early 1960s. Yet Braverman's account of Russian society was simply wrong. If Russia was on the way to socialism, then why did the Russian workers turn against the 'workers' state'?

Like many of his generation, Harry Braverman believed that the world was coming to be dominated by huge bureaucratic entities, militarised states and monopoly capital. Socialists in the Workers' Party, including Hal Draper, responded to this new situation by describing the Russian working class as a slave class, and identifying American Communists as agents of the Comintern. Supporters of the *American Socialist* were more positive in each respect, regarding Russia as a complex, but only partly degenerated workers' state, and American Stalinism as a legitimate workers' movement. If Draper's politics were one alternative to the SWP's, the Socialist Union chose an opposite route out. Braverman's Marxism was less dogmatic than the US SWP's, but it was yet more prone to a reconciliation with Stalinism. The intellectual pessimism of the Socialist Union explains Braverman's inability to express the potential (or even the limits) of workers' resistance against capitalism. Despite the great power of *Labour and Monopoly Capital*, Harry Braverman fits awkwardly within the dissident Marxist tradition. He shared its sympathy with the plight of the working class, but not its optimism that capitalism could be overthrown.

A superb, but flawed book

I have criticised Harry Braverman's *Labour and Monopoly Capital* in some detail. In the process I have concentrated on its weakest points, and have understated the enormous polemical power of the book. *Labour and Monopoly Capital* was a cry of protest against the degradation of work. It described in detail the processes by which work becomes something alien to the worker, is planned and directed from elsewhere, and is reduced to a series of repetitive and mindless tasks. Braverman stood on the side of the worker against the manager, and wrote for the worker, and as such deserves reading today. If his account was also flawed, and crucially failed to consider in detail how workers could fight back, this is only because Braverman was a product of his time. He reached his political maturity when the US and Soviet states both seemed mighty and invincible. From his political allies he drew the conclusion that social machinery, bureaucracies and states were of greater significance than ordinary people. By contrast, the best of his contemporary Marxists maintained that structures are the products of people, and changing people have the power to change the structures. As Marx wrote in his *Theses on Feuerbach*, and in rejection of mechanical materialism, 'The materialist doctrine of history concerning the changing of circumstances and upbringing forgets that circumstances are changed by men and that the educator must himself be educated.'[44] Capital can be endured, or it can be resisted, but the greatest hope comes when people fight back.

9

Samir Amin: theorising underdevelopment

As the literature studied in this book approaches the present, we move towards the concerns of today's anti-capitalists. One such article was published by the Egyptian economist Samir Amin in 1990, 'The Social Movements in the Periphery'. Amin began this essay by describing the crisis of the left. The fall of the Berlin Wall had swept away a set of linked strategies that had held the hearts of radicals for the previous hundred years. In the West, workers had assumed that change could only come about through electing a left-wing party, whose economics were Keynesian and whose social policies would extend the welfare state. The self-styled Communist societies of the East had promised to achieve socialism through policies of state-led industrialisation. As for the South,

> In African and Asia the history of the past century had been that of the polarisation of the social movement around the struggle for national independence. Here the model was that of the unifying party, setting itself the objective of buying together social classes and various communities in a vast movement that was disciplined ... and effective in its action towards a single goal. The regimes that emerged after independence became badly stuck in this heritage, the single-party state denying its legitimacy solely from the achievement of the goal of national independence.

The embedded politics shared by socialists all over the globe included a belief in 'the party' as the custodian of the movement. There was also an idea that development could only occur through the expansion of industry, with the state leading this process. Such politics were described as the only logical consequence of Enlightenment thinking; indeed they were identified with human rationality itself. 'Today', Amin wrote, 'the models of managing social life in these organisational forms seem to have exhausted their historical effectiveness.' In place of these models, Amin argued for a more democratic, bottom-up strategy, a peoples' rebellion, with self-consciously anti-capitalist politics.[1]

Reading passages such as these, it is easy to see the links that bind Samir Amin's ideas to the strategies of the Seattle movement. Such campaigns as Jubilee 2000 or the meetings at Porto Alegre started from a belief that the problems of the developing world are more urgent than any residual poverty in the global West or North. Anti-capitalists often distinguish between an old party-based politics and the new social movements. The critique of state-led industrialisation is also timely. The old Third World dominated the production of such commodities as gold and diamonds, and of all sorts of industrial materials, but to little good effect. The notion of democracy versus global capitalism also links to a common slogan of the new movement, 'People not Profit'. The fact that Samir Amin's ideas connect to the new anti-capitalism should not surprise us. Amin has taken part in many of the most important events, and is the director of the Forum Tiers Monde (Third World Forum) in Dakar, Senegal. He even led off the anti-WTO conference at Beirut in autumn 2001. The more important point is that Amin was writing down these thoughts as early as 1990. Ten years later they have become part of the common sense of a generation. What was it about Samir Amin that has given his ideas such relevance?

A life of letters

Samir Amin is best known today as the author of many books, including *Accumulation on a World Scale*, *Neo-Colonialism in West-Africa*, *Imperialism and Unequal Development*, *The Law of Value and*

Historical Materialism, *The Future of Maoism*, *Eurocentrism* and *Spectres of Capitalism*.[2] His work includes economic theory, centred around development and underdevelopment; critiques of subaltern politics, including Nasserism and mainstream African nationalism; and many theoretical books exploring capitalism and the possibilities of resistance against it. Yet as Aidan Foster-Carter points out, in his study of 'the empirical Samir Amin', even such a list is incomplete. Amin actually made his name as the author of monographs dedicated to the countries of North, West and Central Africa.[3] The range of his writing makes it impossible for any one short study to do full justice to his work.

Samir Amin was born in Cairo in 1931. The best source for his early life is an autobiographical memoir he published in 1996, *Re-reading the Postwar Period*.[4] His parents were both doctors. Having achieved his high-school diploma in 1947, Amin left the Middle East for Europe to study. For the next ten years he lived mainly in France, and attended universities there. Eventually, Amin took three degrees in Paris, at the Institute of Political Studies (1954), at the Institute of Statistics (1955) and a Ph.D. in Economics (1957). What distinguished him already was his politics. Amin claims to have called himself a Communist from the age of eleven. 'I recall how I followed the battle of Stalingrad with anguish, then delight at its outcome.'[5] Slowly, Amin's precocious Communism was filled out by more reading. Jules Verne was followed by Zola, then Balzac and then Marx (*The Eighteenth Brumaire of Louis Bonaparte*, *The Civil War in France*), and Lenin (*State and Revolution*, and *Imperialism, the Highest Stage of Capitalism*). Even in his late teens, Amin was already convinced of the truth of Marx's economic theories:

> Reading *Capital* had immediately persuaded me of the fundamental position of the Marxist law of value in the critique of bourgeois economics. To me it was not a question of a concept reduced to its positive aspect (the amount of socially necessary labour), as Ricardo posited it, but a critical holistic concept revealing the character of commodity alienation peculiar to capitalist society. Value determined not only capitalist economics, but all forms of social life in the system.[6]

In Paris, Amin planned to study higher mathematics, and this choice took him then to economics (via law). 'I immediately joined the Communist Party and became active in the school cell.'[7] Later

Amin joined the overseas student movement, contributing to its paper *Étudiants Anticolonialistes*. Around this time, Amin spent a year in England. One London friendship was with a fellow émigré and a future leader of the Zanzibar revolution, Abdulrahman Mohamed Babu. Amin's memories of Babu are one of the most substantial autobiographical documents that he has produced. 'We were both very active among African students in Britain and France trying to start a unified movement, or unifying various movements, of students from various African and Asian countries.... In working together we discovered that we had the same views.' Both shared the idea that full independence could only be achieved under socialism.

> National liberation cannot have any meaning if it is not led by a Communist Party, by Marxism and socialist forces associated with it. We were among the first readers of Mao Tse Tung's *New Democratic Revolution* which was published in French and English in 1950 or 1952.[8]

The same debates that influenced Walter Rodney were also played out in Asia and the Middle East. As far as Amin was concerned, there were only two possible positions that anyone could take:

> There was the Indian line presented by Nehru and the Congress Party (which was similar to and came from the same tradition as the Egyptian position) – national liberation or the struggle for independence with a view to participating on a more equal footing in the same global capitalist system; and there was the Chinese line which was followed by the Vietnamese.... Most of the organisations we belonged to – particularly the Africans and the people from the Middle East – were rather of the Nehru line. We were a minority but we had a strong impact and Babu played a major role in that. Our position was that national liberation cannot be separated from socialism because no other social forces than those with an objective interest in going beyond capitalism ... could achieve national liberation.

Does Samir Amin still hold this position? 'Perhaps we were exaggerating (as history has proved) because the role of the bourgeoisie had not completely ended, but I think looking back after forty years that we were not fundamentally wrong.'[9] His ideas appeared in print first as articles published in the left-wing French and Egyptian press.[10]

From development to underdevelopment

Samir Amin's first full-length pieces of writing were his published theses. The first was a statistical study of savings and their use in Egypt between 1938 and 1952.[11] The second was a much more original piece of work, a study in the mechanisms which have shaped the position of the developing economies. This was completed in 1957,[12] which was also the year that Amin married Isabelle, in Paris. For its time, Amin's doctoral thesis was an extraordinary piece of work. It took on major issues which most economists had preferred to leave quiet, including above all the question: how had this rich economic system allowed the majority of the world's population to remain poor?

In order to understand the novelty of Amin's thesis, we should place it within the context of the evolution of economic theory. The big names of political economy had all concerned themselves with the question of *why* commercial and industrial development took place. Such ideas had been considered by Adam Smith and David Ricardo. Karl Marx considered the processes by which capitalism spread itself unevenly across the globe, in volumes two and three of *Capital*. Yet as the nineteenth century wore on, there was a tendency for economic theory to become more limited. Amin's near contemporary Sidney Pollard suggests that mainstream economists wanted to separate monetary choices from their social context, busying themselves with the very much narrower questions of how quantifiable needs were met.[13] The conventional approach tended to ignore the existence of inequality inside or between nations. Such prejudices lasted long. As late as 1945, most economists preferred to write as if all of humanity lived within a wealthy, advanced capitalist society. It was only after the end of the war that economists turned their concerns towards Asia, Africa and Latin America. Decolonisation was an important spur to action, as indeed was the formation of the United Nations and allied agencies. There was now an institutional basis for development politics, outside the university system.

Early development theory was an extension of conventional economic theory, which equated development with growth and industrialisation. A 'stages' mentality of economic development dominated discussions. Alexander Gerschenkron and W.W. Rostow both maintained that all countries passed through exactly the same process of economic growth.[14] First agricultural societies developed trade, then market relationships paved the way for industrial take-off. Over time, the early industrial societies became mature economies. The underdeveloped countries were merely at an earlier stage in this linear historical process. One of the first of the postwar thinkers to break decisively with this approach would be Raúl Prebisch – although his arguments were only fully developed a decade after Amin's thesis. The 'dependency' theory formulated by Prebisch suggested that the world had been divided into a 'centre' and a 'periphery'. The nations of the Third World were the producers of raw materials for First World manufacturers, and were forced into a dependent role. This condition was not fixed, however. According to Prebisch, some degree of protectionism could enable these countries to enter a path of self-sustaining development. Historical examples of industrialisation, such as Soviet Russia, were held up as proof that there was more than one path to development, if the state was willing.[15]

The focus of Amin's theory was the relationship between the centre and the periphery. Amin placed the polarisation between regions at the heart of his view of history. In the modern age, capital has been accumulated in the centre through unequal trade, high wages and militarism. The economies of the periphery were impoverished, even as they joined the capitalist world. They adapted to the role set for them in the emerging world order, as suppliers of raw materials and low-cost labour for the centre.

Amin's emphasis on the importance of development and underdevelopment was no passing insight. Similar themes have recurred in his writing ever since. If this was his critique of capitalism, then what did Amin offer in its place?

Reversing underdevelopment

An article by Gernot Kohler published in 1994 addressed the socialist content of Amin's thinking. According to Kohler, Amin's preferred world system is democratic, socialist and federalist. The overall task is (in Amin's words) 'the construction of a global political system which is not in the service of the global market but which defines its parameters.' For the shape of such an alternative world system, Amin has insisted on two general ingredients: that the world must become 'more authentically democratic', and that its state system must be polycentric, which requires 'reorganisation ... on the basis of large regions'. Such regions would include Europe, Africa and so on. In different places, Amin has spoken of the need for global disarmament, a world parliament (or institutions which would represent social interests on a global scale), the liquidation of the World Bank, the International Monetary Fund and GATT, and equal, sustainable access to the planet's resources. How could all this be achieved? According to Amin, 'The transformation of the world system always begins with struggles at its base.' He is not explicit about what forms the struggle should take.[16]

There are some unusual aspects to Amin's socialism. Although he was committed to political activism from the early 1950s, Amin located much of what he wrote in a genre – the economics of development – far removed from the language of the rural and urban poor. From 1957 to 1960 he worked as an economist in the Economic Development Organization, a planning unit associated with the Egyptian government. 'My duties kept me in close touch with the manner in which the new public sector was managed, and with the discussions among company boards.'[17] From 1960 to 1963, Amin worked as an economic consultant to the government of Mali. This was also the period when his first books appeared, an Arabic-language study of monetary flows in Egypt, and a French-language survey of Mali's national accounts.[18] He later taught for several years as a university lecturer in France. Between 1970 and 1980, Samir Amin was director of the United Nations Africa Institute for Economic Development and Planning. His audience was not originally the African working poor, but the decision-makers, the officials of the less developed countries and the United Nations.

Samir Amin's writings developed as the decade turned. In the 1960s, his work was primarily economic. Its subject was the African national economy, with studies appearing of the Ivory Coast, Senegal, Ghana, The Gambia, Morocco, Chad, the Congo and Egypt. The contents of these studies were statistical, detailed and empirical. They were not obviously political, although Amin's sympathies are evident to any reader.[19] One passage from *The Development of Capitalism in the Ivory Coast* provides an early statement of Amin's belief in self-managed, autonomous growth:

> The Ivory Coast [experiences] 'growth without development': that is to say, growth created and maintained from the outside, without the structures thus established permitting one to foresee any automatic evolution towards the further stage of self-centred national development, moved by its own internal dynamism.[20]

In the 1970s, such judgements multiplied. Amin's writings took on a different character, becoming more polemical. Two major books stand out. The first was *Accumulation on a World Scale*, published in 1970; the second was *Unequal Development*, published three years later, a more popular study on the same theme.

Like many other political economists (including Karl Marx), Samir Amin reached his economic conclusions through a critique of previous arguments. *Accumulation on a World Scale* was conceived in part as a rejection of the economic theories of W.W. Rostow, a leading theorist of economic development in the early post-war period. Rostow's arguments have already been mentioned in this chapter. Amin's criticism was that in his hands, the process of underdevelopment was made to appear almost 'natural'. It was simply a stage through which all societies had to go, in their progress towards capitalist plenty. Was it purely coincidental that Rostow had worked as an adviser to the US government, Amin asked? Samir Amin preferred the claim that underdevelopment was made by the action of fully self-conscious individuals. The poverty of whole nations was not fixed, but changed over time. 'The development of underdevelopment … is jerky and made up of phases of extremely rapid economic growth … followed by sudden blockages.' Underdevelopment was the intended consequence of the world's unequal economic and political systems.[21] His creative argument has been summarised in the following terms:

1. The world capitalist system, consisting of social formations in the centre and periphery, is integrated into a single world system primarily through relations of exchange and unequal specialization of production.

2. There exists in this global system a hierarchical structure of modes of production/sectors, with uneven productivity and heterogeneous relations of production.
3. Modes of production/sectors of the periphery are: (a) articulated with capitalist social formations at the centre, but (b) disarticulated with regard to social formations at the periphery.
4. This structure of articulation/disarticulation is the result of the centuries-old evolution of forms of international specialization, dictated by the internal dynamics of capitalist social formations and imposed on the periphery by the centre.
5. Transfer of value/economic surplus takes place from peripheral capitalist to central social formations as a result of primitive accumulation. This process survives the pre-history of capitalism; its persistence to the present constitutes the essence of the problem of accumulation on a world scale.[22]

Amin's argument stands as a powerful critique of the inequalities upon which the international economy is based. The idea is impressive in its full development. It can also be expressed succinctly, in the most precise terms. As Amin later wrote: 'I argued that development and underdevelopment were two sides of the same coin: capitalist expansion.' Yet if underdevelopment and mass poverty were the processes on which capitalism thrived, then what alternatives were there to such a market system?

First and Third World Maoism

We have seen that Amin identified with the Chinese Revolution from an early stage. He was 18 when Beijing fell, and 21 when he and his comrades in London were arguing for Mao's ideas among their friends. There is a gap between his experience and that of the contemporary left. Today's activists have grown up in a society where the revolutionary content of the Chinese state seems to be quite exhausted. The Chinese Communist Party awards its medals these days to the thrusting members of a model bourgeoisie. Long gone also are the days when Chinese arms could be found in the hands of insurgent Vietnamese or Indian peasants. The one country in the world where Maoism remains a mass force is Nepal.

Even more distant are the images of mass Maoist parties in the West – but Maoism was an important force in the 1974 Portuguese Revolution, and after that it influenced the American, French and German lefts.

To understand the appeal of this ideology, we need to say something about the history of Maoism in the West, as well its Chinese form. Western Maoism took many forms. In terms of organisation, we can distinguish between (1) those Communist Parties such as the French, which prevaricated between Russian and Chinese-style socialism, allowing representatives of both wings to speak, at least until the time of the Sino–Soviet split; (2) 'hard' Maoist parties, which followed every twist and turn of the Cultural Revolution in a spirit of utter fidelity to the Chinese state; and (3) 'soft' Maoist groups, which shared little of Mao's philosophy beyond a general belief that the world was decided by human action, and that 1960s-era Stalinism was too deterministic.

Maoism was subject to many different interpretations. In Britain, the Committee to Defeat Revisionism published strait-laced books with titles like *On Khrushchev, Fertilizer, and the Future of Soviet Agriculture*.[23] By contrast, a 'soft Maoist' formation, Big Flame, was in existence for four years before coming out in favour of China. Before then, its supporters were not sure whether they agreed more with Stalin, Trotsky or Mao.[24] Part of its appeal was that Maoism seemed to combine (to different degrees) elements of support for the peasantry, loyalty to the Chinese model, and a vague, philosophical belief in 'action'. The latter stemmed from the attempts made at rapid industrialisation in the 1960s. At this time China was copying the Russian experience of 1929. This leap into the unknown had to be defended as a choice of conscious human beings who refused to be cowed by the heavy hand of economic laws. Such 'idealism' or even 'anti-dogmatism' played well to an audience of Western socialists.

Samir Amin was by no means the only prominent Maoist economist writing in the 1960s. The one-time left-Keynesian Joan Robinson praised the Cultural Revolution and North Korea after visiting in the late 1960s. At an abstract level, Maoist strategy seems to make good sense. Self-sufficiency could only assist poor, dependent and heavily indebted countries. Reducing the gap between town and countryside should lessen conflict and help raise cooperation and thus productivity. According to Amin, the first four years of Chinese development paved a path to socialism, 'The nationalisation of the great enterprises, the achieving of agrarian reform, the struggle against the tendencies of private capitalism, the ideological re-education of the intellectuals, and the blocking of American aggression in Korea, mark this period as the construction of the new society.'[25]

Yet is this the only way in which Chinese history can be read? We could just as well argue that Maoism was the politics of crash-industrialisation taken from Russian experience and adapted to local conditions. This is a point made by Nigel Harris in *The Mandate of Heaven*, his classic study of Chinese Communism. Harris begins by rejecting the claim that the rulers of Beijing represented any form of working–class or even 'popular' rule:

> In 1978, as in 1949, the most important role of the workers of China was not as the leadership of the country but as the primary source of the surplus which sustains the State and national accumulation. The mass of the peasants have been permitted to retain a larger share of their very much smaller product; but again, by no stretch of the imagination can they be seen as collectively directing the Chinese state.

If not the workers or the peasants, then who ruled? Harris argued that in conditions of rising state spending right across the world, the leaders of Chinese Communism were able to do much the same job as that attempted (successfully) by the Russian bureaucracy in 1929, and that tried (unsuccessfully) by the leaders of African socialism in the 1970s. The task was to accelerate the production of heavy industrial goods. In favourable conditions, rapid industrialisation was achieved, but without social justice:

> China was more backward than Russia, and needed more time for development. It was not possible to eliminate the small property owners without jeopardizing the security of the State. Each acceleration in the pace of accumulation prompted counteraction from both workers and peasants. The regime went into reverse, permitting the reappearance of the 'rich peasant' economy, the old unregenerate small-holder. Indeed, in the rural areas the boundary between party and rich peasants tended to disappear. Then the party leadership, in alarm at the disintegration of its power, was compelled to purge or at least chastise the rural cadres,

to try to reopen the gap between the bureaucratic and small propertied middle classes. Throughout the shifts and zigzags of party policy as the regime tried to propel China towards industrialization, none of the factions of the party challenged the need for rapid accumulation.[26]

One criticism that can be made of this passage is that it fails to do justice to the tremendous excitement that such industrialisation created – not in China, but in other underdeveloped countries. Harris portrayed the Cultural Revolution as one swing of the pendulum as the leadership vacillated between private property and 'the disintegration of its power'. Perhaps this is what it meant for people living in China. Yet in Europe, the Cultural Revolution was represented as a major step forward in the liberation of the Third World from colonial rule. As a student living in London, Samir Amin believed that he had found the secret of successful development in Africa. He was wrong to believe the myths – but they were there.

Amin in the African context

For activists of Samir Amin's vintage, the choice of Maoism was justified as a move *to the left* away from the ideas of the old and bureaucratised Communist Parties. According to Amin himself, 'Maoism offered a critique of Stalinism from the left, while Khrushchev made one from the right.'[27] Maoist politics were at their most radical outside China, in Africa, India and the rest of the Third World. Amin interpreted the Chinese–Soviet debate as an argument about how to achieve socialism in the developing countries. 'Among other things there was the question of the so-called non-capitalist road, or was it a capitalist road with its own specificities, its own contradictions with other capitalist roads and interests but belonging to the family of capitalist roads?' How could activists maintain the socialist content of the national revolts, and what indeed should socialists make of those states where redistribution had not happened, but whose leaders had allied with the USSR?

> Even if those contradictions create the conditions in which we can consider the regimes anti-imperialist and therefore support them in their struggle we should not forget that they are very strongly aware of

the danger that is represented by an autonomous organisation of the popular classes.... The Soviet Union was supporting them and the Soviet Union was right from an overall perspective of a major struggle, East–West, the Cold War, but also capitalism versus socialism in general; but you need to qualify them as nationalist bourgeois, nationalist populist, nothing more, with all the internal contradictions implicit in this.[28]

The touchstone for Amin was still at the time Egypt, 'I was at that point very critical of Nasserism and it created some problems for me for quite a long period.' The early 1960s were 'a crucial point in history at least from the Egyptian point of view, after the radicalisation of 1956 but before the defeat of 1967, a time of close Soviet–Egyptian relations.' All over Africa people were adopting radical nationalist, even Marxist, politics. Was this enough?

> It was also the glorious time of Ghana with Nkrumah, of Guinea with Sekou Toure, there was the victory of Algeria. In other words, there were a number of points in the map of Africa where there seemed a potential for radicalisation going beyond nationalist populism.... Is it possible and if so under what conditions for nationalist populism to move to the left? Not because the leaders move to the left by themselves, not because they develop a socialist rhetoric from time to time, not because the Soviets gave them a certificate of socialism, but provided the popular classes organised independently go into conflict with the system and go ahead.[29]

Such problems occurred when regimes employed a populist rhetoric, but the grassroots activists failed to put sufficient pressure on the leadership of the movement. In 1972, Samir Amin and his allies organised a large meeting in Dar es Salaam. Many different liberation movements were represented, including organisations from South Africa, Angola, Mozambique and Zimbabwe. The debate there concerned the question of how to move away from the narrow targets of achieving independent statehood, towards another line. As Amin recalls, 'The meeting did not please everybody.'[30]

In 1975, Samir Amin helped to establish the Third World Forum. His thinking was strategic. Through the 1960s and early 1970s, the power system had been confronted with a major challenge. Now, he believed, popular forces were in danger of exhaustion. In their absence, the likely victors were local ruling

classes, entirely loyal to foreign, imperialist interests. These groups
he characterised as a 'comprador' bourgeoisie. Even today, Amin
blames the weakness of African development on decisions taken in
the 1960s, including the choice of the Soviet model over the
Chinese example:

> When we think of the historical limitations of nationalist populism and
> Soviet socialism we realise that in the two cases where we have a vision
> of capitalism without capitalists, the target is to reproduce a society
> which is very close to the reality of a capitalist society with a view to
> 'catching up' or reducing the historical gap which is a result of im-
> perialism and unequal development till it is reduced to the point of the
> countries becoming equal partners ... If it is normal capitalism, we in
> Africa are bound to be more mediocre, because ... we are still produc-
> ing raw materials, agricultural and mineral, and not moving into indus-
> trialisation.... This latest chapter in the history of Africa has come to
> such a disastrous point that it has led to the crystallisation of such
> things as ethnicity, civil war, religious illusions etc.[31]

Towards the present

We saw in the last section that Samir Amin long remained loyal to
a model of Chinese-style socialism. Yet life has taken some of the
sheen off this model. As early as the 1970s, China began a process
of rapprochement with America. Foreign policy links were followed
by trade. Today, China's rulers are as enthusiastic about business
as rulers anywhere. In his recent book, *Re-reading the Postwar
Period*, Amin complains that China, North Korea and Cuba are all
aiming 'for a capitalism that purports to control its relations with
the dominant world system'. He also argues that, although from
1960 to 1975 he 'entirely shared the Maoist view', there have been
periods of development in his thinking. 'From 1980 to 1985 I
began to challenge this problematic.'[32] If so, then the process began slowly. In 1982, Amin's *The Future of Maoism* argued that of
all nations China was the only one to have transcended capitalism.[33]
Elsewhere, he no longer argued that China was 'building socialism',
only that its society stood outside mainstream capitalist development, and that:

> The goal of socialist construction, such as it had been formulated in the
> ideology of Chinese Marxism ... was not possible, but that the long

popular national phase on which it was embarked, and from which it will not emerge for many decades, constitutes not a stage in capitalist expansion, but the necessary form of transcendence from the peripheries of the system.[34]

There are other places in which Amin's Maoism appeared much softer, more in the form of a loose philosophical identification than as a precise programme. In his 1970 book, *The Maghreb and Modern World*, Amin described his ideal as 'a peasant radicalism which would pursue the struggle to the bitter end'. In this quote, Maoism stood for Indian or African peasant insurrection, not Chinese socialism as such. In the same work, Amin described the limitations of state industrialisation. 'The establishment of an administrative or para-administrative elite necessarily entailed a widening of social inequalities, as did the seizure of colonist land by a fraction of the labouring peasantry and by new proprietors.' Such passages seem to transcend the limits of the political tradition in which he was raised. They offer a more compelling explanation of the origins of a local ruling class:

> To insist upon acceleration of production at all costs leads only to an impasse. This 'economist' version of a simplistic Marxism is the linchpin of the bureaucrat's argument: social inequality, expressed in inequalities of income and power, is a 'necessary' and 'positive' stage of development. The actual consequence of such a policy, in the present conditions of the Third World, is to reinforce parasitic social groups incapable of promoting the accelerated development they want, and to increase the disillusionment and mute opposition of the masses.

Elsewhere Samir Amin developed this approach, arguing for the delinking of Third World nations from the global capitalist economy.[35] Only a strategy of independent economic development could secure social justice. Yet for this strategy to hold, the educators would still have to be educated. The peasant masses still needed to watch their leaders closely, and to govern their decisions by the maximum of direct democracy. In other words, Samir Amin's theoretical approach to the dilemmas of Third World liberation corresponds closely to the practical approach grasped by Walter Rodney. The best alternative to what Amin termed 'dependent state capitalism' was the self-organisation of the mass movement.[36]

Orientalism

This chapter began with a passage written by Samir Amin in 1990, in which he described the crisis of radical thought following the fall of the Berlin Wall. Such ideas did not emerge haphazardly or by chance. Through the 1980s, most people of the left could see that the Soviet Union was in trouble. This process caused many writers to consider their relationship to the ideas of Marx. Amin has described his own attempt at re-evaluation, 'By the mid-1980s I had reached a new conclusion: historical Marxism had under-estimated the gravity of the problems caused by global polarisation and posed the issue of the transition in the incorrect terms of bourgeois revolution or socialist revolution.' The real goal, he concluded, 'was a very long evolution beyond capitalism, of a national and popular character, based on delinking and a recognition of the genuine conflict between the trend toward capitalism and the aspiration for socialism.'[37] One key idea here is the notion of 'delinking'. Amin has argued that national economies can operate outside the capitalist value system, provided that the benefits of growth flow equally to all classes.[38]

In several places, Samir Amin has spoken of the need to test Marxism against 'the challenge of actually existing capitalism'. This point connects to the main argument of this book – that any socialist ideas only have validity in so far as they are continuously checked against the test of the present. Amin has put the argument himself, persuasively:

> History did not come to a halt in 1880, nor in 1917, nor in 1945. In each decade, new facts indicate new developments *unsuspected at previous stages.* The outcome of previous struggles determines at each moment new alternatives which are both unforeseen and unforeseeable. So it is necessary at each stage to take seriously the task of integrating new facts into the analysis. And yet there will always be individuals searching for absolute certainties who ... prefer the reassuring religious vision of an apocalyptic catastrophe and a golden age miraculously created at a single stroke, instead of the disturbing prospect of perpetually changing conditions which necessitate continuous rethinking.[39]

In his book *Eurocentrism* Amin argues that Marxism 'remains an unfinished construct'. It is 'a still incomplete search for another culture, capable of serving as the basis for a social order that can surmount the contradictions that capitalism has never overcome and can never resolve'. Here Amin confronts the perceived traces of a racist mindset even inside his own socialist tradition. Amin observes that Marxists had employed a stages theory of history in which all humanity was expected to evolve from primitive communism to slave society, and via feudalism to capitalism and then socialism. It followed that the West was predetermined to become capitalist first. 'The European model is applied to the entire planet, forcing everyone into an iron corset.' Marx was also wrong to think that capitalism would spread throughout the world, 'The global expression of capitalism has never made it its task to homogenise the planet. On the contrary, this expansion created a new polarisation, subjecting social forms prior to capitalism to the demands of the reproduction of capital in the central formation.'[40]

The task of rethinking Marxism compels us to challenge every argument advanced in its name. Karl Marx himself swore by the motto 'doubt everything'. It is worth asking how far Amin's insights take us forwards. For example, the notion of five stages in human development is not to be found in Marx, but rather in Stalin.[41] It ignores all sorts of societies described by Marx, as well as his account of different moments or phases in capitalism.

The idea that Marxism reduces all of human history to a single pattern of development makes little sense of the many alternative theories which different Marxists have produced over the years. For example, a hundred years ago, the Russian socialist Leon Trotsky described the world using a different language of 'combined and uneven development'. His insights were close to Marx, and indeed to Amin himself, but different from Stalin's didactic socialism. Trotsky suggested that Russia was both an underdeveloped society and one in which there were examples of the most modern techniques of production. The industrial proletariat of pre-revolutionary Petrograd was just as large and as highly concentrated as the working class of Paris or Berlin. Underdeveloped societies were capable of borrowing the most advanced economic techniques from their more developed rivals, and for this reason development could be a very rapid process indeed.[42]

Another point Trotsky made was that any one state should never be seen in total separation from those around. Both he and Lenin argued that no country could survive in isolation from a world economic system that remained capitalist. The creation of socialism in Russia therefore depended on the success of revolutionaries to make their cause spread. The isolation and underdevelopment of Russia could be transformed if Germany and France also turned socialist. A socialist federation of Europe would solve the poverty of Russia. Amin accuses Marx of expecting the global periphery to wait for socialism to happen in the centre. Yet in Trotsky's Marxism we find almost entirely the opposite approach. Indeed such politics became the dominant ideology of the Soviet state in its first few years. The Communist International was established, and Russia was renamed the Union of Soviet Socialist Republics. More such republics were expected to follow suit, and soon. In both these moves we see the working through of an idea of development, in which the West was charged with 'catching up' with a more radical South or East.

For several reasons, Samir Amin's relationship to the Trotskyist tradition has been largely hostile. He suggests that Trotsky's admirers have always believed, deep down, that the centre of resistance remains the workers of the First World. Such a strategy, he claims, 'is not Leninist: it denies the worldwide nature of the system'.[43] Yet I have tried to suggest here that Amin's critique is based on a misreading of Trotskyism. The implication of Trotsky's theory is precisely that there is no singe 'centre of resistance'. Wherever they are, workers should fight. Wherever they are, they should cause the struggle to spread.

Amin has rejected these arguments, suggesting at times that there was no possibility of *any* useful development happening in the West. In *Accumulation on a World Scale*, Amin argued (loosely following Baran and Sweezy)[44] that capitalist crisis was a thing of the past, and that Western workers therefore had no interest in thinking or acting against the system.[45] There is a hint in that argument of defeatism. For if there was no potential alliance between Third and First World workers, then how could Third World workers resist the combined offensive of First and Third World capitalism? In response to such criticism, Amin would no doubt argue that plenty of social theorists have already dedicated their life to the cause of the Western proletariat. It is only time that more looked to the South.

In Amin's *Eurocentrism* we find this and another idea, that capitalism had failed to spread. Such an insight might at first appear surprising. Is not one of the most common ideas associated with today's anti-capitalism that a process of globalisation is taking place in which the authentic cultures of the developing world are being reduced by the intrusion of a homogenous global culture? Given how often Amin is associated with anti-globalisation activism, you might expect him to share this insight. It seems even odder that anyone should want to describe the economic conditions of Syria or Senegal as pre-capitalist. The problem is rather the dominance of unequal market relationships. Yet, in terms of Amin's socialism, there are good reasons to characterise the developing world as 'social forms prior to capitalism'. It would follow from this argument that each underdeveloped society should begin its own process of industrialisation, under the leadership of an authentic national class. Delinking from global capitalism means self-sufficient economic growth. By emphasising the pre-capitalist nature of the developing world, Amin means to suggest the continuing validity of a Chinese-style or similar socialism.

If the anti-globalisation activists are right that the world has been tyrannised by the spread of a single pattern of capitalist development, then the freedom to manoeuvre of any single, national bloc is reduced. As long ago as 1970, Samir Amin described capitalism as a global system. The language he used then seems even truer now. Amin began by listing the different forms of developed and underdeveloped societies. He continued:

> All these countries are integrated, though to varying degrees, in a world-wide network of commercial, financial and other relations such that none of them can be thought of in isolation – that is leaving these relations out of account – in the way that one can think of the Roman Empire and Imperial China, as ... unaware of each other.[46]

Amin's argument in this passage casts doubt on his own strategy of delinking. Transnational corporations may exist as global entities (Microsoft, Coca-Cola, Pepsi), or as bloc of merged business, mirroring the development of regional economies (Airbus). It is possible to see how their goods might be annexed by socialists organised beyond the level of the nation-state. In national units, though? The success of this tactic is hard to conceive now.

Over the years, Amin's work has come in for varied criticism. Nigel Harris has concentrated on one passage in which Amin suggested that the source of unequal trade was to be found in the role played by Western trade unions. Harris interprets him as arguing that the only means for the Third World to advance was at the expense of First World workers. If so then Amin's politics meant self-sacrifice and guilt, not socialism.[47] Henry Bernstein, the one-time editor of the *Journal of Peasant Studies*, has suggested that Amin's theories depend on a false synthesis of irreconcilable elements, not least Marxism and development theory. They constitute 'an encyclopaedic tangle of categories and method which is self-reinforcing and results in a series of mutually contradictory propositions'.[48] Sheila Smith has criticised Amin's categorisation of peripheral economies as non-capitalistic. Yet she joins this point to an unduly complex theory of market relationships, the main theme of which appears to be the non-definable character of the system.[49] Aidan Foster-Carter is a more sympathetic judge. In one passage, he complains of Amin's doctrinaire qualities. 'A Luther, in some respects, he attacks Pope and Vatican – or rather, *this* Pope, *this* Vatican.'[50] In Amin's work, Chinese socialism was long above criticism. Even recently, when he has claimed to go beyond Maoism, there is still a striking continuity between the political strategies he argues now, and the one that he defended in the past. Amin's engagement with Marx is a creative dialogue held within just one current of the Marxist tradition, when the argument of this book is that the most exciting thinking has happened *between*.

Beyond the present

In a number of recent articles, Samir Amin has sketched out what he sees as the major contradictions facing the world today. As you would expect, the tone of his argument is critical, its method is strategic, and the conclusions breathe a spirit of hope. They begin, always, with the latest forms taken by capitalism. Amin associates contemporary globalisation with 'five new monopolies' that distort the patterns of global trade in favour of the dominant powers; they are 'the control of technology; global financial flows; access to the planet's natural resources; media and communications; and weapons of mass destruction. The twenty-first century, he writes, will not be 'America's century'. 'It will be one of vast conflicts, and the rise of social struggles that question the disproportionate ambition of Washington and of capital.' Blocs of capital tend to compete. Expect the USA and Japan to clash, and the USA and Russia. 'If the European Left could free itself from its submission to the double dictate of capital and Washington, it would be possible to imagine that the new European strategy would be articulated on those of Russia, China, India and the Third World in general, in the perspective of a necessary multipolar construction effort.' If this alliance fails, 'the European project itself will fade away'.[51]

In a recent book, *Spectres of Capitalism*, Samir Amin has described a world not so different from the one which Karl Marx envisaged, all those years ago. 'We are once again in one of those moments when the gluttons hold their orgy. But this momentary triumph of unrestrained capital is not accompanied by a brilliant new expansive surge for capitalism but by the deepening of its crisis!' The boundless appetite of capital reveals only 'the absurd irrationality of this system'. Capitalism 'expands consumption in a distorted manner by favouring wholesale waste by the rich, but this in no way compensates for the poverty to which it condemns the majority of workers and peoples, who become ever less successfully integrated into its system of exploitation'. The system creates its antagonists. 'This paradoxical victory of capital giving rise to its prolonged crisis is only apparent if we cool off by reading the *Communist Manifesto* and recall to our memory the plain reason for this: capitalism is incapable of overcoming its fundamental contradictions.'[52] It is easy to imagine a world without bosses. A society without labour, however, would have no future at all.

David Widgery: the poetics of propaganda

David Widgery was a political writer. He devoted his life to communicating the ideas of Marxism, that society could be organised from below, and that workers could run the world. In his writing, he explained, he challenged and he persuaded. His articles described the relationship between things, the connection between unemployment and racism, the link between crisis and capitalism, raising in Lenin's phrase 'many ideas', so that the world could be understood as a single whole. Some of the breadth of his work can be seen in the range of papers and magazines that he wrote for. His own anthology of his work, compiled in 1989, includes articles published in *City Limits*, *Gay Left*, *INK*, *International Socialism*, *London Review of Books*, *Nation Review*, *New Internationalist*, *New Socialist*, *New Society*, *New Statesman*, *OZ*, *Radical America*, *Rank and File Teacher*, *Socialist Worker*, *Socialist Review*, *Street Life*, *Temporary Hoarding*, *Time Out* and *The Wire*. Any more complete list would also have to include his student journalism and regular columns in the *British Medical Journal* and the *Guardian* in the 1980s. Widgery was also an activist, a doctor and an author.[1] He attended the Ruskin Conference (the founding event of British women's liberation), and edited *OZ*, after its main editors were tried for indecency in 1971. He chaired the Campaign to Save Bethnal Green Hospital, and compiled three anthologies of radical prose. He was an active supporters of Britain's first 'history from below' movement, the History Workshop. Widgery was also among the first of his generation to grasp the significance of the gay rights struggles of the early 1970s.

Better than any one else, David Widgery expressed in his life the radical diversity of which the left was capable, as it came under the influence of the 1968 revolts. While many socialists could claim to have played a more decisive part in any one area of struggle – trade-union, gender or sexual politics, radical journalism or anti-racism – none shared his breadth of activism. Widgery had a re-markable ability to 'be there', contributing to the early debates of the student, gay and feminist movements, writing for the first new counter-cultural, socialist and rank-and-file publications. The peaks of his activity corresponded to the peaks of the movement. Just 18 years old, Widgery was a leading part of the group that established Britain's best-known counter-cultural magazine, *OZ*. Ten years later he helped to found Rock Against Racism, parent to the Anti-Nazi League, and responsible for some of the largest events the left has organised in Britain. RAR was the left's last great flourish, before Margaret Thatcher became prime minister, and the movement entered a long period of decline, from which even now it is only beginning to awake.

Widgery also had a talent for friendship. His partners included Sheila Rowbotham and Marsha Rowe, editor of *Spare Rib*. Other friends included the journalists Paul Foot and Tariq Ali;[2] radical designers and photographers Ruth Gregory, Syd Shelton, Red Saunders, Andy Dark and Roger Huddle; children's author Michael Rosen; first New Leftist Peter Sedgwick; the biographer of Britain's underground press Nigel Fountain; gay activists Bob Cant and Jeffrey Weeks; left-wing historians Raphael Samuel, E.P. Thompson and Dorothy Thompson, Barbara Winslow and Sally Alexander. Widgery was also a member of a revolutionary party, the Inter-national Socialists, the predecessor of today's Socialist Workers' Party (not to be confused with the American party of the same name). The succession from the Thompsons and Raphael Samuel and their allies to the next generation of socialists, including Sheila Rowbotham, David Widgery, Tariq Ali and Paul Foot, expresses some of the contrast between the British left of 1956 and the second wave of 1968, between a class-based left, and a second group, more determinedly Marxist, but broadening their activism so that all aspects of human life could be changed.

1947–68: to be young was very heaven

Born in 1947 to a Quaker family, Widgery wrote very little about his early life. Sheila Rowbotham describes his father as socially ambitious, but his mother as a more typical member of the public-sector middle class.[3] More decisive than this parental contrast was a period of illness. David Widgery nearly died in the 1956 polio epidemic, and spent the next five years graduating as he described, 'from wheelchair and callipers to my first pair of shop-bought shoes'. It was a horrific experience for a young child to go through, trapped in a hospital without his parents and with the children 'crying, as I so clearly remember, ourselves to sleep at night with our nurses in tears at their inability to comfort us'. The experience did have one valuable result: it gave Widgery his admiration for the National Health Service, and may even have contributed to his later decision to become a doctor.[4]

Having survived this ordeal, Widgery was then sent off to grammar school, where he became quickly contemptuous of its rituals, 'My school even invented a Latin song we sang about the school's airy position above the railway sidings, which we sang like so many housewives being introduced to Royalty.'[5] He joined CND and took part in the Aldermaston march, and also wrote for the national school students' *U Magazine*. At the age of 15, Widgery read Jack Kerouac's great novel *On the Road* and discovered in it 'a coded message of discontent'. Later he would claim that Neal Cassady, the hero of the novel, was the 'Leon Trotsky of his time'. Widgery bunked off after hours from school to listen to jazz bands at the Rikki-Tik club in Windsor. He was expelled from his grammar school, appropriately enough, for publishing an unauthorised magazine, *Rupture*.[6] In 1965, he interviewed Allen Ginsberg for *Sixth Form Opinion*, and was seduced by him, before escaping on his Lambretta. Later that year, Widgery spent four months travelling across the United States. He arrived as Watts, the black district of Los Angeles, exploded in riots. Widgery then journeyed to Cuba

and later to the West Coast, taking part in anti-Vietnam protests
called by members of Students for a Democratic Society.[7]

Widgery came of age in the middle of the 1960s, surrounded by
sex, dope and psychedelia, yet also cynical about his generation's
myths of cultural revolt: 'All you need is love, but a private income
and the sort of parents who would have a Chinese smoking jacket
in the attic help.' 'Against Grown-Up Power', an article he wrote
in 1967, spurned the values of the older generation, publicly
attaching its author to the spirit of anger and revolt that would
manifest itself in the student protests of the following year's events:

> Yours is the generation which calls concentration camps 'strategic ham-
> lets' and supporting the oil sheiks 'a peacekeeping role'. 'Democratic
> breakthroughs' are things like letting workers at Fairfields actually talk
> to their boss or stopping students standing up when lecturers enter the
> room.... Politics becomes the business of managing a given industrial
> system to reward those it exploits at intervals which more or less
> coincide with elections. The bad joke at Westminster represents the
> people, and together with the TUC, the CBI and the bankers becomes
> something called 'The National Interest'.[8]

David Widgery found a place among the underground papers
that sprang up to celebrate their vision of the 1960s. Richard
Neville, the editor of *OZ*, describes meeting Widgery by chance
while listening to Bob Dylan at the Isle of Wight festival in August
1969. David 'had weaselled his way there as a Trotskyite rep of the
electricians' union'.[9] They exchanged pleasantries, with Neville
expressing surprise that a busy revolutionary could find the time to
waste at a gig. 'If one per cent of this celestial crowd devoted itself
to throwing yoghurt bombs at the Queen or undressing in court',
Widgery replied, 'we'd all be a lot better off.' Neville and Widgery
remained on good terms, and close enough for Widgery to imper-
sonate Neville on a Saturday night episode of TV's *Frost Report*.[10]

Although he had been (very briefly) a member of the Communist Party and then the ultra-orthodox Trotskyist organisation the
Socialist Labour League (SLL) in the early 1960s, it was only in
1968 that David Widgery decisively attached himself to the revolutionary left, by joining the International Socialists (IS), today's
Socialist Workers' Party (SWP).[11] In one book, Widgery claimed
(tongue-in-cheek) to have joined the IS because they were the only

party to publish an obituary of the surrealist André Breton. Whatever the reasons for his early conversion, he was to remain a member of the IS and then the SWP for the rest of his life. Widgery was not the only young radical to become a socialist in 1968. Thousands moved to the left under the impact of the Tet offensive, when Vietnamese forces scored extraordinary victories against the greater military forces of the United States, under the influence of the Russian invasion of Czechoslovakia in August, and inspired by the student protests and the general strike which broke out in France in May '68. Widgery himself describes walking round London 'with a transistor radio in my ear to catch the latest news'. In Mexico, five thousand troops fired on demonstrators, killing over a hundred people, while in Germany a generation of activists were won to the tactic of immediate, violent action against the state. The nearest that English students came to events in France and Washington was at the London School of Economics in Holborn, where David Widgery bunked medical school and joined in the protests, which culminated in January 1969 when hundreds of students and local building workers tore down steel gates which has been installed by the college principal to prevent them from occupying the university buildings.[12]

Paul Foot describes meeting David Widgery for the first time in 1968: 'His eyes were shining and he had a grin on his face as though it were fixed there forever. I was off to speak on socialism at York University – he had just come from there. "It's great", he said. "Great. An enormous middle-class fun palace." Suddenly his expression changed, and he glowered at me. "They don't need you there", he said. "Not another of us. They need the proletariat."' Widgery was a rare member of his generation to use the latter term spontaneously and unselfconsciously. Foot continued:

> David Widgery believed above all else in the struggle for socialism. He knew for certain that individuals can't get socialism on their own, and he committed himself all his life to the organisation which, he believed, tried hardest to adopt and raise its theory of socialism to the level of doing something to get it.[13]

Widgery was also attracted to the open spirit of discussion and debate within the party. Inside the IS, David Widgery found a hero in Peter Sedgwick, a member of the 1956 generation, best known for having popularised the works of the dissident former Bolshevik Victor Serge, but also the author of *Psychopolitics*, an early foray into left-wing psychoanalysis.[14] Widgery made clear the emotional debt he owned to his hero:

> Almost uniquely among the many Marxist intellectuals of the 1956 vintage, he didn't just write about the left but made it, shaped it and served it as an active member of first the 'Socialist Review' group, then the International Socialists, and until the mid-1970s the SWP.... Sedgwick's politics were of Bolshevism at its most libertarian and Marxism at its most warm-hearted and witty. He also dressed like a Basque beatnik, wrote footnotes on his own footnotes, collected tins of mulligatawny and was founding editor of *Red Wank: Journal of Rank and File Masturbation*, whose second (and unpublished) issue was to feature 'Great autoerotic revolutionary acts' and 'Coming out as a worker: problems in a TU Branch'.[15]

Underground overground left

David Widgery's most important political work in this period was his journalism for *OZ*. Widgery's role within the main editorial group was to act as the conscience of the magazine, denouncing *Private Eye* and the Sunday broadsheets, mourning the loss of Jack Kerouac, and describing what might happen 'When Harrods was looted'. This article appeared in violet, printed on green, beside a complicated diagram presenting the affinity of William Morris's art with Rosa Luxemburg's socialism, and inside a front cover made of detachable dayglo stickers. The presentation was typical of the graphic eclecticism of *OZ*. Meanwhile Widgery's article was an earnest attempt to translate the traditional concerns of revolutionary Marxism into the language of the new underground left,

> Without these roots into and connections with working-class life, the most scintillating critique of bourgeois ideology, the fullest of blueprints for student power, and the grooviest of anti-universities could all be paid for by the Arts Council for all the danger they present. To wait for revolution by Mao or Che or comprehensive schools or BBC2 is to play the violin while the Titanic goes down, for if socialists don't take their theory back into the working class there are others who will.[16]

David Widgery also reminded *OZ* writers that if the magazine's language of 'free love' was to have any real meaning then it must take into account the sexism which was a definite part of the male hippie dream. Here he was influenced by his close friend Sheila Rowbotham, one of the leading voices of the new movement for women's liberation, who was briefly a member of IS, and later helped to organise the famous Ruskin Conference, which took place in Oxford in February 1970.[17] Reviewing Richard Neville's book *Playpower* for *OZ* that year, David Widgery demonstrated that Neville's vision of sexual freedom for men meant that he was in reality a 'raving reactionary' towards women. Neville, he pointed out, had not learned even the ABC of feminism:

> Women are doubly enslaved, both as people under capitalism and women by men. The hippie chick has always been one of the most unfree of women; assigned to be ethereal and knowing about Tarot and the moon's phases but busy at cooking, answering the phone and rolling her master's joints ... Neville's view of the sexual transaction is not so much advanced as insulting, and it is all the more sad he doesn't even notice it.[18]

David Widgery's critique of hippie misogyny was distinctive, and well ahead of its time. The first *Women's Newsletter* appeared in Britain in May 1969. Germaine Greer's *Female Eunuch* was only published in 1971, while Sheila Rowbotham's major works *Women, Resistance and Revolution*, then *Woman's Consciousness, Man's World* and *Hidden from History* appeared in 1972 and 1973.[19] The point is not just that Widgery saw problems early. Some of his quality can be seen through a contrast with fellow *OZ* contributor Germaine Greer. Greer's book *The Female Eunuch* is vividly alive to the oppression of the 'castrated female'. Hers is a developed critique of the commercialisation of the body; it is a finished argument, and in that sense her book is far in advance of anything that Widgery wrote at this time. Yet all you need to see are Greer's chapter titles – 'Bones', 'Hair', 'Puberty', 'Abuse', 'Misery', 'Resentment', 'Rebellion' – and it becomes clear that much of her specific critique of women's oppression could be extended into a general condemnation of the fact that all human bodies have been diminished by a society in which profit is king. Such a call would not need to have been less radical. It could be more angry, a point

Greer herself acknowledged in the introduction to her book. 'The most telling criticisms will come from my sisters of the left, the Maoists, the Trots, the IS, the SDS, because of my fantasy that it might be possible to leap the steps of revolution and arrive somehow at liberty and communism without strategy or revolutionary discipline.'[20]

The most telling criticism of Germaine Greer came not from Widgery but from another *OZ* contributor, Michelene Wandor, and her critique was not located on Leninist terrain. Wandor rejected Greer's tendency to titillate *OZ* audiences with articles on the joys of lesbianism. 'The movement doesn't seek the replacement of penis power by cunt power', she wrote, 'or any generalized power. It seeks the involvement of all women cutting across the class structure.' Michelene Wandor then went on to cite the six hundred women 'sick of doing the dance of the ovaries' at the Ruskin Conference, and asked 'Where was Germaine?' Greer was at home, working on the proofs of the book that would make her name.[21]

Meanwhile Widgery developed his political interests from gender to sexuality, attempting to interest the editors of *Socialist Worker* in a review of Don Milligan's pamphlet *The Politics of Homosexuality*. The piece finally appeared in *Gay Left*, endorsing Milligan's contention that the source of sexual oppression lay in the capitalist family, and its solution lay in social revolution. 'A male worker who sneers at queers, just like one who talks of niggers and slags, is finally only sneering at himself and at his class.'[22]

In the spring of 1971, Widgery acted as a court representative for Neville when *OZ* went on trial, and defended the magazine to the best of his abilities, until Neville insisted on replacing him, as Widgery's final medical exams drew near.[23] Writing for *Socialist Worker* during the trial, under the pseudonym 'Gerry Dawson', David Widgery made it clear that he had his own vision of rebellion, which went beyond the narrow masculine sexual radicalism that *OZ* championed. He expressed his reservations with Neville's project, but went on to defend it, as one expression of a greater desire for revolutionary change,

> There is a sort of erotic reformism which suggests that quite literally 'all you need is love'. Its attractiveness is as considerable as its ineffectuality. But in reacting against it, socialist puritans are in danger of

ignoring one of the most intimate of capitalism's contradictions. Engels was right when he pointed out 'that with every great revolutionary movement, the question of free love comes to the foreground'.[24]

Widgery was invited to edit *OZ* after the trial, as an exhausted Neville took a break. The magazine now was in decline, undercut by the rising left press, and unsure where to turn. Unwilling to reproduce its earlier staple photographs of glamorous underdressed hippie women, the magazine had less to say, and folded in 1972. Widgery penned *OZ*'s obituary,

> Whether *OZ* is dead, of suicide or sexual excess, or whether *OZ* is alive and operating under a series of new names is unclear at the moment. What is clear is that *OZ* bizarrely and for a short period expressed the energy of a lot of us. We regret his passing.[25]

Leaving *OZ* as the magazine slowly died, David Widgery became more active elsewhere as a journalist. He increasingly felt that the underground press had failed. As he told *Time Out* in 1973, the hippie papers had not succeeded in pushing their cultural radicalism into the hearts of the working class. 'At the core of the shabby myths and collective dishonesties of the underground was the belief that the class struggle had had it, that the workers had been hopelessly bribed, bamboozled and betrayed.' Yet the bohemian milieu was impotent to change society on its own, and because of its indifference to workers it was unable to win over the one force that could transform society. Thus the underground had become an empty vessel, incapable of turning its fine words into revolutionary actions. Widgery was to return to this theme in a later interview:

> Occasionally, you'd meet shop stewards at conferences who were interested in the underground press, or got stoned, or were interested in radical music. That was always very fruitful. Otherwise there wasn't much apparent link between the workers' struggle and this psychedelic flowering. The former was pragmatic and fairly empirical, predominantly concerned with money and making excuses for Harold Wilson. The latter was almost wholly an imported problem, which is what made the 'off with the pigs' rhetoric so flimsy.[26]

The two years between 1972 and 1974 saw some of the sharpest conflicts of the entire post-war period. David Lyddon and Ralph Darlington have described the workers' struggles of 1972, when miners, dockers and printers struck to defeat the Tories' Industrial Relations Act. The protests threatened to become an unofficial general strike. Heath dropped the Act, and his government finally collapsed in 1974, following its inability to stop a second, national miners' strike.[27] Life itself seemed to have demonstrated the truth of the claim that workers possessed a special power to challenge the dominance of capital. This was also the period when Rowbotham and Widgery were at their closest, before rival attachments would get in their way.[28] Widgery's anthology *The Left in Britain* includes a warm statement of thanks to Rowbotham, who 'peeled oranges, made rude remarks, wrote file cards for newspapers and put up with them and me'.[29]

Widgery and Orwell

I have described David Widgery's early activism in some detail, because it is important to understand where his voice as a writer came from. Influenced by his love of beat poetry and jazz, and shaped by his own active involvement in the underground press, David Widgery was a remarkably open writer, ready to borrow from different styles and forms, and determined to put his message across in the most persuasive way possible. He understood better than anyone else of his generation that language is for expressing and not for concealing or hiding thought. Widgery consciously read and copied the popular writers of the past. Like George Orwell, Widgery loved Jonathan Swift, but his heroes were many. *Preserving Disorder* includes articles on the political writers Fernando Claudin, Sylvia Pankhurst, C.L.R. James and Lenin, as well as pieces on Widgery's other influences, Norman Mailer, John Lennon, Jack Kerouac, Bessie Smith and Billie Holiday.

In a famous essay, 'Politics and the English Language', George Orwell attempted to map out the rules of effective political writing. The point of the essay was to criticise the hack political writing of the 1930s and 1940s, and consequently most of his suggestions were negative. Propagandists should not lapse into dogma; neither should they parrot any party line. They should also avoid tired or dying metaphors and also lazy clauses, 'verbal false limbs'. Orwell

thought that six rules in particular would cover most of the traps
into which bad political writing then fell:

i.   Never use a metaphor, simile or other figure of speech which you
     are used to seeing in print.
ii. Never use a long word where a short one will do.
iii. If it's possible to cut a word out, always cut it out.
iv. Never use a passive where you can use the active.
v.   Never use a foreign phrase, a scientific word or a jargon word where
     you can think of an everyday English equivalent.
vi. Break any of these rules rather than say anything outright
     barbarous.[30]

Like Orwell, Widgery wrote in a style that treasured originality
and creativity. He was aware that communication took place through
the reader's imagination and not just through passive acceptance of
the printed word. His writing style played with sounds and images
to create meaning. It was a very simple, musical language. Indeed,
if positive rules could be taken from Widgery's writing to set against
Orwell's negative rules, they would include at least the following
two broad statements of advice.

The first rule would be *always write for your audience*. David
Widgery wanted many people to understand him, and was not
afraid to experiment. He used visual metaphors, experimented with
grammar, and wrote in a language which copied the rhythms of
speech. Any of these techniques he employed, provided they made
his meaning easier to understand. Widgery grasped that cultural
forms were changing, and insisted to his comrades that they should
watch and follow.

The second rule would be *don't just write for your audience –
challenge them*. Widgery asked his readers questions. He did not
lecture, but involved his audience in a process of questioning. He
prompted them to see for themselves the connections between
different events. Writing about the death of Steve Biko, in the
Rock Against Racism magazine *Temporary Hoarding*, Widgery
began with the events of the Soweto uprising, and proceeded to
describe the repressive apparatus of the South African state. Only
then did he turn his readers' gaze to the role played by their own
Labour administration:

The British government voted in the United Nations, yet again, against business sanctions contra South Africa ... Britain is still South Africa's largest trading partner and investor. Almost a quarter of South Africa's exports go to Britain and 4 per cent of British exports are destined for South Africa.... The state that killed Steve Biko is, despite the diplomatic talk, deeply connected to Britain. To help black Africa to freedom, we will have to free ourselves.[31]

There are other ways in which a comparison with George Orwell finds in David Widgery's favour. Cut off from any large political movement, Orwell returned from Spain a revolutionary, but became isolated and fell into cynicism. After 1945, the majority of his political contacts were moving to the right, and Orwell was unable to maintain a consistently left-wing anti-Stalinism. Demoralised, he allied with right-wingers, and failed when he sought to justify his remote position:

In our time it is broadly true that political writing is bad writing. Where it is not true, it will generally be found that the writer is some kind of rebel, expressing his own private opinions, and not a 'party line'. Orthodoxy, of whatever colour, seems to demand a lifeless, imitative style.[32]

Unlike Orwell, Widgery was no maverick. Everything he wrote was the collective property of his family and friends. Juliet Ash describes Widgery showing articles to her, and to her children:

Every time he wrote anything, he would test it out. Even when my daughter was young, 6 or 7, he would test things out on her. I remember him testing articles on me, and on my son. He had a way of talking that teased things out of people. He used humour, and made people laugh. He never left anyone out.[33]

Beyond his immediate acquaintances, Widgery also benefited from contact with movements of protest, and with the SWP. Linked to a political party, but free within it, Widgery was as good a writer as Orwell, and a more successful activist.

Like any writer of quality, Widgery in his enthusiasm would sometimes push an argument too far, as when he maintained that the left relied too heavily on newspapers and books. The 1973 introduction to his book *The Left in Britain* regretted committing the memories of real people to the sole care of books and dusty paper:

In fact, because such a small group of people actually find written words convincing I half wish that it wasn't a book at all but some species of talking poster which might express what the modern socialist movement feels like from within – its humour and music and oratory and colours and the intellectual sensations of its mentors and inventors, the autumn and granite of E.P. Thompson, the whiskey and ice of Alasdair MacIntye or the hurdy gurdy of Tony Cliff.[34]

I think the musical quality of this passage disproves its own argument. Widgery's idea of a talking book–poster plays on the reader's imagination and lasts with them. It is a forceful image, and no less powerful for being expressed through the medium of the written word.

Doing time

After the exuberance of 1972–74, the period of the 1974–79 Labour government was a time of decay and cynicism, during which society shifted to the right, preparing the ground for the Tories' election victory in 1979. Although it was elected with a left-wing manifesto and significant support, following the mass strikes of 1972–74, in power Labour was a massive disappointment. The government squeezed wages and cut public spending while also bringing the trade-union leaderships into close contact with the government. Bitter struggles continued through the five years of Labour rule, but the overall result was to reduce the levels of militancy within society. The number of strikes fell rapidly, while the government held the line on its compulsory incomes policy. The International Socialists were riven by a bitter faction fight, and there was no mass movement to which its members could relate. Between 1974 and 1976, David Widgery published an anthology, *The Left in Britain* (1976), and started work on *Health in Danger* (1979). He also threw himself into his new job, as an East End GP. In retrospect, however, it seems clear that Widgery was marking time, easing before a further burst of activity. Paul Foot describes these years well:

> David hated orthodoxy. As the SWP turned for survival to its own orthodoxy in the long years of the 'downturn', David became restless. He ventured outside the party walls, returning often to lecture us at

Skegness on the campaign against abortion [*sic*] in the 1930s or the gay liberation movement in the 1970s. 'You've got to listen to those gays', he told us in 1977.[35]

Although the mid-1970s were quieter for Widgery than the previous decade, it was not long before there was a mass movement, and his ideas could once more be put to the test.

The challenge came initially from the British far right. While the left was in disarray, the party which gained most from the failure of the Labour government was the National Front. First set up in 1967 as an alliance of different racist organisations, the NF only took off under Labour. In 1976, the Front received 15,340 votes in Leicester. The following year, it achieved 19 per cent of the vote in Hackney South and Bethnal Green, and 200,000 votes nationally. The strength of the organisation was on the streets. According to Ken Leech, working as a priest in London's East End, 'Between 1976–8 there was a marked increase in racist graffiti, particularly NF symbols, all over Tower Hamlets, and in the presence both of NF "heavies" and clusters of alienated young people at key fascist locations, especially in Bethnal Green.' By 1976–77, the National Front had more activist members than ever before. Its cadres waged a violent race war, and thirty-one black people were killed in racist murders in Britain between 1976 and 1981.[36]

Members of the NF attempted to build in various milieux, among football supporters and the young unemployed. One battle was over music. These were the years of punk, when the stadium bands of the early 1970s lost touch with their audience, and a new music sprang up, libertarian and anarchistic, stripped down of the pomposity of Led Zeppelin or Queen. Caroline Coon described the anger of punk music at its birth:

> The musicians and their audience reflect each other's street cheap ripped-apart, pinned-together style of dress.... The kids are arrogant, aggressive, rebellious.... Punk rock sounds simple and callow. It's meant to. The equipment is minimal, usually cheap. It's played faster than the speed of light.... There are no solos. No indulgent improvisations.... Participation is the operative word.[37]

NF members attempted to tap into this new punk style. They were helped by traces of ambiguity which punk displayed towards fascism. The style was anarchistic, but politically vague and individualistic. The sound of punk, with its jagged three-chord repetitions, was the antithesis of 1970s' reggae; in Jon Savage's phrase, 'the style had bled Rock dry of all black influences'. Members of the Sex Pistols wore swastikas, as if the symbol could be a fashion statement, while one of their last singles pronounced that 'Belsen was a Gas'.[38]

With the National Front in the ascendant, several well-known figures expressed themselves openly in favour of some version of its racist message. In August 1976, Eric Clapton interrupted a Birmingham concert to make a speech supporting Enoch Powell, the racist Tory MP. Until then Clapton was best known for having produced a cover version of the reggae classic 'I Shot the Sheriff?' Clapton's speech led directly to the formation of Rock Against Racism (RAR), and David Widgery was one of the leading lights in this movement. Two former mods, Red Saunders and Roger Huddle, wrote a letter, which was published in the *New Musical Express*, *Melody Maker*, *Sounds* and *Socialist Worker*:

> When we read about Eric Clapton's Birmingham concert when he urged support for Enoch Powell, we nearly puked. Come on Eric.... Own up. Half your music is black. You're rock music's biggest colonist.... We want to organise a rank and file movement against the racist poison music. We urge support for Rock Against Racism. P.S. Who shot the Sheriff Eric? It sure as hell wasn't you!

The letter set the tone of the new organisation. RAR published its own paper, *Temporary Hoarding*, and artists, musicians and writers participated in the creation of a musical and literary style, which drew its influence from French surrealism, Marxist politics and the best of punk. The message was angry, exciting and compelling, educational without sermonising, effective at reaching the young. David Widgery's editorial in the first issue of *Temporary Hoarding* was RAR's first manifesto: 'We want Rebel music, street music. Music that breaks down people's fear of one another. Crisis music. Now music. Music that knows who the real enemy is. Rock against Racism. Love Music Hate Racism.'[39]

Part of RAR's political radicalism lay in its total acceptance of punk's rough working-class sound, the music of white bands like

the UK Subs, Ian Dury or Jimmy Pursey's Sham 69. By adopting
this street music as it own, RAR took it out of the hands of the
racists. Yet Rock Against Racism did not simply adapt itself to the
existing punk sound. Rather it sought to change and develop punk
music. RAR brought together white punks and black reggae acts,
Jimmy Pursey with rasta group Misty in Roots, Tom Robinson
with dub act Steel Pulse. As Rock Against Racism developed, so
did the sound of the main RAR bands. The Clash hired a black
producer, Lee Perry, and wrote 'White Man in Hammersmith
Palais'. The Ruts also tried to fuse reggae and punk styles, while
Siouxsie and the Banshees, having worn swastikas in 1976 and
1977, now wrote 'Metal Postcard', based on the collages of the
German anti-fascist Johnny Heartfield.[40] Widgery, with his love of
Jimi Hendrix, reggae and the blues, was an important figure arguing all the while for two-tone music.

Street conflicts between fascists and anti-fascists continued,
reaching an early crescendo on 13 August 1977, when thousands of
anti-fascists, including large numbers of local black youths, prevented the NF from marching through Lewisham. The original
National Front demonstration was publicised as an anti-mugging
march, a crude attempt to intimidate the many Afro-Caribbean
residents in the area. Thousands of anti-fascists gathered in protest.[41] The book David Widgery later wrote as a history of the anti-
racist movement, *Beating Time* (1986), takes up the story of the
Lewisham riot:

> An officer with a megaphone read an order to disperse. No-one did;
> seconds later the police cavalry cantered into sight and sheered through
> the front row of protesters. So, without the organisation, it might have
> ended. Except that people refused to melt away from the police horses
> and jeer ineffectually from the sidelines. A horse went over, then an-
> other, and the Front were led forward so fast that they were quickly
> struggling. Then suddenly *the sky darkened* (as they say in Latin poetry),
> only this time with clods, rocks, lumps of wood, planks and bricks....
> The NF march was broken in two, their banners seized and burnt; only
> thanks to considerable police assistance was a re-formed, heavily pro-
> tected and cowed rump eventually able to continue on its route to
> Lewisham.... The mood was absolutely euphoric. Not only because of
> the sense of achievement – they didn't pass, not with any dignity any-
> way, and the police completely lost the absolute control [they] had
> boasted about – but also because, at last, we were all in it together.

After several hours of street fighting between anti-fascists and the ranks of the Metropolitan Police, one thing at least was clear: the National Front had failed to pass.[42]

The effect of Lewisham was to give a massive boost to anti-racists. In the days that followed, a new anti-racist movement was launched, the Anti-Nazi League. Its founding statement was signed by Brian Clough, the left-leaning football manager; playwright Arnold Wesker; Warren Mitchell, the star of TV's *Till Death Us Do Part*; and several hundred prominent trade unionists, community activists, footballers, musicians and other celebrities. Other vocal members of the Anti-Nazi League included Tariq Ali of the International Marxist Group, and Arthur Scargill, then the Yorkshire President of the National Union of Mineworkers. While the Anti-Nazi League concentrated on confronting the fascists, Rock Against Racism continued to win young people away from the NF. The largest RAR/ANL events were the huge Carnivals, which Widgery helped to organise as a member of the RAR Committee. The first took place on 30 April 1978, and began with a march from Trafalgar Square to Victoria Park, where the Clash, Tom Robinson, Steel Pulse, X-Ray Spex and others played to an audience of at least 80,000 people. The historian Raphael Samuel, a member of the Communist Party in his youth,[43] described Victoria Park as 'the most working-class demonstration I have been on, and one of the very few of my adult lifetime to have sensibly changed the climate of public opinion'.[44] This first Carnival was followed by local Carnivals in many areas. Some 35,000 attended the Manchester Carnival, 5,000 took part in Cardiff, 8,000 in Edinburgh, 2,000 in Harwich, and 5,000 turned out in Southampton. There was a second, larger, London Carnival in the autumn.[45]

Between 1977 and 1979, at least 9 million ANL leaflets were distributed and 750,000 badges sold. Fifty local Labour Parties affiliated, along with 30 AUEW branches, 25 trades councils, 13 shop stewards committees, 11 NUM lodges, and similar numbers of branches from the TGWU, CPSA, TASS, NUJ, NUT and NUPE.[46] The cumulative effect of this campaigning was that the NF was forced onto the defensive, and thoroughly routed. Its activists were unable to put their message across, their graffiti was painted out, and they could not march. In the April 1979 general election, the NF received a mere 1.3 per cent of the vote. Demoralised, the Front split into rival factions and its support crumbled.

For Roger Huddle, writing at the time, the whole point of RAR was that it converted music that was already revolutionary into an organisation which could live up to its radicalism: 'RAR's fight is amongst the youth whose life style is rebellious.... Punk is not just the music. It was visual, it revolutionised graphics, it's anti-authority, anarchistic and loud. It has a lot to give RAR and RAR has a lot to give it.'[7] One argument that followed was that the success of the ANL was dependent on the radicalism of its music. It was also the theme of David Widgery's book *Beating Time*,

> The ANL had shown that ... the struggle on the streets set the tempo and the politicians and celebrities support and generalise but do not dictate to it. It demonstrated that an unrespectable but effective unity between groups with wide political differences (the SWP, the organisations of the black communities and the Labour Party) can reach and touch an audience of millions, not by compromise but by an assertive campaign of modern propaganda.[48]

According to David Widgery, it was the radical and cultural mix of RAR which enabled the ANL to succeed:

> It was a piece of double time, with the musical and the political confrontations on simultaneous but separate tracks and difficult to mix. The music came first and was more exciting. It provided the creative energy and the focus in what became a battle for the soul of young working-class England. But the direct confrontations and the hard-headed political organisation which underpinned them were decisive.[49]

This guitar kills fascists

Within Rock Against Racism and the Anti-Nazi League, David Widgery was one of the most consistent voices arguing that all forms of racism had to be opposed. He was the individual who did most to drive Rock Against Racism, contributing under different names to its press, recording its successes, propagandising for RAR within the other milieux in which he was already known. This chapter has already quoted his editorial from *Temporary Hoarding* 1. The same number also featured another Widgery article, titled 'What is Racism?'

Racism is as British as Biggles and Baked Beans. You grow up anti-black, with the golliwogs in the jam, the Black and White Minstrel Show on TV and CSE dumb history at schools. Racism is about Jubilee mugs and Rule Britannia and how we won the War ... IT WOULD BE PATHETIC, IF IT HADN'T KILLED AND INJURED AND BRUTAL-ISED SO MANY LIVES. AND IF IT WASN'T STARTING ALL OVER AGAIN.... The problem is not just the new fascists from the old slime, a master race whose idea of heroism is ambushing single blacks in darkened streets. These private attacks whose intention, to cow and to brutalise, won't work if the community they seek to terrorise instead organises itself. But when the state backs up racialism it's different. Outwardly respectable but inside fired with the same mentality and the same fears, the bigger danger is the racist magistrates with the cold sneering authority, the immigration men who mock an Asian mother as she gives birth to a dead child on their office floor, policemen for whom answering back is a crime and every black kid pride is a challenge.[50]

In just a few lines, this article argued the full ANL and RAR strategy, that racism should be smashed and all the open and covert racists with it, and therefore that the fight against fascism should be turned against the racist institutions of capitalism as well.

The passage is also representative in other ways. More than any other British Marxist, Widgery would defend his politics with arguments drawn from music. How could Widgery prove that all trade-union leaders had the potential to sell out? Look at the careers of their musical counterparts, the Rolling Stones.[51] Or how could you be sure that resistance had the potential to transcend the worst oppression? Just listen to the music of Billie Holiday.[52] In the RAR campaign, Widgery had the opportunity to return the favour, de-manding of socialists that they rise to music's illustrative heights. Indeed in *Beating Time*, Widgery went so far as to claim that reggae, dub and soul *drove* his life and the lives of his friends, their sex lives, their waking time. Music gave his group rhythm and purpose:

Black music was our catechism, not just something we listened to in our spare time. It was the culture which woke us up, had shaped us and kept us up all night, blocked in the Wardour Street mod clubs, fanatical on the Thames Valley R&B circuit, queuing all down Gerrard Street to see Roland Kirk in Ronnie Scott's old basement. It was how we worked out our geography, learnt our sexuality, and taught ourselves history. There was no question of slumming or inverted snobbery, we went for black music because it was so strong rhythmically, there was a passion in it, it was about life and had some point to it. And if white musicians were as good and as exciting (as George Fame, Alexis Korner and the early Stones certainly were) we worshipped them too.[53]

One of the most important tasks facing Widgery's group was to tend Rock Against Racism, and to prevent the new organisation from being swamped by that minority of party activists who would take more from its organisational energy than they would give. This is not to say that Widgery or Huddle or any of their group were 'anti-party', or were even seen as such. The point is more general – that in any united front project which involves people with diverse experiences, active socialists can do as much damage by pushing the 'right' line over-enthusiastically, as they can by permitting less useful or duller voices to be expressed.

Members of the Socialist Workers' Party also disagreed among themselves when it came to the direction in which the new movement should travel. Because RAR was aimed at punks, and not at existing socialists, there were many party members who regarded Widgery's group with suspicion. John Shemeld, an activist from South London, was part of the anti-RAR trend: 'I was thirty, and conscious of my age…. The general problem was that there wasn't enough politics talked to the audience. We tended to surf a wave, rather than building a permanent organisation.' Keith Flett agrees that the SWP failed to build a relationship with the thousands of people involved in RAR,

> The emphasis, correctly, was on activity and also a horror, again correct I think, of continuing a campaign for the sake of it once it had done its job. Yet the ANL never had its own paper and we simply forgot quite quickly many of the people who were involved if they didn't join.

Ian Birchall suggests that tensions between Rock Against Racism and the SWP were a reflection of a wider debate within the latter party. Several members of the party's leadership, including Chris Harman, felt that their paper, *Socialist Worker*, was too preoccupied with the concerns of young punks and failed as a result to put across a full Marxist politics. The RAR comrades replied that the SWP leadership had underestimated the potential of punk.[54]

One set-piece debate took place following the first ANL

Carnival. The SWP's magazine *Socialist Review* duly wrote up this event. David Widgery, Roger Huddle and others argued in a letter to the magazine that the coverage there had failed to express the energy and politics that Rock Against Racism had actually unveiled: 'Atrocious articles on Carnival. Mr Calico Nickers wants to harness and channel the energy of "Youth" who have ten times more idea of what's going down than your pretty average Marxist Editor ... Working class kids NOW are political and having fun without having to make five minute speeches to prove it.'[55] More mainstream comrades would get their revenge when Widgery's *Beating Time* appeared in the mid-1980s. Pat Stack told the readers of *Socialist Review* that its author had exaggerated the success of Rock Against Racism

> The first thing that struck me about the book was that the style of design and layout was dated, photographs thrown around the pages in chaotic style. A style, which like the fanzine, belongs now to another era.... For most of those active at the time there is little doubt that the ANL was key to the growth of RAR yet Widgery tends to put things the other way around.[56]

It would be wrong to exaggerate the divisions. While there were differences of emphasis and rows, such were signs of a healthy, growing movement. In all important respects, Widgery's tactics won out, and the movement was stronger for the role he played.

The process of arguing for the autonomy of RAR and ANL was not purely defensive. David Widgery, Red Saunders, Ruth Gregory and Syd Shelton hoped to use RAR to generate a new political language, less verbal and more visual, more youthful and populist than the socialism which they had inherited. Some of their politics can be seen from a one-off magazine, *Rentamob*, published by the self-appointed 'Agitprop bulletin of the SWP and supporters' in 1977, in other words at the height of the RAR phenomenon. Posters, street theatre, bands and graffiti, all were promoted, with the longest article dedicated to the success of a single badge, 'Stuff the Jubilee'. Beneath the slogan, 'Down with Slogans', *Rentamob* set out a vision of how RAR could bring fanzine culture to the left,

> Go to the average left-wing meeting – a dull pub room, a speaker who may be good, but followed by a generally lifeless question-and-answer

session and a list of exhortations from the chair. Yet the struggle for socialism is the struggle to tap the immense creative, imaginative ability of working people, the enthusiasm that is crushed by class society.[57]

In a later article, drawing on the lessons of RAR, Widgery chides his comrades for their occasional humourlessness. Thatcher was in power. Many good activists sought to make a virtue of their isolation:

> If socialism is transmitted in a deliberately doleful, pre-electronic idiom, if its emotional appeal is to working class sacrifice and middle class guilt, and if its dominant medium is the printed word and the public procession, it will simply bounce off people who have grown up this side of the 1960s watershed. And barely leave a dent behind.[58]

This is a key passage, the nearest Widgery came to a full statement of his mature beliefs. Strongly implied in the rejection of conventional British practices of self-denial was a conception of socialism as physical pleasure, as genuine self-emancipation, which is close to the Epicurean idea of human liberation found in the philosophical works of the early Marx,[59] and close also to the emphasis on socialism as play that appears in *The Right To Be Lazy*, the classic work of Paul Lafargue, Karl Marx's utopian son-in-law.[60]

So was David Widgery really a Leninist, or some kind of philosophic anarchist? The International Socialists were increasingly Leninist, having undergone a conversion towards such politics as late as 1970. In 1978, Widgery was charged with reviewing the third (penultimate) volume of Tony Cliff's biography of Vladimir Lenin for the SWP publication *Socialist Review*. He suggested that the true Lenin would be found somewhere between the staid reformism of British Eurocommunism, damned by Widgery as 'Len Murray, *Crossroads* and the Morning Star', and the obscure wilds of 'liberal anarchism (the other big late-1970s political growth industry)'. Lenin was celebrated above all for his *Philosophical Notebooks*, for having the courage to rip up his earlier admiration for Kautsky, and for having led the Soviet insurrection of 1917. The article was given a just title: 'Alternative Lenin'. Certainly Widgery's argument owed more to the confident utopianism of *The State and Revolution* than it did to the party-builders manual, *What Is To Be Done?*[61]

The success of Rock Against Racism and the Anti-Nazi League ensured that the late 1970s was David Widgery's finest moment. One of the founders of Rock Against Racism, he later became the movement's first historian. He wrote regularly for the RAR paper *Temporary Hoarding*, and helped to organise the hugely successful carnivals. The intervention of RAR, which involved Widgery along with many others, changed the sound of popular music, and helped to turn the racist tide in society, not just crushing the National Front, but also turning millions of young people decisively against all forms of racist prejudice. David Widgery was absolutely the prophet of the hour.

1979–92: keeping on keeping on

In the 1980s, the ascendancy of Margaret Thatcher in Britain and Ronald Reagan in America combined with a sustained offensive by capital. There was a sharp downturn in class struggle. In Britain, where strikes occurred, they were lost. One by one, the engineers, the steel workers, the dockers, the miners and the print workers were crushed. Meanwhile the allies of the working class also went into retreat, and by the end of the decade the socialist organisations, the women's movement, the campaigns for black liberation and for gay rights had all been reduced to a shell. Here is Widgery on Thatcher, from an article written in 1980:

> Mrs Thatcher's new philosophy was really very old – that the economy can only function if the rich are given more wealth and power. It follows that welfare has outlived its usfulness and it is now kind to be cruel. A new morality tale is announced, morally squalid, but, it is said, economically inevitable; profit is life's true motive, the market the final arbiter, welfare a corrupting influence on the poor, and respect for law best derived by force. Any objectors were pointed first at the evident disarray of Callaghan, then at the scale of the world slump and at length sweetly told 'There is simply no alternative.'[62]

Ironically, the cultural values of the left became more popular than ever, but with few exceptions the ideas lacked forces to carry them. Few socialists prospered. Some former activists were demoralised, others retreated into their private lives to escape. Meanwhile Widgery seems to have suffered increasing pain as a result of the polio he had suffered as a child. With one leg shorter than the other, he had been unable in the 1970s to take part in many of the marches he had helped to organise. By the 1980s, Widgery's illness was clearly much worse; he admitted to Ruth Gregory that he was 'in a lot of pain, a lot of the time'. David Widgery drank more and smoked, and was often rude or worse when drunk. According to Syd Shelton, 'he knew no moderation in anything'.[63]

Increasingly absorbed by his work life as a GP in the East End, David Widgery took his anger and his continuing inspiration from the lives of the people that he met through his work. The first essay he wrote about his doctoring began with a description of a typical twelve-hour day, 'Forty-three consultations, 430 decisions, 4,000 or 5,000 nuances, eye muscle alterations and mutual mis-understandings have left me emotionally drained.... But don't pity me. I get paid quite well, by my patients' standards. Pity the patients instead.'[64] The patients would also be the theme of the articles Widgery wrote from the mid-1980s for the *British Medical Journal*. David Widgery used this platform to condemn the priva-tisation of psychiatric care, to describe the East End from the perspective of the region's single parents, and to criticise the nation's psychiatrists for listening in silence to a dull homily from Prince Charles.[65] As his long-time partner Juliet Ash recalls, Widgery was proud to have followed Peter Sedgwick in writing about health, and proud to write for the *BMJ* – 'a socialist writing within such a terribly establishment body'.[66]

Three of Widgery's books, *Health in Danger* (1979), *The National Health: A Radical Perspective* (1988), and *Some Lives* (London: Sinclair-Stevenson, 1991), were also primarily devoted to the politics of the National Health Service. In *The National Health*, Widgery described how as a doctor he was continually reminded of just how important free health care was. There was some romanti-cising of his own class background (which was as much private-sector as public-sector middle class). Widgery was completely honest, though, when he expressed his dedication to the values of free health care:

> I had to write this book because I do care about what happens to the NHS, and I do not want to see its idealism squandered by Treasury accountants. I am an Attlee child, part of the generation shaped by

Beveridge and Bevan; I got the chance to train as a doctor because of postwar education and the grammar schools; I survived childhood illness in NHS hospitals; I know what even those quite modest reforms have meant to the qualities of people's lives; their health and human development. I cannot sit quietly by while the health service is dismantled before my eyes.[67]

Radical in the NHS

The narrative of *The National Health* is still in parts an institutional history of the NHS. In David Widgery's last book, *Some Lives*, though, the patients moved right to the front of his account. He described with care the lives of noisy kids and gay cruisers, cancer victims, newsagents with strike collection boxes on their counters, drunk night cleaners with daughters living in Chigwell, feuding neighbours and delicate babies, lonely grandparents and coughing dockers. Although these were his patients, they were the subject and not the object of the book, and Widgery's East Enders emerge as people with life and dignity:

> What always strikes me about those condescending documentaries about the poor East Enders, ignorant, ill and probably racist into the bargain, is exactly the reverse: how well the modern Cockneys do in circumstances which their 'betters' would find impossible. How much better they would do if their material conditions were hoisted a few notches up the class system. And yet how much more common decency, respect for humanity, honour and humour they possess than so many of the middle and upper classes who despite lip service to collective interests in fact approach life in a spirit of naked self-interest.[68]

Some Lives is an extraordinary social history of health and East London, and indeed London itself was now one of Widgery's greatest loves.[69] The book is remarkable for the ease with which Widgery moves from the detail to the general, from specific accounts of one patient's life to broader questions of politics and class. Widgery wrote about the politics of health with an insight and an eye for detail which have hardly been matched.

Some Lives is no dry exercise in social statistics. The arguments for democratic control of free health care are made almost accidentally. Conventional socialist authorities, both people and famous moments, appear, but never with the meaning that you might expect. Jenny Marx is quoted, a lurid passage in which she described her own suffering following her child's premature death. The Anti-Nazi League reappears, but only as an optimistic codicil at the end of a long discussion of the heart attacks, stomach ulcers and diabetes suffered by the victims of anti-Asian racism. One of the most extraordinary passages is devoted to the simple-seeming wonder of human birth:

> 'Delivered' through the biggest door that is ever opened in life. Such joy and physical creativity after the vomiting, piles and stretched pains of pregnancy, the dreadful force of labour and the blood and shit and waters of birth. To the final shock and delight of suckling the immaculate, slippery, vernix-coated living being: the proof that bodies aren't just wonderful ideas but they *work*.[70]

Central to David Widgery's book is a method that rooted more theoretical arguments in the physical reality of people's lives. In the above passage, blood and shit are creative forces that enable the body to function, and the resulting vitality serves as a reminder that people can turn all social obstacles to dust. The method of the book seemed to go far beyond the device of historical metaphor or allegory. People's bodies are no longer used as a means to explain another argument; they have become the most important part of the story.

Even the book's cover had a purpose, metamorphosing between hardback and paperback from an image of Widgery himself to the monstrous phallic symbol of Canary Wharf. The rise of this huge tower block, completed in 1990s, stood in *Some Lives* for the spread of private enterprise into socialised health care, where it could bring only harm. In the last pages of his book, Widgery allowed himself to leave behind the method of allusion, and state clearly his rejection of business involvement in health.

> The despoilation of our cities concerns me not just now as a Londoner but as a doctor.... I see the social cost which has been paid for it in the streets of the East End: the schizophrenic dementing in public, the young mother bathing the newborn in the sink of a B-and-B, the pensioner dying pinched and cold in a decrepit council flat.... These were the years when hospital after hospital was boarded up in the East End and the Prime Minister told us that the health service 'was safe in her hands' while waltzing off to private hospitals when she got ill.[71]

Against Thatcherism stood the values of collective action and public initiative that enabled a system of free health care to work. The two ideals were portrayed as antagonistic, irreconcilable. Yet Widgery made no attempt to predict the outcome of their conflict.

Widgery's Marxism

David Widgery died at home following a freak accident in 1992. The episode was not foreseen, and caused enormous sadness to his family. Afterwards, several large memorial meetings were held in his name. Two incidents from this time demonstrate the regard in which Widgery was held by his friends. The first was a speech given at the official memorial meeting by Darcus Howe, journalist and activist and follower of C.L.R. James.

> Darcus Howe said that he had fathered five children in Britain. The first four had grown up angry, fighting forever against the racism all around them. The fifth child, he said, had grown up 'black in ease'. Darcus attributed her 'space' to the Anti-Nazi League in general and to David Widgery in particular.[72]

It is a powerful compliment, yet not the most striking that David would receive. The second moment was less formal, but no less resonant in its symbolic meaning. At David Widgery's funeral, Michael Fenn, who had been a leading activist among the dockers whose strikes brought down Heath's Industrial Relations Act in 1972, appeared with the London Royal Docks shop stewards' committee banner, 'Arise Ye Workers', which he had kept from that time. Finding the banner, bringing it to Widgery's funeral – it is hard to imagine a more powerful epitaph.[73]

David Widgery's premature death brought several obituaries. Different friends remembered Widgery in different ways. For most members of Widgery's party, it was impossible to separate his life from the story of the SWP. According to Paul Foot, who worked alongside Widgery as a journalist on *Socialist Worker*,

> David was a restless man. He was always driving his body further than it could go in feverish pursuit of something unattainable. He was quite unlike the popular image of a revolutionary. He was the opposite of David Spart[74] or Citizen Smith.[75] He was not one for party exclusivity.

Most of his friends were outside the party. If he disagreed with the party, he said so. Indeed, so terrified was he of the image of the party hack that he would often say he disagreed when he didn't.[76]

In his obituary for the Socialist Workers' Party's magazine, *Socialist Review*, Bob Light pointed to the tensions between Widgery and the party to which he belonged:

> We need, we will always need, comrades like Widgery and Sedgwick to remind us that socialism starts and finishes with human beings and their needs. We need to be reminded that there is a world outside industrial sales and contact visiting. But what Dave only fitfully understood was that without the humdrum work of organisation and routine, the world will be condemned to stay a shithole for ever.[77]

Ian Birchall was the author of the Breton obituary which first motivated Widgery to join the IS. Later, he sparred with the younger man over his history of Rock Against Racism, *Beating Time*. Birchall admires Widgery's writing, but suggests there was a flightiness to his politics,

> I knew David Widgery right back from '68. A man of enormous talent, wonderful speaker, wonderful writer, but a man who was moving so quickly that he never bothered to correct his mistakes. All his books are brilliant, and they're all riddled with inaccuracies. If you write like that, in his sort of way, then checking the spelling of the Leighton Buzzards isn't the most important thing.

I asked Birchall how might Widgery have responded to this charge? His reply: 'He called me the sniffer dog of orthodox Trotskyism.'[78]

David Widgery's relationship to his own party was complex. The key episode was undoubtedly his involvement in Rock Against Racism. In this movement, Widgery and his friends were required to play a dual role. They themselves had been educated into a revolutionary tradition, and they hoped that some variant of their politics could inform this young campaign. Yet there was an equal challenge to prevent other, overenthusiastic comrades from jumping in, and stifling the united character of the project. It is in this context that Bob Light described Widgery as 'A radical humanist intellectual on permanent loan to revolutionary socialism'. There is no better summary of his political life.

This point raises in turn the question of lasting influence. To be a loyal critic within your own party is a lonely role. There is no lasting organisation or journal associated with Widgery's legacy, in the style (for example) of the library for Victor Serge in Moscow. Even those projects that have been mooted in memory of Rock Against Racism have mostly failed to get off the ground. If Widgery's lonely situation was not at fault, then the long industrial and political downturn that followed Thatcher's victory in 1979 should be blamed. Only in the last few years has a new generation of activists begun to break through, and even were they to be attracted to Widgery's politics it is unlikely that the exact pattern of his interests would be repeated. Widgery was too close to the present-day campaigns of his contemporaries to have his works blasted out of time.

Those from more historical backgrounds have tended to recall his work as a writer. Raphael Samuel remembered Widgery for *Some Lives*. 'The book confronts one as a kind of giant temporary hoarding on which East End lives have inscribed themselves as so many graffiti, often obscene, always harrowing (because this is a book of sufferings), yet also comic.' Samuel enjoyed Widgery's gallows humour,

> As a good libertarian, he rejoices in the Dionysiac and the transgressive. The stories usually begin staccato, as though culled from a doctor's casebook, and this no doubt was much of their original base. He amplified them with extended passages of oral testimony – and scraps of correspondence – which clearly go beyond the needs of the case. It is as though he was acting as an archivist for the future.[79]

Sheila Rowbotham remembered Widgery's preference for emotion over fact, 'The historian's guilt at inaccuracy was merely bizarre to him.'[80] Most of all Juliet Ash recalls David Widgery's restlessness. She recalls that he was always doing five things at once. 'He packed all his life in, when he was a doctor and on call, he would be writing a book. He packed more into 45 years than most people manage in 70.'[81]

This chapter is not a full biography, but merely an account of David Widgery's work as a writer. I have described his political background, the way in which it shaped his work, and the impact

of his writing, which set the tone for the entire anti-racist movement in the late 1970s. I have neglected his career as a doctor, most
of his essays and his journalism, and I have hardly mentioned at all
the anthologies, or the other powerful books he wrote in the political downturn of the 1980s. What I hope, though, is that the brief
account here gives a feel of Widgery dissident Marxism, which was
not just an abstract project of theoretical renewal, but linked instead to a mass movement that changed the lives of millions. If the
ideas of revolutionary socialism are ever to become living forces,
then they must be carried in people's hearts, and for that to happen the ideas must find their champions, people who have the
talent to persuade. David Widgery was one.

The dissident tradition

At the end of this book, it is appropriate to return to the themes with which the argument began. Early on, I referred to John Molyneux's characterisation of the 'real Marxist tradition'. This he identified as sharing three strands: a goal of revolutionary change, a scientific method, and an approach which connected theory and practice. This definition remains the best starting guide to the politics of revolutionary Marxism. Above all, it is a dynamic model, in which the final test has been to ask which writers and activists related their ideas to their practice, *in a living way*. This book has attempted to elaborate that final clause. A distinction has been made between 'orthodox' thinkers, who used their Marxism to defend existing projects, and dissidents, who reapplied Marxist categories, holding on to what was central, but who were not afraid to think for themselves. The purpose of this distinction has been to emphasise the point that in the period between the mid-1920s and 1989 this was a rare position. Especially because Marxism was used to justify the tyranny in Russia, so the revolutionary tradition was hidden beneath a muck of lies. It was difficult to be a dissident; such Marxists were reviled, slandered and worse. Although this book has described two monoliths, Stalinism and social democracy, more of the focus of this book has been on the negative consequences of the former. This is not because either pole was better or worse. In global terms, how could you choose between a social democracy that was corrupted by its collusion with Washington, and so-called Communism in Moscow? If this book has concentrated on the negative consequences of Moscow, it has done so for the reason that the corrosive effects of Stalinism were felt on the Marxist tradition itself. Precisely because the Stalinists were more ready to term themselves revolutionary socialists, precisely because in so many countries they were opponents of poverty and inequality, so their mistakes and worse did more damage to the left.

One advantage of this approach is that it clarifies who the Marxists were. It is not enough to assume that all deserved it who used the name. By concentrating on Molyneux's conception of revolutionary Marxism, a number of figures are already excluded from the tradition. The first category are those who turned against the working class, including Stalin and Mao and their followers in Russia and China. The second group would be those who ignored the workers, the academic Marxists, such as the Frankfurt School or their many descendants in the universities today. By insisting on dissidence, a further category of self-defined Marxists also fall out of the picture, namely those Maginot Marxists who used socialism purely as a defensive project, without subjecting it to the test of life.

Yet the question remains of whether the Marxist dissidents constitute a *tradition*? Throughout this book, I have used the word loosely, to refer to those who felt a common purpose with other Marxists of their type. Yet there has been more evidence of a tradition than this loose use of the term would imply. When Marxists have conceived of a revolutionary tradition, they have tended to view it as the possession of an organisation, often the socialist party. Typical is that axiom, associated with Lenin, 'the party is the memory of the class.' Inside a party, militants would meet to discuss the consequence of their interventions. Out of their deliberations, a collective knowledge would emerge. In this scheme, socialist parties should have been the prime means through which a Marxist continuity was established. Yet the dissident Marxists lived in a situation shaped by the *failure* of the workers' parties, the Communists and socialists who had seemed capable of transforming the world but became shells. At the start of the twenty-first century, there are few parties left which come in any way close to Lenin's ideal. Yet despite the utter failure of the social-democratic and Stalinist models, other parties and movements have been built, and more are constantly being rebuilt, from small beginnings, as must be done. Examples of more successful interventions by Marxist parties have been discussed in previous chapters, and there is no need to repeat them here.

The best sign of a continuity between the writers discussed in this book is the presence of 'carriers', a set of writers whose work became a common property among the dissidents. In a previous book, I have described how a generation of dissident Marxists in the 1930s – including Daniel Guérin, Victor Serge, Antonio Gramsci, August Thalheimer and especially Leon Trotsky – came to a common, dialectical theory as to how fascism should be opposed.[1] The dissidents described in this book have included David Widgery, who learned from Peter Sedgwick, who translated Victor Serge. Karl Korsch corresponded with the great German dramatist Bertolt Brecht. Korsch and Serge both contributed to the debates in American journals over the spread of managerial society. Indeed it is from this well that much of Harry Braverman's distinctive Marxism sprung. Braverman learned from Leon Trotsky, Hal Draper and C.L.R. James. James was a friend of Torr's protégé, Edward Thompson. The economic arguments of Paul Baran, Paul Sweezy and Samir Amin intersected at several points. Henein and Amin were both shaped by wartime Cairo. The strategies of Amin and Rodney were nigh-on identical. Georges Henein reported deriving inspiration from the novels of Victor Serge,[2] while as a group the Egyptian Trotskyists were influenced by André Breton. Breton also worked with Serge, as Sedgwick did with Tony Cliff, Dona Torr with E.P. Thompson, Trotsky with Guérin, and so on. The connections that bound together the various dissidents were every bit as dense as a knotted string.

The most vital politics in the present are those of the anti-capitalist movement. It is a diverse mix of protesters, some of whom have backgrounds in classical Marxist parties, while others are dissidents. Single-issue protesters march alongside socialists, anarchists, 'light' and 'deep' greens. The aesthetic of the movement is cut from the same cloth as Widgery's *OZ*, dayglo stickers and all. Yet what brings together the hippies and the politicos is a sense of totality. Corporate America seeks to remake everything, destroy all. Previously unity could be forged around specific, local campaigns. We have spent too long chasing small exploiters and let the real monsters – the World Bank and the IMF – go free.

Perry Anderson, in one of his books, criticises the Marxists of his own generation for their failure to live up to the high standards of the socialist past. Writing of post-war Marxism, he states that 'It is impossible to point out any single body of writing in these years which reveals, even faintly, the kind of conceptual attack, the combination of political resolution and theoretical imagination that marked the great interventions of Luxemburg or Lenin, Trotsky or Parvus.'[3] Anderson's criticism can be read as a lament, but would be better taken as a challenge. The dissidents who are re-membered in the future will be those who related their ideas to class, those Marxists who found a mass audience, and those who were not afraid to think for themselves. It is in the movements that we cannot yet know, and in the great rebellions to come, that such dissidents are most likely to emerge, and the revolutionary politics of Marxism will again be renewed.

Notes

Introduction

1. N. Klein, *No Logo* (London: Flamingo, 2000), pp. 107–27.
2. A point made by R. Huq, 'The Right to Rave: Opposition to the Criminal Justice and Public Order Act 1994', in T. Jordan and A. Lent (eds), *Storming the Millennium: The New Politics of Change* (London: Lawrence & Wishart, 1999), pp. 15–35.
3. For the relationship between Seattle and the traditions of the left, see J. Charlton, 'Talking Seattle', *International Socialism Journal* 86 (2000), pp. 3–19.
4. D. Renton and J. Eaden, *The Communist Party of Great Britain since 1920* (London: Palgrave, 2002).
5. The account here is based on J. Molyneux, 'What Is the Real Marxist Tradition?', *International Socialism Journal* 20 (1983), pp. 3–55.
6. P. Sedgwick, 'The Pretenders: An Answer to R. Emmett', in J. Higgins (ed.), *A Socialist Review* (London: Pluto, 1965), pp. 163–7.
7. I. Deutscher, *Marxism, Wars and Revolutions* (London: Verso, 1984), p. 245; also, I. Deutscher, *Marxism in Our Time* (London: Jonathan Cape, 1972), p. 18.
8. This is the argument of D. Renton, *Classical Marxism* (Bristol: New Clarion Press, 2002).
9. Although at least one recent book interprets Orwell as a 'literary Trotskyist', suggesting that his interests were close to the politics discussed here. J. Newsinger, *Orwell's Politics* (London: Macmillan, 1999).
10. H. Draper, *The Two Souls of Socialism* (London: Bookmarks, 1996 edn).
11. 'An Open Letter to Leszek Kolakowski', in E.P. Thompson, *The Poverty of Theory and Other Essays* (London: Merlin, 1987), pp. 92–192, here p. 123.

Chapter 1

1. S. Kotkin, *Magnetic Mountain: Stalinism as a Civilization* (Berkeley: University of California Press, 1997); S. Kotkin, *Steeltown, USSR* (Berkeley: University of California Press, 1991).
2. Cited in M. Haynes, *Russia: Class and Power 1917–2000* (London: Bookmarks, 2002), p. 11.
3. The role played by such dissident Marxists in the struggle against fascism is described in D. Renton, *Fascism: Theory and Practice* (London: Pluto, 1999).
4. R. Luxemburg, *The Junius Pamphlet* (Colombo: Young Socialists, 1992 edn), p. 8.
5. There is a useful summary of these theories in A. Westoby, 'Conceptions of Communist States', in D. Held et al., *States and Societies* (Oxford: Blackwell, 1983), pp. 219–42.
6. L. Trotsky, *The Revolution Betrayed: What Is the Soviet Union and Where Is it Going?* (New York: Pathfinder, 1972 edn).
7. C.L.R. James, *The Black Jacobins: Toussaint l'Ouverture and the San Domingo Revolution* (London: Allison & Busby, 1980).
8. J. Molyneux, *Leon Trotsky's Theory of Revolution* (London: Macmillan, 1982).
9. J.-P. Sartre, *Critique de la raison dialectique* (Paris: Gallimard, 1960).
10. There is a useful potted history in M. Kenny, *The First New Left* (London: Lawrence & Wishart, 1995).
11. S. Rowbotham, *Women in Movement: Feminism and Social Action* (London: Routledge, 1992), p. 259.
12. J. P. Cannon, *The I.W.W.* (New York: Pioneer Publishers, 1956), p. 31.
13. H. Braverman, 'Marx in the Modern World', *American Socialist*, November 1957, p. 5; cited in M.G. Livingstone, 'Harry Braverman: Marxist Activist and Theorist', paper given to the conference 'Explorations in the History of US Trotskyism', September–October 2000.

Chapter 2

1. V. Serge, ' La Vie Intellectuelle en Russie (1): Mayakovsky', *Clarté* 67 (1924), pp. 504–8, 504.
2. 'The Streets Are Our Palettes: A Tribute to Vladimir Mayakovsky', in D. Widgery, *Preserving Disorder* (London: Pluto, 1989), pp. 88–96, 89.
3. Serge, ' La Vie Intellectuelle en Russie (1)', p. 506.
4. Widgery, 'The Streets Are Our Palettes', p. 90.
5. P. Edwards (ed.), *Blast: Vorticism 1914–1918* (Aldershot: Ashgate, 2000), p. 18.
6. Widgery, 'The Streets Are Our Palettes', p. 90.
7. Serge, ' La Vie Intellectuelle en Russie (1)', 507.
8. S.A. Smith, *Red Petrograd* (Cambridge: Cambridge University Press, 1983).
9. L. Trotsky, *Literature and Revolution* (London: Redwords, 1991), p. 182.
10. Widgery, 'The Streets Are Our Palettes', p. 91.
11. Serge, ' La Vie Intellectuelle en Russie', 508.

12. Widgery, 'The Streets Are Our Palettes', p. 93.
13. 'The Work of Art in the Age of Mechanical Reproduction', in W. Benjamin, *Illuminations* (London: Fontana, 1992 edn), pp. 211–44.
14. Several of the documents of early left Bolsheviks are reproduced in R. Kowalski, *The Russian Revolution 1917–1921* (London: Routledge, 1997).
15. Cited in S. Fitzpatrick, *The Commissariat of Enlightenment: Soviet Organization of Education and the Arts under Lunacharsky: October 1917 to 1921* (Cambridge: Cambridge University Press, 1970), p. 125.
16. L. Trotsky, *On Literature and Art* (New York: Pathfinder, 1977), p. 112; cited in B. Watson, *Art, Class and Cleavage: Quantumlumcunque Concerning Materialist Esthetix* (London: Quartet, 1998), p. 58.
17. M. Lewin, *Lenin's Last Struggle* (London: Faber & Faber, 1969).
18. M. Rosen and D. Widgery, *The Chatto Book of Dissent* (London: Chatto & Windus, 1991), pp. 87–8.
19. Widgery, 'The Streets Are Our Palettes', p. 95.
20. Serge, ' La Vie Intellectuelle en Russie (1)', p. 508.
21. V. Serge, *Memoirs of a Revolutionary 1901–1941* (Oxford: Oxford University Press, 1963), p. 268
22. I. Deutscher, *The Prophet Unarmed: Trotsky 1921–1929* (Oxford: Oxford University Press, 1959), p. 187.
23. A.D.P. Briggs, *Vladimir Mayakovsky: A Tragedy* (Oxford: Meeuws, 1979), p. 2.
24. Widgery, 'The Streets Are Our Palettes', p. 89.
25. F. Engels, *Socialism: Utopian and Scientific* (London: Bookmarks, 1993 edn), p. 67.
26. A. Kollontai, *The Autobiography of a Sexually Emancipated Woman* (New York: Herder, 1971), p. 9.
27. The account here is based on A. Holt, 'Introduction', in A. Kollontai, *Selected Writings* (London: Allison & Busby, 1977), pp. 13–27.
28. B. Farnsworth, *Aleksandra Kollontai: Socialism, Feminism and the Bolshevik Revolution* (Stanford, CA: Stanford University Press, 1980), pp. 16–18.
29. L. German, *Sex, Class and Socialism* (London: Bookmarks, 1989), pp. 229–30.
30. C. Rosenberg, *Women and Perestroika: Present, Past and Future for Women in Russia* (London: Bookmarks, 1989), p. 79.
31. C. Porter, 'Introduction', in A. Kollontai, *Love of Worker Bees* (London: Virago, 1977), pp. 7–20, 13.
32. A. Kollontai, 'Women's Labour in Economic Development' (1924), cited in T. Cliff, *Women's Struggle and Women's Liberation: 1640 to the Present Day* (London: Bookmarks, 1984), p. 140.
33. Rosenberg, *Women and Perestroika*, p. 81.
34. Farnsworth, *Aleksandra Kollontai*, p. 184.
35. Kollontai, *Love of Worker Bees*.
36. 'Communism and the Family', in A. Kollontai, *On Women's Liberation* (London: Bookmarks, 1998), pp. 35–48, here 43, 45, 38
37. M. Liebman, *Leninism under Lenin* (London: Merlin Press, 1975).
38. R. Service, *Lenin: A Biography* (Cambridge, MA: Harvard University Press, 2000); O. Figes, *A People's Tragedy: The Russian Revolution 1891–1924* (London: Jonathon Cape, 1996).

39. V.I. Lenin, 'What Is To Be Done? Burning Questions of Our Movement', in *Collected Works*, Volume 5 (London: Lawrence & Wishart, 1961), pp. 347–530.

40. C. Porter, *Alexandra Kollontai: A Biography* (London: Virago, 1980), p. 344.

41. Holt, 'Introduction', p. 20.

42. Cited in S. Rowbotham, *Women, Resistance and Revolution* (Harmondsworth: Penguin, 1972), p. 138.

43. Rosenberg, *Women and Perestroika*, pp. 87–95.

44. Holt, 'Introduction', pp. 22, 25.

45. A.L. Tait, *Lunacharsky: Poet of the Revolution (1875–1907)* (Birmingham: Birmingham Slavonic Monographs, 1985), p. 105.

46. I. Deutscher, 'Introduction', in A. Lunacharsky, *Revolutionary Silhouettes* (London: Penguin, 1967), pp. 9–26, here 19.

47. Tait, *Lunacharsky: Poet of the Revolution*, p. 5.

48. Deutscher, 'Introduction', p. 13.

49. V.I. Lenin, 'Materialism and Empirio-Criticism', in *Collected Works*, Volume 14 (London: Lawrence & Wishart, 1972), pp. 17–362.

50. Tait, *Lunacharsky: Poet of the Revolution*, p. 2.

51. Deutscher, 'Introduction', p. 17.

52. S. Fitzpatrick, *The Commissariat of the Enlightenment: Soviet Organization of Education and the Arts under Lunacharsky 1917–1921* (Cambridge: Cambridge University Press, 1970), p. 9

53. Deutscher, 'Introduction', p. 18.

54. Fitzpatrick, *The Commissariat of the Enlightenment*, p. xv; also L. Kirschenbaum, *Small Comrades: Revolutionising Childhood in Soviet Russia 1917–1933* (Melbourne: Routledge Falmer, 2001).

55. L. Trotsky, *Writings of Leon Trotsky* [1933–34] (New York: Pathfinder, 1972), p. 185.

56. Tait, *Lunacharsky: Poet of the Revolution*, p. 3.

57. Deutscher, 'Introduction', p. 21.

58. Fitzpatrick, *The Commissariat of the Enlightenment*, p. 2.

59. Lunacharsky, *Revolutionary Silhouettes*, pp. 10, 43, 65, 75, 134.

60. Fitzpatrick, *The Commissariat of the Enlightenment*, p. 59.

61. Deutscher, 'Introduction', p. 20.

62. 'Theses on the Problems of Marxist Criticism', in A. Lunacharsky, *On Literature and Art* (Moscow: Progress Publishers, 1965), pp. 11–27, here 11, 12, 22.

63. R. C. Tucker, *Stalin in Power: The Revolution from Above* (New York: W.W. Norton, 1990), p. 309.

64. S. Weissman, *Victor Serge: The Course is Set on Hope* (London and New York: Verso, 2001), p. xi.

65. Serge, *Memoirs of a Revolutionary*, p. 34.

66. The account of the trials here is based on Serge's *Memoirs*. Meanwhile, Richard Parry has suggested that Serge played a less creditable part, distancing himself from the 'bandits' on trial, in a way that he had not done in print. R. Parry, *The Bonnot Gang* (London: Rebel Press, 1987), pp. 33–6, 156, 180–2.

67. V. Serge, *Year One of the Russian Revolution* (London and New York:

Bookmarks, Pluto and Writers & Readers, 1992), p. 369.

68. D. Guérin, *Anarchism: From Theory to Practice* (New York: Monthly Review Press, 1970), p. 97; there is a useful discussion of the role of the anarchists in the revolution in A. Rosmer, *Lenin's Moscow*, trans. and ed. I. Birchall (London: Bookmarks, 1971), pp. 114–19.

69. Serge, *Memoirs*, p. 128; Serge's shifting views on Kronstadt constitute a major theme in D. Cotterill (ed.), *The Serge–Trotsky Papers: Correspondence and Other Writings between Victor Serge and Leon Trotsky* (London: Pluto, 1994).

70. Serge, *Memoirs*, p. 222.

71. V. Serge, *Littérature et Révolution* (1932); Ian Birchall describes Serge's sympathy for the French ultra-left supporters of proletarian culture, notably Henry Poulaille, in I. Birchall, 'Proletarian Culture', *Critique* 28–9 (1997), pp. 75–98.

72. Serge, *Memoirs*, p. 315.

73. V. Serge, *Destiny of a Revolution* (London: Hutchinson, n.d.).

74. Serge, *Memoirs*, p. 348.

75. The crossing is described in C. Lévi-Strauss, *Tristes tropiques*, trans. J. and D. Weightman (Harmondsworth: Penguin, 1976), pp. 26–7.

76. V. Gorkin, 'The Last Years of Victor Serge', *Revolutionary History* 5/3 (1994), pp. 199–208.

77. R. Greeman, 'Memoirs of a Revolutionary', *International Socialism* 94 (2002), pp. 103–14.

78. L. Trotsky, *The Revolution Betrayed: What is the Soviet Union and Where is it Going?* (New York: Pathfinder, 1972 edn).

79. V. Serge, *Seize fusillés: où va la Révolution Russe?* (Paris: Spartacus, 1936).

80. V. Serge, 'Le dernier livre de Trotski: Staline', unpublished manuscript dated 1946, Serge Archive, Yale University, quoted in R. Greeman, 'Communism's Collapse: The Political Heritage of Victor Serge', *Rethinking Marxism* 7/2 (1994).

81. C.L.R. James and R. Dunayevskaya, *The Invading Soviet Society* (New York: Johnson–Forest Tendency, 1947); T. Cliff, *State Capitalism in Russia* (London: Pluto, 1955 edn).

82. R. Hilferding, 'State Capitalism or Totalitarian Economy?', *Left*, September 1947; A. Ciliga, *The Russian Enigma* (London: Ink Links, 1979). Susan Weissman argues strongly that Serge saw Russia as 'bureaucratic collectivist', in S. Weissman, 'On Stalinism', *Critique* 28–9 (1997), pp. 197–222, and Weissman, *Victor Serge*.

Chapter 3

1. G. Plekhanov, *The Role of the Individual in History* (London: Lawrence & Wishart, 1951 edn), p. 54; K. Kautsky, *The Materialist Conception of History* (Yale: Yale University Press, 1988 edn), p. 482.

2. J. Rees, *The Algebra of Revolution: The Dialectic and the Classical Marxist Tradition* (London: Routledge, 1998), pp. 135–43.

3. P. Goode, *Karl Korsch: A Study in Western Marxism* (London: Macmillan, 1979), pp. 70–71. Korsch was familiar with Lenin's, 'On the Significance of Militant Materialism' (1922), which is quoted in K. Korsch, *Marxism*

and Philosophy (London: Pluto, 1970 edn), p. 9. However, Lenin's most important philosophical work, the Philosophical Notebooks, were not published until after his death. They can be read today in V.I. Lenin, *Collected Works*, Volume 38 (Moscow and London: Progress Publishers and Lawrence & Wishart, 1976 edn). ''On the Significance of Militant Materialism' is located in V.I. Lenin, *Collected Works*, Volume 36 (Moscow and London: Progress Publishers and Lawrence & Wishart, 1966 edn), pp. 227–36.

 4. E. Gerlach, 'Karl Korsch's Undogmatic Marxism', *International Socialism* 19 (1963), pp. 22–7; Korsch, *Marxism and Philosophy*; K. Korsch, *Three Essays on Marxism* (London: Pluto, 1971); D. Kellner (ed.), *Karl Korsch: Revolutionary Theory* (Austin: University of Texas Press, 1977); K. Korsch, *Karl Marx* (New York: Humanities Press 1963 edn).

 5. Goode, *Karl Korsch*, p. 11.

 6. For a fuller treatment of Korsch's views on factory councils, see Goode, *Karl Korsch*, pp. 58–9; Kellner, *Karl Korsch*, pp. 18–24.

 7. H. Korsch, 'Memories of Karl Korsch', *New Left Review* 76 (1972), pp. 34–46; Kellner, *Karl Korsch*, pp. 40–48.

 8. M. Jay, *The Dialectical Imagination: A History of the Frankfurt School and the Institute of Social Research 1923–1950* (London and Boston: Little, Brown, 1973).

 9. Korsch, *Marxism and Philosophy*, pp. 58–9.

10. Ibid., pp. 54–60.

11. Ibid., pp. 84–5; F. Engels, *Ludwig Feuerbach and the End of Classical German Philosophy* (Peking: Foreign Languages Publishing House, 1976 edn); there is also a useful discussion of Marxism as a negation of philosophy in T. Eagleton, *Marx and Freedom* (London: Phoenix, 1998), pp. 3–16.

12. For Korsch's influence on Brecht, B. Brecht, *Letters* (London: Methuen, 1990), pp. 133, 145–6, 153, 165–7, 238, 296, 352, here 296.

13. K. Korsch, 'The Present State of the Problem of "Marxism and Philosophy"', in *Marxism and Philosophy*, pp. 89–128.

14. Korsch, *Three Essays*, pp. 61, 68.

15. Goode, *Karl Korsch*, p. 111.

16. Kellner, *Karl Korsch*, pp. 163.

17. Ibid., pp. 147, 166.

18. Korsch, *Karl Marx*, p. 110.

19. Ibid., p. 79.

20. Ibid., p. 136.

21. Ibid., p. 229.

22. M. van Elteren, 'Karl Korsch and Lewinian Social Psychology: Failure of a Project', *History of the Human Sciences* 5/2 (1992), pp. 33–62; the results of the research are published as K. Korsch and K. Lewin, 'Mathematical Constructs in Psychology and Sociology', *Journal of Unified Sciences* 9 (1939).

23. K. Korsch, 'Human Nature: The Marxian View', *Journal of Philosophy* 42/26 (1945), pp. 712–18, p. 718; K. Korsch, 'The World Historians', *Partisan Review* 9/5 (1942), pp. 354–71. There is a full list of these articles in the bibliography in Goode, *Karl Korsch*, pp. 218–28.

24. K. Korsch, 'Ten Theses on Marxism Today (1950)', *Telos* 26 (1975–6), pp. 40–41.
25. Gerlach, 'Karl Korsch's Undogmatic Marxism', pp. 22–7; F. Halliday, 'Karl Korsch: An Introduction', in Korsch, *Marxism and Philosophy*, pp. 7–23, p. 22; Goode, *Karl Korsch*, pp. 186–7; P. Anderson, *Considerations on Western Marxism* (London: New Left Books, 1976), pp. 29–30, 49–50.
26. E.J. Hobsbawm, *Revolutionaries* (London: Quartet, 1977), p. 160.
27. D. Kellner, 'Korsch's Revolutionary Historicism', *Telos* 26 (1975–6), pp. 170–93; L. Kolakowski, *Main Currents of Marxism, Its Origins, Growth and Dissolution*, Volume 3: *The Breakdown* (Oxford: Oxford University Press, 1981), pp. 308–23; H. Sheehan, *Marxism and the Philosophy of Science: A Critical History*, Volume 1: *The First 100 Years* (Princeton and London: Princeton University Press, 1985), pp. 255–73, p. 273.
28. Korsch, *Karl Marx*, p. 38
29. Goode, *Karl Korsch*, p. 82.
30. Ibid., p. 147.
31. Korsch, *Karl Marx*, p. 197.
32. G. Lukács, *History and Class Consciousness* (London: Merlin, 1971 edn); also, for an analysis of Lukács's Marxism as it developed over time, see Rees, *Algebra of Revolution*, pp. 202–61.
33. Including G. Lukács, *The Historical Novel* (London: Penguin, 1981 edn); G. Lukács, *The Destruction of Reason* (London: Merlin, 1980).

Chapter 4

1. A. Callinicos, *Trotskyism* (Milton Keynes: Open University Press, 1990), pp. 1–2.
2. Paris: Corti, 1938.
3. Paris: Éditions de Minuit, 1947.
4. Paris: Corti, 1949.
5. Paris: Mercure de France, 1956.
6. The notion of 'literary Trotskyism' is explored in J. Newsinger, *Orwell's Politics* (London: Macmillan, 1999).
7. J. Berque et al., *Hommages à Georges Henein* (Paris: Le Pond de L'Épée, 1974); S. Alexandrian, *Georges Henein* (Paris: Seghers, 1981).
8. A. Abdalla, *The Student Movement and National Politics in Egypt 1923–73* (London: Al Saqi, 1985); J. Beinin, *Was the Red Flag Flying There? Marxist Politics and the Arab–Israeli Conflict in Egypt and Israel 1948–65* (Berkeley: University of California Press, 1990); J. Beinin and Z. Lockman, *Workers on the Nile* (Princeton, NJ: I.B. Tauris, 1988); E.J. Goldberg, 'Tinker, Tailor, Textile Worker: Class and Politics in Egypt 1930–54', Ph.D. thesis, University of California, 1983; P. Frank, *The Fourth International: The Long March of the Trotskyists* (London: Ink, 1979); R.J. Alexander, *International Trotskyism 1929–85: A Documentary Analysis of the Movement* (Durham and London: Durham University Press, 1991), p. 249; S. Botman, *The Rise of Egyptian Communism 1939–70* (New York: New York University Press, 1988), pp. 12–16.
9. For a balance sheet on the Third World revolutions, see T. Cliff, *Deflected Permanent Revolution* (London: Socialist Workers Party, 1986 edn).

10. W. Ghali, *Beer in the Snooker Club* (London: Serpents Tail, 1987); A. Aciman, *Out of Egypt* (London: Random House, 1996).

11. Alexandrian, *Georges Henein*, pp. 9–15.

12. M. Richardson and K. Fijalkowski, *Surrealism Against the Current: Tracts and Declarations* (London: Pluto, 2001), pp. 203–4.

13. See http://melior.univ-montp3.fr/ra_forum/fr/jacquier_c/reynaud_paligot_surreal.t.html; Richardson and Fijalkowski, *Surrealism Against the Current*, pp. 117–9.

14. G. Perrault, *A Man Apart: The Life of Henri Curiel* (London: Zed Books, 1987).

15. The authors of this statistic were the Henein group. 'Egypte: Un Manifeste Programmatique des Trotskystes Égyptiens', *Quatrième Internationale*, July–August 1947. The arguments in this section are largely based on A. Alexander, 'From National Liberation to Social Revolution: Egypt 1945–53', in K. Flett and D. Renton (eds), *New Approaches to Socialist History* (London: New Clarion Press, 2003), pp. 92–104.

16. J. Heyworth-Dunne, *Religious and Political Trends in Modern Egypt* (London: Near and Middle East Monographs, 1950), p. 63.

17. R.P. Mitchell, *The Society of the Muslim Brothers* (London: Middle East Monographs, 1969), pp. 308–9.

18. Perrault, *A Man Apart*, pp. 62–3.

19. 'Note on Communist Policy for Egypt', undated document (1951), in the Communist Party of Great Britain archive (CP) in the National Museum of Labour History in Manchester: CP/CENT/INT/56/03.

20. Botman, *The Rise of Egyptian Communism 1939–70*, pp. 12–16.

21. L. Soliman, *Pour une histoire profane de la Palestine* (Paris: La Découverte, 1989), p. 92.

22. Anwar Kamal (1919–1973) was a poet. Ramses Younan was a graphic artist who later acquired fame as a champion of abstraction. See www.imarabe.org/temp/expo/coll-kinda/coll-kinda-dossp.html. Lotfallah Soliman (1919–1995) was a writer and journalist. He was later briefly an adviser to the FLN in Algeria, 'Loutfallah Soliman', *Cahiers Léon Trotsky* 61 (1998), pp. 123–4.

23. The group was more Egyptian than any of its rivals on the left, but a small number of its cadres were taken from Egypt's minorities. Both Henein and Younane were Copts, born into the Christian minority. This should not be surprising; members of oppressed or marginalised groups have often provided revolutionary movements with their leadership.

24. Botman, *The Rise of Egyptian Communism 1939–70*, p. 14.

25. J. Damien, *Qui est monsieur Aragon?* (Cairo: Éditions Masses, 1944), p. 10. There is a useful discussion of surrealism and anti-Stalinism in the essays collected as 'The International Federation of Independent Revolutionary Artists', *Revolutionary History* 7/2 (1999), pp. 203–18. Also M. Nadeau, *The History of Surrealism*, trans. R. Howard, intro. R. Shattuck (London: Jonathan Cape, 1968 edn).

26. Botman, *The Rise of Egyptian Communism 1939–70*, p. 14; at various times there have been copies of *al-Tatawwur* in Dar al-Kutub, the national library in Cairo; there are also copies in Harvard.

27. From *al-Tatawwur* 3 (March 1940), quoted in Alexandrian, *Georges*

Henein, p. 30.

28. Interview with Alex Acheson, published as 'The Wartime Agitation of a Trotskyist Soldier', in S. Bornstein and A. Richardson, *War and the International: A History of the Trotskyist Movement in Britain 1937–49* (London: Socialist Platform, 1986), pp. 246–7. Alec Acheson (1912–1996) was a supporter of the Revolutionary Socialist League, and later the RCP. For his obituary, see *Revolutionary History* 6/4 (1998), pp. 242–3. Iqbal Alaily's book was *Vertu de l'Allemagne* (Cairo: Éditions Masses, 1940). The introduction to her collection is republished in translation in P. Rosemont, *Surrealist Women: An International Anthology* (Austin: University of Texas Press, 1998), pp. 192–5.

29. Botman, *The Rise of Egyptian Communism 1939–70*, p. 15.

30. Perrault, *A Man Apart*, pp. 93–4.

31. Botman, *The Rise of Egyptian Communism 1939–70*, p. 15; this journal is referred to in RCP, 'News On Sections', Internal Bulletin, March 1945, copy in the Jock Haston papers (DJH), in the Brynmoor Jones Library, University of Hull: DJH/15A/21/y, and in Alexandrian, *Georges Henein*, p. 34; I have not been able to locate any surviving copies of the original paper.

32. As one consequence of this activity, the young Israeli Trotskyist Tony Cliff considered emigrating to Egypt. He has described asking the sister of one comrade to find out about the group. 'Sadly, the report I got from my friend after visiting Egypt was very disappointing indeed. According to her, the tiny Trotskyist group was made up of dilettantes. One person told her, "If you want to find the Trotskyists in Cairo, look around until you find three or four Rolls Royce cars in the street together; you'll know then the Trotskyists are meeting." (Of course this was a big exaggeration.)' See T. Cliff, *A World to Win: Life of a Revolutionary* (London: Bookmarks, 2000), pp. 34–5.

33 A copy of the Palestinians' letter was printed in the paper *Workers International News*, December 1944; Soliman, *Pour une Histoire Profane*, pp. 92–4; Beinin, *Was the Red Flag Flying There?*, pp. 144–60.

34. 'Egypt', *Fourth International* 8/7 (July–August 1947).

35. Magdi Wahba, in Berque et al., *Hommages à Georges Henein*, p. 110.

36. 'Report on the Egyptian General Elections', internal RCP document, January 1945, DJH/15G/8; RCP, 'News on Sections', Internal Bulletin, March 1945; Alexandrian, *Georges Henein*, p. 34.

37. G. Henein to A. Keen, 30 July 1945, DJH/15F/8.

38. G. Henein to A. Acheson, 22 October 1945, DJH/15F/8.

39. S.V. Bardell to CP, 25 January 1946, CP/CENT/INT/56/03.

40. G. Henein to RCP, 22 December 1945, DJH/15B/58/1. The pamphlet was A. Kamal, *For a Classless Society* (Cairo: Éditions Masses, 1945).

41. *Grades Largeurs*, Autumn–Winter 1981, pp 78, 86, 100.

42. Beinin and Lockman, *Workers on the Nile*, p. 348. There is a vivid description of the events of 9 February in the left-Wafdist paper *al-Wafd al-Misry*, 10 February 1948, copies in Dar al-Kutub, Cairo.

43. '4th International' to J. Haston, undated, February 1946, DJH/15B/58/1.

44. Quoted in 'Activities of Egyptian Trotskyists', *Socialist Appeal*, 24 May 1946.

45. S.V. Bardell, 'The Conflict in Egypt', unpublished document, April 1946, CP/CENT/INT/56/03; 'Terror in Egypt: Trotskyists lead in Egyptian Struggle', *Socialist Appeal*, Mid-July 1946; 'Egypte: Les Trotskystes dans la Lutte Contre le Gouvernement', *Quatrième Internationale*, August–September 1946.

46. For Acheson, see Bornstein and Richardson, *War and the International*, pp. 246–7; for the controversy between the IKD and the International Secretariat of the Fourth International, see Alexander, *International Trotskyism*, pp. 425–30.

47. Jock Haston to 'Lout., Georges, Ramsis, Ibrahim', 17 April 1946, DJH/15B/58/1.

48. Henein actually remained in Egypt. For example in 1947 his visitors included the poet Henri Michaux, see the account at www.magazine-litteraire.com/archives/ar_mich2.htm.

49. Haston to RCP, 24 April 1946, DJH/15B/58/1; Henein to Nicholas Calas, 10 January 1948, quoted in Berque et al., *Hommages à Georges Henein*, p. 42.

50. J. Deane, 'Summary from Files', 10 February 1947, MRC/325/29/D47 (5).

51. L. Soliman, 'Egyptian Notes', *Fourth International* 7/11 (November 1946); A. Schwartz (Bookshop Culture) to *Socialist Appeal*, 3 December 1946, DJH/15B/58/1; 'Egypt', *Fourth International* 8/7 (July–August 1947); 'Loutfallah Soliman', *Cahiers Léon Trotsky* 61 (1998), pp. 123–4.

52. Richardson and Fijalkowski, *Surrealism Against the Current*, pp. 46–8; G. Henein, *Carnets 1940–1973: L'Esprit Frappeur* (Paris: Écrits, 1980), pp. 42, 67.

53. G. Henein, La Prestige de la Terreur (Cairo: Éditions Masses, 1945). Text available at http://pages.globetrotter.net/charro/hermes4/henein.htm.

54. The last line is almost untranslatable. 'Il n'est que temps de redorer le blason des chimères.' Literally, 'It is only time to paint again with gold the crest of chimeras.'

Chapter 5

1. For a discussion of the politics of the Communist Party Historians' Group, see E. Hobsbawm, 'The History Group of the Communist Party', in M. Cornforth (ed.), *Rebels and Their Causes: Essays in Honour of A.L. Morton* (London, 1978), pp. 21–48; V. Kiernan, 'Making Histories', *Our History Journal* 8 (1984), pp. 7–10; D. Parker, 'The Communist Party and its Historians 1946–89', *Socialist History* 12 (1997), pp. 33–58; and B. Schwarz, '"The People" in History: The Communist Party Historians' Group', in R. Johnson et. al. (ed.), *Making Histories: Studies in History-Writing and Politics* (London: Hutchinson, 1982), pp. 44–95. The minutes of the party historians are held among the Communist Party files (CP) in the National Museum of Labour History, in Manchester, at CP/CENT/CULT/5/11.

2. Interview with Dorothy Thompson, 23 September 1998.

3. R. First and A. Scott, *Olive Schreiner* (London: Andre Deutsch, 1980).

4. D. Thompson, *Outsiders: Class, Gender and Nation* (London: Verso, 1993), pp. 10–11; interview with Dorothy Thompson, 23 September 1998. For Brigadier William Wyndham Torr, see *Who's Who*, 1956.
5. Thompson, *Outsiders*, pp. 10–11; J. Callaghan, 'The Communists and the Colonies: Anti-imperialism between the Wars', in G. Andrews, N. Fishman and K. Morgan (eds), *Opening the Books: Essays on the Cultural History of the British Communist Party* (London: Pluto, 1995), pp. 4–22, 8; letter from Chimen Abramsky to the author, 28 September 1998; interview with Brian Pearce, 4 October 1998.
6. Karl Marx and Friedrich Engels, *Correspondence 1846–95: A Selection with Commentary and Notes* (London: Lawrence & Wishart, 1934); K. Marx, *Capital*, Volume 1 (London: George Allen, 1938); F. Engels, *The Origins of the Family, Private Property and the State* (London: Lawrence & Wishart, 1940); K. Marx, *On China 1853–60: Articles from the 'New York Daily Tribune'* (London: Lawrence & Wishart, 1951); D. Torr, *Marxism, Nationality and War* (1940); D. Torr and M. Davison (trans.), *Dimitroff's Letters from Prison* (London: Victor Gollancz and Martin Lawrence, 1935). Letter from E.J. Hobsbawm to the author, 23 October 1998.
7. C. Hill, *The English Revolution 1640* (London: Lawrence & Wishart, 1940); D. Torr to B. Pearce, 14 January 1948. I am grateful to Brian Pearce for giving me access to surviving copies of their correspondence. The Hill controversy is also discussed in Schwarz, 'The People in History', p. 51. The discussion flared up again within the Historians' Group in 1948, and also provides the backdrop to the later debate in *Past and Present* in response to Maurice Dobb's book, *Studies in the Development of Capitalism*. This latter controversy is collected in R. Hilton (ed.), *The Transition from Feudalism to Capitalism* (London: Lawrence & Wishart, 1976).
8. E.P. Thompson, *William Morris* (London: Lawrence & Wishart, 1955); G. Thomson, M. Dobb, C. Hill and J. Saville, 'Foreword', in J. Saville (ed.), *Democracy and the Labour Movement: Essays in Honour of Dona Torr* (London: Lawrence & Wishart, 1954), pp. 7–9.
9. D. Torr, *Tom Mann and His Times* (London: Lawrence & Wishart, 1956), p. 16; D. Torr, *Tom Mann* (London: Lawrence & Wishart, 1936), p. 47; E.P. Thompson, 'Tom Mann and His Times', *Our History* 26–7 (1962), p. 38.
10. Letter from Victor Kiernan to the author, 30 September 1998.
11. Interview with Dorothy Thompson, 23 September 1998.
12. E.P. Thompson, 'The Secret State within the State', *New Statesman*, 10 November 1978.
13. E.P. Thompson, *The Making of the English Working Class* (Harmondsworth: Penguin, 1968 edn). T. Steele, *The Emergence of Cultural Studies: Cultural Politics, Adult Education and the English Question* (London: Lawrence & Wishart, 1997), p. 150.
14. This formula would make Althusser the grandfather of post-structuralism, and thus the great-grandfather of postmodernism.
15. P. Anderson, 'Origins of the Present Crisis', in R. Blackburn, (ed.), *Towards Socialism* (London: New Left Books, 1965); T. Nairn, 'The British Political Elite', *New Left Review* 23 (1964), pp. 19–25; T. Nairn, 'The

English Working Class; *New Left Review* 24 (1964), pp. 45–57; T. Nairn, 'The Anatomy of the Labour Party', *New Left Review* 27 (1964), pp. 48–65, and *New Left Review* 28, pp. 33–62.

16. E.P. Thompson, 'The Peculiarities of the English', in *The Poverty of Theory and Other Essays* (London: Merlin, 1978), pp. 35–147, 56.

17. P.Q. Hirst, *Marxism and Historical Writing* (London: Routledge, 1985), p. 1. The phrase is lifted, rather unjustly, from Thompson's critique of Althusser. Thompson's use was more careful. Behind Althusser stood the massed ranks of the French Communist Party, organically tied as it was to the world Communist movement. The 'police action' mentioned was not entirely rhetorical. Behind Thompson there were no forces more threatening than the social clubs of the British New Left. For Thompson's use, see 'The Poverty of Theory: or an Orrery of Errors', in *The Poverty of Theory and other Essays*, pp. 193–398, 326.

18. F. Inglis (ed.), *E.P. Thompson: Collected Poems* (Newcastle: Bloodaxe Books, 1999), p. 121.

19. The text of this debate is provided in R. Samuel (ed.), *People's History and Socialist Theory*, History Workshop Series (London Routledge & Kegan Paul, 1981), pp. 375–408.

20. B. Schwarz, 'History on the Move', *Radical History Review* 57 (1993), pp. 202–20.

21. M. Newman, *John Strachey* (Manchester: Manchester University Press, 1989), p. 70; there is also a useful life of Havelock Ellis in S. Rowbotham and J. Weeks, *Socialism and the New Life: The Personal and Sexual Politics of Edward Carpenter and Havelock Ellis* (London: Pluto, 1977).

22. I am grateful to Anne Alexander for suggesting the comparison.

23. 'Love/Welfare of the Object', CP/IND/TORR/01/01.

24. 'Pity and Gratitude', CP/IND/TORR/01/01.

25. Ibid.

26. Schwarz, 'The People in History', p. 84.

27. Thompson, 'The Poverty of Theory', p. 322.

28. The notes of the group in 1956–57 are held at CP/CENT/CULT/5/12.

29. Thompson, 'The Poverty of Theory', p. 324.

30. Ibid., p. 325.

31. Ibid., pp. 326–7.

32. A. MacIntyre's, 'Notes from the Moral Wilderness', in K. Knight (ed.), *The MacIntyre Reader* (Cambridge: Polity, 1998), pp. 31–49.

33. The point is furthest developed by Marx in his criticism of an early programme of the German Social Democratic Party. See 'Critique of the Gotha Programme', in K. Marx and F. Engels, *Collected Works*, Volume 24 (London: Lawrence & Wishart, 1989), pp. 75–99, 86–7.

34. M. Shaw, 'From Total War to Democratic Peace: Exterminism and Historical Pacifism', in H.J. Kaye and K. McClelland (eds), *E.P. Thompson: Critical Perspectives* (Temple, Philadelphia: Temple University Press, 1990), pp. 233–52, 249.

35. Interview with Dorothy Thompson, 23 September 1998.

36. Thompson, *Making of the English Working Class*, p. 13.

37. Ibid., pp. 9–10.

38. B.D. Palmer, *Objections and Oppositions* (London: Verso, 1994), p. 94.

Chapter 6

1. P. Baran, *The Political Economy of Growth* (London: Penguin, 1973 edn).
2. P. Baran, *Marxism and Psychology* (New York: Monthly Review Press, 1960).
3. This account is based on P.M. Sweezy and L. Huberman, *Paul A. Baran (1910–1964): A Collective Portrait* (New York: Monthly Review Press, 1965), pp. 29–47, esp. 31.
4. P.M. Sweezy, *Four Lectures on Marxism* (New York and London: Monthly Review Press, 1981), p. 13.
5. The only problem with seeing the 1930s as a Keynesian moment is that Keynes's theories were still incomplete at this time. The most common approach maintains that booms began only after Keynes thought of them and governments followed. It is much more useful to see him as taking the actual practice of the 1930s and (slowly) converting this into economic theory.
6. J.B. Foster, 'Remarks on Paul Sweezy on the Occasion of His Receipt of the Veblen–Commons Award', *Monthly Review*, September 1999.
7. The politics of the article are discussed in D. Renton, 'Albert Einstein's Socialism', *Rethinking Marxism* 13/2 (2001), pp. 132–45.
8. US Supreme Court, 'Sweezy v. New Hampshire', October Term, 1956, *US Reports* 354 (1957), pp. 234–70; Foster, 'Remarks on Paul Sweezy'.
9. One important debate which cannot be covered here is Sweezy's contribution to the Marxist theory of the emergence of capitalism. To some extent, this debate pre-empted the controversy over monopoly theory. Sweezy's importation of Keynesian concepts came in for the most devastating root-and-branch critique, especially from British Marxist historians. Yet even his fiercest critics would suggest that Sweezy's intervention was a valuable stimulus to new thought. See R. Hilton (ed.), *The Transition from Feudalism to Capitalism* (London: Verso, 1976).
10. 'Happy Birthday Paul', *Monthly Review*, April 2000.
11. Sweezy, *Four Lectures*, p. 15.
12. A. Davies, *Where Did the Forties Go? A Popular History. The Rise and the Fall of the Hopes of a Decade* (London: Pluto Press, 1984), p. 86.
13. Historicus, 'Fascism in America', *Monthly Review*, October 1952.
14. P. Baran, 'The Commitment of the Intellectuals', *Monthly Review*, May 1961, cited in Sweezy and Huberman, *Paul A. Baran*, p. 10.
15. The starting point in this always-rightward odyssey was J. Burnham, *The Managerial Revolution* (Harmondsworth: Penguin, 1960 edn).
16. Sweezy and Huberman, *Paul A. Baran*, p. 41.
17. Ibid., p. 47.
18. P. Binns and M. Gonzalez, 'Cuba, Castro and Socialism', *International Socialism Journal* 8 (1980), pp. 1–36, here 8–9; also R. Blackburn, 'Class Forces in the Cuban Revolution: A Reply to Peter Binns and Mike Gonzalez', *International Socialism Journal* 9 (1980), pp. 81–94.
19. J.L. Anderson, *Che Guevara: A Revolutionary Life* (New York: Bantam Books, 1997).
20. R. Blackburn, Introduction to R. Debray, *Strategy for Revolution* (London: New Left Books, 1970), pp. 10–11; cited in P. Binns, A. Callinicos, M.

Gonzalez, 'Cuba, Socialism and the Third World: A Rejoinder to Robin Blackburn', *International Socialism Journal* 10 (1981), pp. 93–105.

21. P.A. Baran and P.M. Sweezy, *Monopoly Capital: An Essay on the American Economic and Social Order* (New York: Monthly Review Press, 1966), p. 4.

22. Baran and Sweezy, *Monopoly Capital*, p. 43.

23. P.M. Sweezy, 'Monopoly Capitalism', in J. Eatwell, M. Milgate and P. Newman (eds), *The New Palgrave: Marxian Economics* (London: Macmillan, 1987), pp. 297–303.

24. J.B. Foster, 'Monopoly Capital at the Turn of the Millennium', *Monthly Review*, April 2000; also for the original discussion of surplus, see Baran and Sweezy, *Monopoly Capital*, p. 125.

25. K. Marx, *Capital*, Volume 3 (London: Lawrence & Wishart, 1959), pp. 211–31.

26. Not surprisingly, therefore, a whole sub-branch of Marxist economics has developed along these lines, asking what has happened to profit rates in the past hundred years. See, for example, C. Harman, 'Footnotes and Fallacies: A Comment on Robert Brenner's "The Economics of Global Turbulence"', *Historical Materialism* 4 (1999), pp. 95–104.

27. These very themes are discussed in P. Sweezy, *The Theory of Capitalist Development* (New York: Oxford University Press, 1942).

28. There is a superb short summary of the 'transformation problem' in A. Callinicos, *The Revolutionary Ideals of Karl Marx* (London: Bookmarks, 1996 edn), pp. 145–6.

29. Foster, 'Monopoly Capital at the Turn of the Millennium'.

30. C. Harman, *Explaining the Crisis: A Marxist Re-appraisal* (London: Bookmarks, 1984 edn), pp. 148–54.

31. These examples are all taken from 'Happy Birthday Paul'.

32. Baran and Sweezy, *Monopoly Capital*, p. 9.

33. Baran, *Political Economy*, p. 241.

34. Ibid., p. 267.

35. Ibid., pp. 276, 403, 416.

Chapter 7

1. M. Mamdani, 'A Critique of the State and Civil Society Paradigm in Africanist Studies', in M. Mamdani and E. Wamba-dia-Wamba (eds), *African Studies in Social Movements and Democracy* (Dakar: CODESRIA, 1995), pp. 602–16, here 609.

2. J.S. Saul, 'Ideology in Africa: Decomposition and Recomposition', in G.M. Carter and P. O'Meara, *African Independence: The First Twenty-Five Years* (Bloomington: Indiana University Press, 1985), pp. 300–29, 312.

3. B. Moore, *Queen's College Reunion Journal*, July 2000, cited in I.C. Fraser, 'Dr. Walter Rodney: Scholar, Historian, Politician', www.kaieteur.com/qcsite/heroes/walter_rodney.htm.

4. R. Lewis, *Walter Rodney's Intellectual and Political Thought* (Detroit: Wayne State University Press, 1999).

5. The thesis was eventually published as W. Rodney, *A History of the Upper Guinea Coast* (Oxford: Clarendon Press, 1970), here pp. 18, 21, 71, 72, 259, 262–4, 270.

6. A. Mazrui, 'Africa between Ideology and Technology: Two Frustrated Forces of Change', in Carter and O'Meara, *African Independence*, pp. 275–99, 295.
7. A. Creighton, 'The Walter Rodney Factor in West Indian Literature' *Stabroek News*, 18 June 2000, www.guyanacaribbeanpolitics.com/wpa/rodney_literature.html.
8. C.L.R. James, *Walter Rodney and the Question of Power* (London: Race Today, 1983), p. 2.
9. L.T. Hector, 'Fan the Flame', www.candw.ag/~jardinea/ffhtm/ff970620.htm.
10. P. Gilroy, *The Black Atlantic: Modernity and Double Consciousness* (London: Verso, 1993).
11. W.E.B. Du Bois, *Black Reconstruction in America 1860–1880* (Cleveland: World Publishing, 1969), p. 48.
12. C.L.R. James, *Minty Alley* (London: Secker & Warburg, 1936).
13. C.L.R. James, *World Revolution 1917–1936: The Rise and Fall of the Communist International* (London: Secker & Warburg, 1937).
14. C.L.R. James, *The Black Jacobins: Toussaint L'Ouverture and the San Domingo Revolution* (London: Secker & Warburg, 1938).
15. C.L.R. James, *Nkrumah and the Ghana Revolution* (London: Allison & Busby, 1977). There is a useful discussion of this book in R.D.G. Kelley, 'The World the Diaspora Made: C.L.R. James and the Politics of History', in G. Farred (ed.), *Rethinking C.L.R. James* (Oxford: Blackwell, 1996), pp. pp. 103–30.
16. See 'French Intellectuals and Democrats in the Algerian Revolution', in F. Fanon, *Toward the African Revolution* (Harmondsworth: Penguin, 1970), pp. 86–101.
17. F. Fanon, *Black Skin, White Masks* (New York: Grove Press, 1967).
18. D.K. Orwa, *The Congo Betrayal: The UN–US and Lumumba* (Nairobi: Kenya Literature Bureau, 1985).
19. Cited in R. Segal, *African Profiles* (London: Penguin, 1962), p. 260.
20. N. wa Thiong'o, *The First Walter Rodney Memorial Lecture* (London: Friends of Bogle, 1987), p. 6.
21. James, *Nkrumah and the Ghana Revolution*, pp. 103, 157, 169, 177.
22. A. Cabral, 'Revolution in Guinea', cited in R.H. Chilcote, *Amílcar Cabral's Revolutionary Theory and Practice: A Critical Guide* (Boulder and London: Lynne Rienner, 1991), p. 29. There is also an extraordinary description of Cabral in B. Davidson, *The Liberation of Guiné: Aspects of an African Revolution* (Harmondsworth: Penguin, 1969).
23. A. Cabral, 'Unity and Struggle', cited in Chilcote, *Amílcar Cabral's Revolutionary Theory*, p. 15.
24. For witness accounts of the Mozambique revolution at its height, see C. Searle, *We're Building the New School! Diary of a Teacher in Mozambique* (London: Zed Books, 1981); also Saul, 'Ideology in Africa', pp. 300–329.
25. W. Rodney, *How Europe Underdeveloped Africa* (London: Bogle-L'Ouverture Publications, 1972), pp. 2, 80.
26. Ibid., pp. 7, 13, 27.
27. W. Rodney, *West Africa and the Atlantic Slave Trade* (Lagos: Afrografika, 1969), p. 7.

28. W. Rodney, *The Groundings with My Brothers* (London: Bogle-L'Ouverture Publications, 1970).

29. E. Williams, *Capitalism and Slavery* (London: André Deutsch, 1964).

30. Hector, 'Fan the Flame'.

31. W. Rodney, 'The African Revolution', in P. Buhle (ed.), *C.L.R. James: His Life and Work* (London: Allison & Busby, 1986), pp. 30–48, 30, 37, 39, 40–41, 46–7.

32. Ironically, this is precisely the point that the impeccably non-Marxist Eric Williams made in his major work, *Capitalism and Slavery*.

33. E. Bernstein, *Evolutionary Socialism*, trans. E.C. Harvey (London: Independent Labour Party, 1909), pp. 160, 170, 177, 196, 198.

34. Z. Bacchus, 'Walter Rodney', www.guyanajournal.com/page23c.html.

35. W. Rodney, *People's Power: No Dictator* (Georgetown: Working People's Alliance, 1979), p. 1.

36. Socialist Forum, *'And Finally they Killed Him': Speeches and Poems at a Memorial Rally for Walter Rodney* (Lagos: Socialist Forum, 1980), p. 10. This notion of situation has its counterpart in the literary theories of Ngugi wa Thiong'o, who describes the liberation author's 'quest for relevance', in Ngugi wa Thiong'o, *Decolonising the Mind: The Politics of Language in African Literature* (London: James Currey, 1986), p. 87.

37. W. Rodney, *Signs of the Times* (London: Working People's Alliance Support Group, 1978), p. 12.

38. Rodney, *People's Power*, p. 21.

39. M. Seenarine, 'Gender, Culture and Class in Walter Rodney's Writings on Guyana', www.saxakali.com/Saxakali-Publications/moses6.htm.

40. W. Rodney, *A History of the Guyanese Working People, 1805–1905* (New York: Johns Hopkins University Press, 1981), pp. 141, 204.

41. Ibid., pp. 205–7.

42. Ibid., p. 179.

43. Hector, 'Fan the Flame'.

44. Although the analysis in this chapter is closest to that found in T. Cliff, *Deflected Permanent Revolution*, (London: Bookmarks, 1990).

45. A.P. Maingot et al., 'The Walter Rodney Affair', *New York Review of Books*, 14 May 1981.

46. James, *Walter Rodney and the Question of Power*, p. 12.

47. Rodney, *Signs of the Times*, pp. 1–5.

48. Maingot et al., 'The Walter Rodney Affair'.

Chapter 8

1. 'A Model T is a room with lock inside/ a key is turned to free the world.' C. Raine, *A Martian Sends a Postcard Home* (Oxford: Oxford University Press, 1979), pp. 1–2.

2. S. Sayers, 'The Need to Work', *Radical Philosophy* 46 (1987), pp. 17–26.

3. C. Littler, *The Development of the Labour Process in Capitalist Societies* (London: Heinemann Educational, 1982), p. 26.

4. H. Braverman, *Labour and Monopoly Capital: The Degradation of Work in the Twentieth Century* (New York and London: Monthly Review Press,

1974), pp. 5–7; also U. Pagano, *Harry Braverman* (Siena: University of Siena, 1990), pp. 1–2.

5. J.P. Cannon, *The Struggle for Socialism in the 'American Century'* (New York: Pathfinder, 1977), p. 200; quoted in T. Cliff, *Trotskyism after Trotsky: The Origins of the International Socialists* (London: Bookmarks, 1998), p. 15.

6. E. Baur et al., 'The Roots of the Party Crisis – Its Causes and Solution', Document Submitted to the Political Committee of the Socialist Workers Party, copy in Socialist Platform library.

7. There is a useful history of James P. Cannon, the leader of the American SWP, in C. Bambery, 'The Politics of James P. Cannon', *International Socialism Journal* 36 (1987), pp. 49–89. Braverman wrote for the SWP's paper and its internal bulletin. Braverman was only in his twenties; his journalism was not yet of a high quality and was criticised from outside the party and also inside the party for its strident and sectarian tone. H. Frankel (Braverman), 'A Defamer of Marxism', *Fourth International*, May 1944, pp. 149–52; J.T. Farrell, Letter, *SWP Internal Bulletin* 6/6 (1944); H. Frankel, 'Comments on the Letter from James T. Farrell', *SWP Internal Bulletin* 6/8 (1944); and J. Campbell. 'The Frankel Article and Our Polemical Method', *SWP Internal Bulletin* 6/11 (1944).

8. A. Johnson, 'The "Special Class" and Social Movement in the Marxism of Hal Draper', paper given to Alternative Futures and Popular Protest Conference, Manchester Metropolitan University, March 1997; there is a more critical examination of Draper's work in S. Wright, 'Hal Draper's Marxism', *International Socialism Journal* 47 (1990), pp. 157–90. Draper's most important work is H. Draper, *Karl Marx's Theory of Revolution*, 4 vols (New York and London: Monthly Review Press: 1977).

9. H. Frankel, 'The New World Reality and the New Confusion, What Hansen's Document Has Revealed', *SWP Internal Bulletin* 15/10 (1953). Cannon replied to these and other statements of the so-called 'Cochranite' minority in J.P. Cannon, 'Background and Issues of the Party Crisis', *SWP Internal Bulletin* 15/12 (1953).

10. L. Proyect, 'Sol Dollinger', *Revolutionary History* 8/2 (2002), pp. 217–21.

11. Baur et al., 'The Roots of the Party Crisis'. The Socialist Union is described in R. Alexander, *International Trotskyism 1929–1985: A Documentary Analysis of the Movement* (Durham and London: Duke University Press: London, 1991), pp. 835–42. Its documents can be read at www.home.inreach.com/soldoll. For an account which makes much of the difference between the young Frankel and the older Braverman, see B. Palmer, 'Before Braverman: Harry Frankel and the American Workers' Movement', *Monthly Review* 50/8 (1999), pp. 33–46.

12. M. Rose, *Industrial Behaviour: Research and Control* (London: Penguin, 1988 edn), p. 315.

13. Braverman, *Labour and Monopoly Capital*, p. 9.

14. 'The Immediate Tasks of the Soviet Government', in V.I. Lenin, *Collected Works*, Volume 42 (London: Lawrence & Wishart, 1969), pp. 68–84, 79–82; A. Gramsci, *Selections from Prison Notebooks*, ed. and trans. Q. Hoare and G. Nowell Smith (London: Lawrence & Wishart, 1971), pp. 277–318.

15. Some Marxists and certain sympathisers did attempt to extend Marxist

categories; see, for example, S. Pollard, *The Genesis of Modern Management* (London: Edward Arnold, 1965); and G. Friedmann, *The Anatomy of Work* (London: Heinemann, 1961).

16. C. Bambery, 'The Promised Land', *Socialist Review* 180 (1994), pp. 23–4.
17. Braverman, *Labour and Monopoly Capital*, pp. 10, 18.
18. Ibid., p. 53.
19. Paul Baran and Paul M. Sweezey, *Monopoly Capital* (New York: Monthly Review Press, 1966).
20. Braverman, *Labour and Monopoly Capital*, pp. 251–6; this point is discussed in A. Rainnie, *Industrial Relations in Small Firms: Small Isn't Beautiful* (London: Routledge, 1989), pp. 38–63, 40–41.
21. Braverman, *Labour and Monopoly Capital*, pp. 85–6.
22. Ibid., p. 102–8.
23. Ibid., p. 113.
24. Ibid., pp. 328–36.
25. The classic statement of such optimism, that computers would transform the way we work, is A. Toffler, *The Third Wave* (London: Collins, 1980).
26. A. Zimbalast (ed.), *Case Studies on the Labor Process* (New York and London: Monthly Review Press, 1979); Brighton Labour Process Group, 'The Capitalist Labour Process', *Capital and Class* 1 (1977), 3–26.
27. P.M. Sweezey, 'Foreword', in Braverman, *Labour and Monopoly Capital*, pp. ix–xiii, xii; Heilbroner's review is quoted in D.M. Gordon, 'Harry Braverman', in J. Eatwell, M. Milgate, and P. Newman (eds), *The New Palgrave: Marxian Economics* (London and Basingstoke: Macmillan, 1990), pp. 65–6.
28. R. Commbs, 'Labour and Monopoly Capital', *New Left Review* 107 (1978), 79–96, 79. For a summary of the debate brought about by *Labour and Monopoly Capital*, see Rose, *Industrial Behaviour*, pp. 347–50; also S. Wood 'Introduction', in S. Wood (ed.), *The Degradation of Work?* (London: Hutchinson, 1982), pp. 11–22; D. Knights, H. Willmott and D. Collinson (eds), *Job Redesign: Critical Perspectives on the Labour Process* (London: Heinemann, 1984), S. Dex, *The Sexual Division of Labour: Conceptual Revolutions in the Social Sciences* (Brighton: Harvester, 1985), W.A.T. Nichols and P. Armstrong, *Workers Divide* (Glasgow: Fontana, 1976); P. Willis, *Learning to Labour* (Farnborough: Saxon House, 1977); S. Hill, *Competition and Control at Work* (London, Heinemann, 1981); T. Watson, *Sociology Work and Industry* (London: Routledge, 1980).
29. Rainnie, *Industrial Relations*, pp. 42–3; also Rose, *Industrial Behaviour*, pp. 314–21.
30. A.L. Friedman, *Industry and Labour: Class Struggle at Work and Monopoly Capitalism* (London: Macmillan, 1977), p. 50; also A. Friedman, 'Responsible Autonomy versus Direct Control over the Labour Process', *Capital and Class* 1 (1977), 43–58; V. Beechey, *Unequal Work* (London: Verso, 1987).
31. Friedman, *Industry and Labour*, pp. 45–55; M. Burawoy, *The Politics of Production* (Verso: London and New York, 1985), pp. 10, 22.
32. Littler, *The Development of the Labour Process*, pp. 105–15.
33. Zimbalast, *Case Studies*, p. ix.
34. S. Cohen, 'A Labour Process to Nowhere?', *New Left Review* 165 (1987), pp. 34–50.

35. J. West, 'Women, Sex and Class', in A. Kuhn and A.M. Wolpe (eds), *Feminism and Materialism* (London: Routledge & Kegan Paul, 1978); Beechey, *Unequal Work*, pp. 73–93.
36. F.R. Eliot, *The Family: Change or Continuity?* (London: Macmillan, 1986).
37. H. Braverman, 'Two Comments', *Monthly Review*, July–August 1976, pp. 119–24, 120.
38. The evolution of women's work is described in L. German, *Sex, Class and Socialism* (London: Bookmarks, 1989), pp. 15–61; and L. German, *A Question of Class* (London: Bookmarks, 1996), pp. 34–9.
39. Braverman, *Labour and Monopoly Capital*, p. 72; H. Braverman, 'Two Comments', pp. 122–3; and Cohen, 'A Labour Process to Nowhere?'
40. P.M. Sweezey, 'Foreword', in Braverman, *Labour and Monopoly Capital*, pp. ix–xiii, xii.
41. P. Thompson, 'The Labour Process and Deskilling', in K. Thompson, *Work, Employment and Unemployment: Perspectives on Work and Society* (Milton Keynes and Philadelphia: Open University Press, 1984), pp. 67–87, 84; also P. Thompson, *The Nature of Work: An Introduction to Debates on the Labour Process* (London: Macmillan, 1989 edn), pp. 106–8.
42. Braverman, *Labour and Monopoly Capital*, p. 22.
43. H. Braverman, *The Future of Russia* (New York: Macmillan, 1963), pp. xi, 155, 158, 162.
44. K. Marx and F. Engels, *Collected Works*, Volume 5 (London: Lawrence & Wishart, 1976 edn), p. 5.

Chapter 9

1. S. Amin, 'The Social Movements in the Periphery: An End to National Liberation', in S. Amin et al., *Transforming the Revolution: Social Movements and the World System* (New York: Monthly Review, 1990), pp. 96–138, 96–7, 97.
2. Samir Amin, *The Maghreb in the Modern World* (London: Penguin, 1970); *Accumulation on a World Scale: A Critique of the Theory of Underdevelopment* (New York: Monthly Review Press, 1970); *Neo-Colonialism in West Africa* (London: Penguin, 1973); *Unequal Development: An Essay on the Social Formations of Peripheral Capitalism* (New York: Monthly Review Press, 1973); *Imperialism and Unequal Development* (New York: Zed Books, 1977); *The Law of Value and Historical Materialism* (London: Harvester, 1977); *The Arab Nation: Nationalism and Class Struggles* (London: Zed Books, 1978); *Class and Nation* (New York: Monthly Review Press, 1980); *The Arab Economy Today* (London: Zed Books, 1982); *Eurocentrism* (London: Zed Books, 1989); *Capitalism in the Age of Globalization* (London: Zed Books, 1997); *Spectres of Capitalism: A Critique of Current Intellectual Fashions* (New York: Monthly Review Press, 1998). This list does not cover all of Amin's books that are available in English, let alone the many texts published in French or Arabic and still untranslated. There is a good bibliography of Amin's early work in *The Arab Economy Today*.
3. A. Foster-Carter, 'The Empirical Samir Amin: A Notice and Appreciation', in Amin, *The Arab Economy Today*, pp. 1–40, 3.
4. S. Amin, *Re-reading the Postwar Period* (New York: Monthly Review, 1994).

5. Ibid., p. 20.

6. Ibid., pp. 175–7.

7. Ibid., p. 23.

8. This may be a reference to Mao Tse-Tung, *The Chinese Revolution and the Communist Party of China* (Peking: Foreign Languages Press, 1950).

9. S. Amin, 'The First Babu Memorial Lecture', *Review of African Political Economy* 25/77 (1998), pp. 475–84; the text is also available at http://ambabu.gn.apc.org/memorial.htm.

10. Such as S. El Masry, 'Où va l'Egypte?', *Democratie Nouvelle*, 1955; also P. Dupont, 'Problèmes actuels de l'économie égyptienne', *Economie et Politique*, 26, 1956.

11. S. Amin, 'Les revenus susceptibles d'épargne et leur utilisation en Egypte 1938–1952', Thèse de Statistiques, ISUP, Paris, 1956.

12. S. Amin, 'Les effets structurels de l'integration internationale des économies precapitalistes: une étude theorique du mecanisme qui a engendré les economies dites sous-développés', Doctorat d'État des Sciences Économiques, Paris, 1957. Passages from the thesis appear in Amin, *Accumulation on a World Scale*.

13. S. Pollard, 'Economic History; a Science of Society?', *Past and Present* 30 (1965), pp. 1–22.

14. A. Gerschenkron, *Economic Backwardness in Historical Perspective* (Cambridge, MA: Harvard University Press, 1962); W.W. Rostow, *The Process of Economic Growth* (New York: W.W. Norton, 1952)

15. See D. Yergin and J. Stanislaw, *The Commanding Heights: The Battle for the World Economy* (Carmichael, California: Touchstone Books, 2002), pp. 232–44.

16. G. Kohler, 'The Future of Global Polarisation', *REVIEW* (Braudel Centre) 17/3 (1994), pp. 337–47, 342, 347.

17. Amin, *Re-reading*, p. 140.

18. S. Amin, *Dirasa fil tayarat al naqdia wal malia fi Misr am 1957* (Cairo: Arab League, 1959); S. Amin, *Comptes économiques de la République du Mali en 1959* (Bamako and Paris: Ministère du plan et de la coordination des affaires économiques et financières, 1959)

19. The classic English language text of this period is Amin, *The Maghreb in the Modern World*.

20. Cited in Foster-Carter, 'The Empirical Samir Amin', p. 12.

21. Amin, *Accumulation on a World Scale*, pp. 299, 608.

22. Amin, *Unequal Development*; Amin, *Accumulation on a World Scale*; Foster-Carter, 'The Empirical Samir Amin', pp. 20–21; C. Ngai-Lung, 'Underdevelopment and the World Capitalist System – An Evaluation of Some Recent Studies', M.Sc. thesis, University of Salford, 1976, pp. 57–97. Samir Amin also offers his own six-point summary of his Ph.D. thesis in Amin, *Re-reading the Postwar Period*, p. 68.

23. Cited in D. Widgery, *The Left in Britain* (Harmondsworth: Penguin, 1976), p. 483.

24. This point is made in P. Thompson and G. Lewis, *The Revolution Unfinished? A Critique of Trotskysim* (Liverpool: Big Flame, 1977), inside back cover. For an interesting counter-critique, see J. Harber, 'Trotskyism and the IS Tradition', *Revolutionary Socialism* 2 (1979), pp. 24–7.

25. S. Amin, *L'Avenir du Maoïsme* (Paris: Editions de Minuit, 1982), p. 66.
26. N. Harris, *The Mandate of Heaven: Marx and Mao in Modern China* (London: Quartet, 1978), pp. 261, 281.
27. Amin, *Re-reading the Postwar Period*, p. 175.
28. Amin, 'The First Babu Memorial Lecture'.
29. Ibid.
30. Ibid.
31. Ibid.
32. Amin, *Re-reading the Postwar Period*, p. 135.
33. Amin, *L'Avenir du Maoïsme*, p. 41.
34. Amin, 'The Social Movements in the Periphery', p. 107.
35. 'The development of the periphery requires the setting up of autocentric national structures', Amin, *Accumulation on a World Scale*, p. 33.
36. Amin, *The Maghreb in the Modern World*, pp. 189, 245.
37. Amin, *Re-reading the Postwar Period*, pp. 167–8.
38. Such an argument begs the question of why class inequality should continue to exist, even in what seems initially a more moderate and limited form?
39. Cited in Foster-Carter, 'The Empirical Samir Amin', p. 36.
40. Amin, *Eurocentrism*, pp. 118–19, 120.
41. It should be noted in passing that Amin has his own stage theory of human development. Society has evolved from the (1) primitive–communal, through (2) early and developed tribute-paying societies (a form which includes feudalism), (3) slave-owning forms, (4) petty commodity production, to (5) capitalism. See Amin, *Accumulation on a World Scale*, pp. 137–68; Amin, *Re-reading the Postwar Period*, p. 218; and Amin, *Unequal Development*, pp. 13–14. Amin's notion of tributary society has gone on to influence a wide range of scholars, suggesting as it does an analytical link between historic European and Asian societies.
42. L. Trotsky, *History of the Russian Revolution* (New York: Pathfinder Press, 1992), pp. 3–15.
43. Amin, *Accumulation on a World Scale*, p. 26.
44. For the many similarities of language, see Amin, *Accumulation on a World Scale*, pp. 9, 22 and throughout.
45. Amin, *Unequal Development*, p. 102.
46. Amin, *Accumulation on a World Scale*, p. 1.
47. N. Harris, *The End of the Third World: Newly Industrializing Countries and the Decline of an Ideology* (Harmondsworth: Penguin, 1986), p. 26.
48. H. Bernstein, 'Sociology of Underdevelopment vs. Sociology of Development?', in D. Lehmann (ed.), *Development Theory: Four Critical Essays* (London: Frank Cass, 1978).
49. See S. Smith, 'The Ideas of Samir Amin: Theology or Tautology?', *Journal of Development Studies* 17/1 (1980), pp. 5–21.
50. Foster-Carter, 'The Empirical Samir Amin', p. 25.
51. S. Amin, 'Not a Happy Ending', *Al-Ahram Weekly* 462 (1999).
52. Amin, *Spectres of Capitalism*, pp. 1–3; also S. Amin, 'The Political Economy of the Twentieth Century', *Monthly Review*, June 2000, pp. 1–17.

Chapter 10

1. D. Widgery, *The Left in Britain* (Harmondsworth: Penguin, 1976); *Health in Danger* (London and Basingstoke: Macmillan, 1979); *The Book of the Year* (London: Ink Links, 1980); *Beating Time* (London: Chatto & Windus, 1986); *The National Health: A Radical Perspective* (London: Hogarth Press, 1988); *Preserving Disorder* (London: Pluto, 1989); *Some Lives* (London: Sinclair-Stevenson, 1991); M. Rosen and D. Widgery, *The Chatto Book of Dissent* (London: Chatto & Windus, 1991). His co-author Mike Rosen's obituary for Widgery can be accessed on the Internet at http://www.gaijin.demon.co.uk/widgery.html.
2. Ali's memories of the 1960s are recorded in many places, not least T. Ali, *Street-Fighting Years: An Autobiography of the Sixties* (London: Collins, 1987). The major project to which Ali contributed was of course *New Left Review*, one of the few left-wing publications that David Widgery appears to have chosen to ignore. Widgery's rather acid view of *NLR* is contained in a passage from his book, *The Left in Britain*. 'Underlying the apparent sophistication of the analyses was the extraordinarily arrogant belief that it is the role of the intellectuals to make the theory, the job of the workers to make the revolution and that what is wrong in Britain is that the latter are too backward to understand the former's instructions.' See Widgery, *The Left in Britain*, p. 513.
3. Interview with Sheila Rowbotham, 13 June 2001.
4. Widgery, *The National Health*, pp. xiv, xv, 56.
5. D. Widgery, 'Against Grown-Up Power', *New Statesman*, August 1967, published in Widgery, *Preserving Disorder*, pp. 3–6, 3. Widgery's contemporary Patrick Cockburn contracted polio in the same year; see P. Cockburn, 'The Summer Plague', *Independent*, 7 August 1999.
6. This episode is described by one of Widgery's school contemporaries at J. Gillatt, 'It's My Life', www.gaijin.demon.co.uk/mylife.htm.
7. R. Neville, *Hippie Hippie Shake: The Dreams, the Trips, the Trials, the Love-ins, the Screw-ups... the Sixties* (London: Bloomsbury, 1996), pp. 173, 271; N. Fountain, *Underground: The London Alternative Press* (London and New York, Comedia, 1988), p. 43; J. Green (ed.), *Days in the Life: Voices from the English Underground 1961–1971* (London: Minerva, 1988), p. 65. For the memories of John Gillatt, a contemporary of Widgery's in Windsor, see www.gaijin.demon.co.uk/mylife.html.
8. Widgery, 'Against Grown-Up Power', p. 5.
9. Contrary to Neville's story, it should be said that Widgery never claimed any links to this union.
10. Neville, *Hippie Hippie Shake*, pp. 73, 162, 184.
11. Widgery described his time in the CP and the SLL in Green, *Days in the Life*, pp. 24, 57.
12. Fountain, *Underground*, p. 56; there is a good history of the IS/SWP in I.H. Birchall, *'The Smallest Mass Party in the World': Building the Socialist Workers Party, 1951–1979* (London: Socialist Workers' Party, 1981); while the events of 1968 in the LSE and internationally are described in C. Harman, *The Fire Last Time: 1968 and After* (London: Bookmarks, 1988).
13. P. Foot, 'David Widgery', *New Left Review* 196 (1992), pp. 120–24, 120.

14. P. Sedgwick, *Psycho Politics* (Pluto: London, 1982).
15. Widgery, *Preserving Disorder*, p. xiii.
16. Widgery, 'When Harrods is Looted', in ibid., pp. 7–13, 13.
17. Rowbotham was to review the experience of her time in the IS in S. Rowbotham, L. Segal and H. Wainwright, *Beyond the Fragments* (Manchester: Merlin, 1979), pp. 21–155.
18. Fountain, *Underground*, pp. 105–6.
19. G. Greer, *The Female Eunuch* (London: Granada, 1971); S. Rowbotham, *Women, Resistance and Revolution* (Harmondsworth: Penguin, 1972); S. Rowbotham, *Woman's Consciousness, Man's World* (Harmondsworth: Penguin, 1973); S. Rowbotham, *Hidden from History: 300 Years of Women's Oppression and the Fight Against It* (London: Pluto, 1973).
20. Greer, *The Female Eunuch*, p. 22.
21. Neville, *Hippie Hippie Shake*, p. 201; Fountain, *Underground*, pp. 106–7.
22. Widgery, *Preserving Disorder*, pp. 101–3.
23. Neville, *Hippie Hippie Shake*, p. 303.
24. G. Dawson [D. Widgery], 'The Politics of Pornography', *Socialist Worker*, 24 September 1971.
25. D. Widgery, '*OZ* Obituary', published in *OZ*, 1972, also in *Preserving Disorder*, pp. 135–8, 138.
26. Fountain, *Underground*, p. 214.
27. R. Darlington and D. Lyddon, *Glorious Summer: Class Struggle in Britain 1972* (London: Bookmarks, 2000), pp. 95–140.
28. Sheila Rowbotham's autobiography ends in 1968, with the movement's beginning, but before Rowbotham's most creative period, and also before her relationship with Widgery. S. Rowbotham, *Promise of a Dream: Remembering the Sixties* (London: Penguin, 2000).
29. Widgery, *The Left in Britain*, p. 15.
30. G. Orwell, 'Politics and the English Language', in S. Orwell and I. Angus, *The Collected Essays, Journalism and Letters of George Orwell*, Volume 4: *In Front of Your Nose* (Harmondsworth: Penguin, 1970 edn), pp. 160–70, 169. For an account of George Orwell's 'literary Trotskyism' which emphasises the continuities between Orwell and writers like Widgery, see J. Newsinger, *Orwell's Politics* (London: Macmillan, 1999).
31. D. Widgery, 'How Did Biko Die?', *Temporary Hoarding*, 1977, in *Preserving Disorder*, pp. 159–61, 161.
32. G. Orwell, 'Politics and the English Language', in *Collected Essays*, Volume 4, p. 165.
33. Interview with Juliet Ash, 5 December 1998.
34. Green, *Days in the Life*, p. 256; Widgery, *The Left in Britain*, p. 14.
35. Foot, 'David Widgery', p. 122.
36. Widgery, *Beating Time* p. 17; K. Leech, *Struggle in Babylon: Racism in the Cities and Churches of Britain* (London: Sheldon Press, 1988), pp. 84–5; Bethnal Green and Stepney Trades Council, *Blood on the Streets* (London: Bethnal Green and Stepney Trades Council, 1978).
37. C. Coon, 'Rebels against the System', *Melody Maker*, 7 August 1976.
38. J. Savage, *England's Dreaming: Sex Pistols and Punk Rock* (London: Faber & Faber, 1991), p. 398.
39. *Temporary Hoarding* 1.

40. Savage, *England's Dreaming*, pp. 487–8.
41. Widgery, *Beating Time*, p. 45.
42. Ibid., pp. 45–7, 45; C. Rosenberg, 'Labour and the Fight against Fascism', *ISJ* 39 (1988), pp. 55–92, 75–9.
43. Incidentally, Samuel was the man who first recruited Peter Sedgwick to the left, some twenty-five years previously. See G. Pearson, 'Red Idols: Ralph Samuel and Peter Sedgwick', *The [Oxford] Isis*, 22 February 1956.
44. R. Samuel, 'David Widgery', *History Workshop Journal* 35 (1993), pp. 283–5, 283.
45. *Rock Against Racism Edinburgh* 1, 1978.
46. Rosenberg, 'Labour and the Fight against Fascism', p. 81; D. Field, 'Flushing out the Front', *Socialist Review*, May 1978.
47. R. Huddle, 'Hard Rain', *Socialist Review*, July–August 1978.
48. Widgery, *Beating Time*, p. 112.
49. Ibid., p. 43.
50. *Temporary Hoarding* 1.
51. Widgery, *Preserving Disorder*, pp. 147–53.
52. Ibid., pp. 76–87.
53. Widgery, *Beating Time*, p. 56.
54. Interview with John Shemeld, 31 July 1998; letter from Keith Flett, 26 December 1998; letter from Ian Birchall, 18 August 1998.
55. D. Widgery, R. Gregory, S. Shelton and R. Huddle, 'Look Get it Straight', *Socialist Review*, July–August 1978; *Socialist Worker*, 7 October 1978; Widgery, *Beating Time*, pp. 83–4. 'Mr Calico Nickers' was the *Review*'s then editor, Alex Callinicos.
56. P. Stack, *Socialist Worker Review*, July–August 1986
57. *Rentamob* 1.
58. 'Rocking Against Racism', in Widgery *Preserving Disorder*, pp. 115–21, 116.
59. The Epicurean side to Marx is examined in John Bellamy Foster's book, *Marx's Ecology: Materialism and Nature* (New York: Monthly Review Press, 2000).
60. P. Lafargue, *The Right to Be Lazy*, ed. and trans. L. Bracken (Ardmore, PA: Fifth Season Press: 1999).
61. Widgery, *Preserving Disorder*, pp. 45–53. Incidentally, *Preserving Disorder* wrongly dates this essay as 1975, before either the book or the magazine existed.
62. Widgery, *The Book of the Year*, p. 3.
63. Interview with Ruth Gregory and Syd Shelton, 6 January 1999.
64. D. Widgery, 'Doctoring', *New Internationalist*, 1983, in *Preserving Disorder*, pp. 186–9, 186. Probably the first article Widgery published on the NHS was D. Widgery 'Unions and Strikes in the National Health Service in Britain', *International Journal of Health Services* 6/2 (1976), pp. 301–8. Although engagingly written, this is a formal, semi-academic history of rank-and-file organisation in the health strikes of 1972–75. The essay is not written in the autobiographical style of *Beating Time* and other work.
65. 'Correspondence', *British Medical Journal*, 12 March 1988; D. Widgery, 'Out East', *British Medical Journal*, 15 July 1989; D. Widgery, 'The Prince and the Psychiatrists', *British Medical Journal*, 21 September 1991.
66. Interview with Juliet Ash, 5 December 1998. Beyond the items listed

above, Widgery's other *BMJ* articles include D. Widgery and A. Livingstone, 'The New General Practice: The Changing Philosophies of Primary Care', *British Medical Journal*, 3 October 1990; D. Widgery, 'Desert Storms', *British Medical Journal*, 11 January 1992; D. Widgery, 'AIDS Farewells', *British Medical Journal*, 5 September 1992; and D. Widgery and S. Cembrowicz, 'Practice Reports', *British Medical Journal*, 14 November 1992. Also see 'Correspondence', *British Medical Journal*, 13 August 1988, 15 April 1989, 12 August 1989, 26 August 1989, 7 October 1989, 27 October 1990, 15 December 1990, 2 November 1991, 29 February 1992, 9 January 1993, 17 April 1993; and the obituary which appeared in *British Medical Journal*, 14 November 1992.

67. Widgery, *The National Health*, p. xiv.
68. Widgery, *Some Lives*, p. 46.
69. D. Widgery, 'Introduction', *A Day in the Life of London* (London: Cape, 1984), pp. 10–13.
70. Widgery, *Some Lives*, p. 51.
71. Ibid., p. 234.
72. Foot, 'David Widgery', p. 122.
73. Interview with Ruth Gregory and Syd Shelton, 6 January 1999; the strikes of the London dockers in the 1970s are described in F. Lindop, 'The Dockers and the Industrial Relations Act, Part 2: The Arrest and Release of the "Pentonville Five"', *Historical Studies in Industrial Relations* 6 (1998), pp. 65–100. The banner can be seen in many photographs of the protests of the 1970s, including the picture of the release of the Pentonville Five which is reproduced on the cover of Darlington and Lyddon, *Glorious Summer*.
74. This imaginary leftist appears in the satirical magazine *Private Eye*.
75. Woolfie (Robert Lindsay) was the leader of the Tooting Popular Front in the television sitcom *Citizen Smith*.
76. Foot, 'David Widgery', p. 123.
77. B. Light, 'The Human Face of Revolution', *Socialist Review*, November 1992.
78. Interview with Ian Birchall, 21 October 1998. For those who have never met Ian, it should be explained that this remark is a *joke*. Even now, the British left possesses all sorts of people who see their role as being to champion a previous orthodoxy. Ian Birchall is not one of them!
79. Samuel, 'David Widgery', p. 284.
80. S. Rowbotham, *History Workshop Journal* 35 (1993), pp. 283–4.
81. Interview with Juliet Ash, 5 December 1998.

Chapter 11

1. D. Renton, *Fascism: Theory and Practice* (London: Pluto, 1999).
2. Henein's opinion of Serge's novel *Midnight in the Century* can be read in a special issue of *Grades Largeurs*, Autumn–Winter 1981, p. 41.
3. P. Anderson, *In the Tracks of Historical Materialism* (London: Verso, 1983), p. 28.

Further reading

The following list serves as a short guide to further reading. It supplements the full bibliographical information given in the notes, to which the reader is directed.

Dissident Marxism 1917–89

Callinicos, A, *Trotskyism* (Milton Keynes: Open University Press, 1990).

Callinicos, A., *The Revolutionary Ideas of Karl Marx* (London: Bookmarks, 1996).

Cliff, T., *State Capitalism in Russia* (London: Pluto, 1955).

Deutscher, I., *Marxism in Our Time* (London: Jonathan Cape, 1972).

Deutscher, I., *Marxism, Wars and Revolutions* (London: Verso, 1984).

Hobsbawm, E., *The Age of Extremes: The Short Twentieth Century 1914–1991* (London: Michael Joseph, 1994).

James, C.L.R., *State Capitalism and World Revolution* (Detroit: Facing Reality, 1969).

Kenny, M., *The First New Left* (London: Lawrence & Wishart, 1995).

Kolakowski, L., *Main Currents of Marxism: Its Rise, Growth and Dissolution*, Volume II: *The Golden Age* (Oxford: Clarendon Press, 1978).

Molyneux, J., *Leon Trotsky's Theory of Revolution* (London: Macmillan, 1982).

Molyneux, J., *What Is the Real Marxist Tradition?* (London: Bookmarks, 1984).

Newsinger, J., *Orwell's Politics* (London: Macmillan, 1999).

Rees, J., *The Algebra of Revolution: The Dialectic and the Classical Marxist Tradition* (London: Routledge, 1998).

Renton, D., *Fascism: Theory and Practice* (London: Pluto, 1999).

Renton, D., and Eaden, J., *The Communist Party of Great Britain since 1920* (London: Palgrave, 2002).

Renton, D., *Classical Marxism: Socialist Theory and the Second International* (Bristol: New Clarion Press, 2002).

Trotsky, L., *The Revolution Betrayed: What is the Soviet Union and Where Is It Going?* (New York: Pathfinder, 1972).

Mayakovsky, Kollontai, Lunacharsky, Serge

Briggs, A.D.P., *Vladimir Mayakovsky: A Tragedy* (Oxford: Meeuws, 1979).

Cotterill, D. (ed.), *The Serge–Trotsky Papers: Correspondence and Other Writings between Victor Serge and Leon Trotsky* (London: Pluto, 1994).

Farnsworth, B., *Aleksandra Kollontai: Socialism, Feminism and the Bolshevik Revolution* (Stanford, California: Stanford University Press, 1980).

Fitzpatrick, S., *The Commissariat of Enlightenment: Soviet Organization of Education and the Arts under Lunacharsky: October 1917 to 1921* (Cambridge: Cambridge University Press, 1970).

Kollontai, A., *Love of Worker Bees* (London: Virago, 1977).

Kollontai, A., *On Women's Liberation* (London: Bookmarks, 1998).

Kollontai, A., *Selected Writings* (London: Allison & Busby, 1977).

Kollontai, A., *The Autobiography of a Sexually Emancipated Woman* (New York: Herder, 1971).

Lunacharsky, A., *On Literature and Art* (Moscow: Progress Publishers, 1965).

Lunacharsky, A., *Revolutionary Silhouettes* (London: Penguin, 1967).

Porter, C., *Alexandra Kollontai: A Biography* (London: Virago, 1980).

Serge, V., *Destiny of a Revolution* (London: Hutchinson, n.d.).

Serge, V., *Memoirs of a Revolutionary 1901–1941* (Oxford: Oxford University Press, 1963).

Serge, V., *Year One of the Russian Revolution* (London and New York: Bookmarks, Pluto and Writers and Readers, 1992).

Tait, A.L., *Lunacharsky: Poet of the Revolution (1875–1907)* (Birmingham: Birmingham Slavonic Monographs, 1985).

Trotsky, L., *On Literature and Art* (New York: Pathfinder, 1977).

Weissman, S., *Victor Serge: The Course Is Set on Hope* (London and New York: Verso, 2001).

Korsch

Goode, P., *Karl Korsch: A Study in Western Marxism* (London: Macmillan, 1979).

Kellner, D., *Karl Korsch: Revolutionary Theory* (Austin: University of Texas Press, 1977).

Korsch, K., *Marxism and Philosophy* (London: Pluto, 1970).

Korsch, K., *Three Essays on Marxism* (London: Pluto, 1971).

Korsch, K., *Karl Marx* (New York: Humanities Press 1963).

Torr and Thompson

Cornforth, M., *Rebels and Their Causes: Essays in Honour of A.L. Morton* (London, 1978).
Saville, J., *Democracy and the Labour Movement: Essays in Honour of Dona Torr* (London: Lawrence & Wishart, 1954).
Steele, T., *The Emergence of Cultural Studies: Cultural Politics, Adult Education and the English Question* (London: Lawrence & Wishart, 1997).
Thompson, E.P., *William Morris* (London: Lawrence & Wishart, 1955).
Thompson, E.P., *The Making of the English Working Class* (Harmondsworth: Penguin, 1968).
Thompson, E.P., *The Poverty of Theory and Other Essays* (London: Merlin, 1978).
Torr, D., *Tom Mann* (London: Lawrence & Wishart, 1936).
Torr, D., *Tom Mann and His Times* (London: Lawrence & Wishart, 1956).

Henein

Alexandrian, S., *Georges Henein* (Paris: Seghers, 1981).
Berque, J., *Hommages à Georges Henein* (Paris: Le Pont de L'Épée, 1974).
Beinin, J., and Z. Lockman, *Workers on the Nile* (Princeton, NJ: Tauris, 1988).
Botman, S. *The Rise of Egyptian Communism 1939–70* (New York: New York University Press, 1988).
Henein, G., *Déraisons d'être* (Paris: Corti, 1938).
Henein, G., *Un Temps de petite fille* (Paris: Éditions de Minuit, 1947).
Henein, G., *L'Incompatible* (Paris: Corti, 1949).
Perrault, G., *A Man Apart: The Life of Henri Curiel* (London: Zed Books, 1987).
Soliman, L., *Pour une histoire profane de la Palestine* (Paris: La Découverte, 1989).

Baran, Sweezy

Baran, P., *Marxism and Psychology* (New York: Monthly Review Press, 1960).
Baran, P., *The Political Economy of Growth* (London: Penguin, 1973).
Baran, P.A. and P.M. Sweezy, *Monopoly Capital: An Essay on the American Economic and Social Order* (New York: Monthly Review Press, 1966).
Sweezy, P.M., and L. Huberman, *Paul A. Baran (1910–1964): A Collective Portrait* (New York: Monthly Review Press, 1965).

Rodney

Fanon, F., *Black Skin, White Masks* (New York: Grove Press, 1967).
James, C.L.R., *Walter Rodney and the Question of Power* (London: Race Today, 1983).

Rodney, W., *A History of the Upper Guinea Coast* (Oxford: Clarendon Press, 1970).

Rodney, W., *West Africa and the Atlantic Slave Trade* (Lagos: Afrografika, 1969).

Rodney, W., *The Groundings with my Brothers* (London: Bogle-L'Ouverture Publications, 1970).

Rodney, W., *How Europe Underdeveloped Africa* (London: Bogle–L'Ouverture Publications, 1972).

Rodney, W., *People's Power: No Dictator* (Georgetown: Working People's Alliance, 1979).

Rodney, W., *A History of the Guyanese Working People, 1805–1905* (New York: Johns Hopkins University Press, 1981).

Braverman

Braverman, H., *The Future of Russia* (New York: Macmillan, 1963).

Braverman, H., *Labour and Monopoly Capital: The Degradation of Work in the Twentieth Century* (New York and London: Monthly Review Press, 1974).

Draper, H., *Karl Marx's Theory of Revolution* (New York and London: Monthly Review Press: 4 vols, 1977).

Littler, C., *The Development of the Labour Process in Capitalist Societies* London: Heinemann Educational, 1982).

Pagano, U., *Harry Braverman* (Siena: University of Siena, 1990).

Amin

Amin, S., *The Maghreb in the Modern World* (London: Penguin, 1970).

Amin, S., *Accumulation on a World Scale: A Critique of the Theory of Under-development* (New York: Monthly Review Press, 1970).

Amin, S., *Unequal Development: An Essay on the Social Formations of Peripheral Capitalism* (New York: Monthly Review Press, 1973).

Amin, S., *The Law of Value and Historical Materialism* (London: Harvester Press, 1977).

Amin, S., *The Arab Economy Today* (London: Zed, 1982).

Amin, S., *L'Avenir du Maoïsme* (Paris: Editions de Minuit, 1982).

Amin, S., *Eurocentrism* (London: Zed Books, 1989).

Amin, S. *Capitalism in the Age of Globalization* (London: Zed Books, 1997).

Amin, S., *Spectres of Capitalism: A Critique of Current Intellectual Fashions* (New York: Monthly Review Press, 1998).

Harris, N., *The Mandate of Heaven: Marx and Mao in Modern China* (London: Quartet, 1978).

Harris, N., *The End of the Third World: Newly Industrializing Countries and the Decline of an Ideology* (London: Penguin, 1986).

Widgery

Neville, R., *Hippie Hippie Shake: The Dreams, the Trips, the Trials, the Love-ins, the Screw-ups... the Sixties* (London: Bloomsbury, 1996).

Fountain, N., *Underground: The London Alternative Press* (London and New York, Comedia, 1988).

Rowbotham, S., *Promise of a Dream: Remembering the Sixties* (London: Penguin, 2000).

Widgery, D., *The Left in Britain* (Harmondsworth: Penguin, 1976).

Widgery, D., *Beating Time* (London: Chatto & Windus, 1986).

Widgery, D., *Some Lives* (London: Sinclair-Stevenson, 1991).

Index